TABLE OF CONTENTS

Top 20 Test Taking Tips.. 4
A Healthy Lifestyle... 5
Family and Emotional Health.. 80
Safety and Prevention 104
Resource Management and Community Health.. 134
Secret Key #1 - Time is Your Greatest Enemy 148
    Pace Yourself 148
Secret Key #2 - Guessing is not Guesswork 148
    Monkeys Take the Test.. 148
    $5 Challenge... 149
Secret Key #3 - Practice Smarter, Not Harder 150
    Success Strategy 150
Secret Key #4 - Prepare, Don't Procrastinate... 150
Secret Key #5 - Test Yourself 151
General Strategies... 151
Special Report: How to Overcome Test Anxiety 157
    Lack of Preparation... 157
    Physical Signals 158
    Nervousness... 158
    Study Steps... 160
    Helpful Techniques 161
Practice Test and Additional Bonus Material... 166

Top 20 Test Taking Tips

1. Carefully follow all the test registration procedures
2. Know the test directions, duration, topics, question types, how many questions
3. Setup a flexible study schedule at least 3-4 weeks before test day
4. Study during the time of day you are most alert, relaxed, and stress free
5. Maximize your learning style; visual learner use visual study aids, auditory learner use auditory study aids
6. Focus on your weakest knowledge base
7. Find a study partner to review with and help clarify questions
8. Practice, practice, practice
9. Get a good night's sleep; don't try to cram the night before the test
10. Eat a well balanced meal
11. Know the exact physical location of the testing site; drive the route to the site prior to test day
12. Bring a set of ear plugs; the testing center could be noisy
13. Wear comfortable, loose fitting, layered clothing to the testing center; prepare for it to be either cold or hot during the test
14. Bring at least 2 current forms of ID to the testing center
15. Arrive to the test early; be prepared to wait and be patient
16. Eliminate the obviously wrong answer choices, then guess the first remaining choice
17. Pace yourself; don't rush, but keep working and move on if you get stuck
18. Maintain a positive attitude even if the test is going poorly
19. Keep your first answer unless you are positive it is wrong
20. Check your work, don't make a careless mistake

A Healthy Lifestyle

Health

Definition of health

Quite simply, health is the state of being sound in mind, body, and spirit. According to the World Health Organization, health is not only the absence of disease, but the presence of physical, mental, and social well-being. When assessing an individual's health, a professional is likely to examine him or her from a physical, psychological, spiritual, social, intellectual, or environmental standpoint. Although every individual has his or her own standard of health, it is common for people to recognize the following characteristics as healthy: an optimistic outlook in life, the ability to relax, a supportive home life, a clean environment, a satisfying job, freedom from pain and illness, and the energy necessary to enjoy life.

Psychological health

According to health professionals, maintaining optimal psychological health is not just a matter of avoiding major disorders or illnesses. In order to achieve excellence in this domain of health, a person has to take active measures to become aware and accept both his or her own feelings and the feelings of others. Achieving optimal psychological health also means developing the ability to express complex emotions, to be independent and not have to rely on anyone else for validation, and to be able to cope efficiently with the normal stress of life. Of course, reaching this state in the psychological domain depends on making progress in the other domains; that is, psychological growth depends on physical, spiritual, social, intellectual, and environmental health.

Physical health

Many health professionals view physical health as a continuum of possible conditions. On the extreme negative end of the continuum is premature death, while at the extreme positive end is optimal wellness. Optimal wellness is defined as the state in which the individual feels and performs at their personal best. Most individuals fall somewhere in between the extremes on the physical wellness continuum. Indeed, health professionals assert that a person will remain somewhere in the middle unless he or she takes active steps to improve his or her physical health. To do this, he or she must eat better, exercise more regularly, avoid dangerous and destructive habits, and protect himself or herself from injury and illness.

Social health

When health professionals refer to social health, they mean the ability of an individual to interact with other people effectively, to develop positive relationships, and to adequately fulfill social roles. Individuals who are socially healthy contribute to the affairs of the community, live peacefully among other people, and are sexually healthy. Social health has major effects on all the other aspects of a person's life. Studies have shown that individuals without strong social ties are more likely to abuse substances, to have heart disease, and even to develop cold infections. Furthermore, individuals who become ill are more likely to recover if they have support from friends and family.

<u>Spiritual health</u>
It is inaccurate to assume that spiritual health means being involved in an organized religion. Many people have a quality spiritual life all by themselves. According to health professionals, an individual has achieved excellent spiritual health if he or she has a defined purpose in life, has learned to experience love, joy, and peace, and is able to help themselves and others achieve these positive feelings. For many people, spirituality is defined as feeling connected to something greater than themselves or their own personal interests. Many recent studies have indicated that the relaxation and behavioral practices associated with spirituality are conducive to physical and psychological health, as well. Many doctors have even gone so far as to classify a lack of religious practice as a risk factor for physical health.

Personal hygiene practices

To stay clean and reduce the risk of disease, students should practice daily basic hygiene. Everyone should wash hair and body daily and should wash the hands more frequently than that. Teeth should be brushed between one and three times daily. Always wash hands before eating, avoid spitting or nose-picking, and cover your mouth when sneezing. Try to avoid coming into contact with any bodily fluids, and keep clothes and living space clean. Finally, avoid putting your fingers in your mouth, and try not to touch any animals before eating.

Besides helping you maintain an attractive appearance, hygiene is essential for keeping you healthy and free of disease. The body is usually covered with a certain amount of bacteria, but if this number is allowed to grow too high, you may place yourself at risk for disease. Individuals who fail to regularly wash their hair are more likely to have head lice, and those who fail to properly clean their genitals are more susceptible to urinary tract infections. Good hygiene also reduces an individual's contagiousness when sick. Hygiene is especially important when dealing with food: failing to wash everything involved in the preparation of a meal can result in the spread of bacterial infections like E. coli and hepatitis A.

Setting goals

Individuals who are most likely to make positive permanent changes in their health set realistic goals along the way. When setting goals, individuals should identify what resources (time, money, and effort) are available to achieve them. Individuals should also identify the potential barriers to success and consider ways to minimize or remove these problems. It is always better to set a number of small, attainable goals rather than goals that may be difficult to achieve.

Achieving health goals

Health professionals say that recognizing negative behavior is the first step toward change. Many individuals will undergo a period of self-observation before deciding to alter their behavior. During this period, they may identify the triggers for the particular behavior and try to discover any underlying psychological reasons. Often a change is more successful if the individual makes his or her goals known or even signs a contract pledging the change. The most important factor in achieving a long-term change, however, is confidence. Study after study shows that individuals who are optimistic about their chances for permanent positive change are more likely to achieve it.

Physical fitness

Physical fitness is the body's ability to perform all of its tasks and still have some reserve energy in case of an emergency. People who are physically fit can meet all of their daily physical needs, have a realistic and positive image of themselves, and are working to protect themselves against future health problems. Physical fitness has three main components: flexibility, cardiovascular fitness, and muscular strength or endurance. Some other factors, like agility and balance, are also often considered when assessing physical fitness. The benefits of pursuing physical fitness throughout life are not only physical but mental and emotional; regular exercise is proven to reduce the risk of disease and increase life expectancy.

Even though the health benefits of physical fitness are universally known, most people still do not exercise enough. There are a number of supposed reasons for this, such as a lack of time or facilities or simply not enjoying exercise. Some out-of-shape individuals become self-conscious about their bodies and athletic performance and avoid exercise. Women are more likely to avoid exercise than men, in some cases because they fear becoming too muscular. However, physiologists have shown that women are unlikely to gain too much muscle mass in a normal fitness regimen. In fact, women consistently score about the same as men in many fitness categories, except upper-body strength.

Reinforcements and self-talk

In a program of reinforcement, an individual rewards him or herself for clear progress toward the goal or punishes him or herself for negative or counterproductive behavior. Research has also shown that individuals can influence their chances of success with their self-talk, meaning the messages they send themselves. An individual who consistently praises him or herself for a job well done is more likely to repeat a positive behavior, while individuals who beat themselves up over every minor mistake or relapse are more likely to commit that negative behavior in the future.

Locus of control

When an individual believes he or she can positively influence his or her own health, that person is said to have an internal locus of control, which is a crucial factor in bringing about change. Individuals who believe external forces (friends, neighborhood, or society as a whole) will determine their health have an external locus of control. Studies have repeatedly shown that individuals with an internal locus of control are far more likely to make long-lasting positive changes. Individuals who have an external locus of control are less likely to seek help and and tend to rate their health more poorly overall.

Wellness

Health professionals refer to the highest state of health as wellness. Wellness has a number of definitions: it may mean enjoying life, or having a defined purpose in life and being able to work towards it, or it may mean deliberately taking the steps necessary to avoid disease and maximize health. Wellness is different from health in that it means actively enhancing health, not just maintaining good health. Total wellness depends on psychological, physical, and social factors. In the general model for wellness, all of these factors combine to produce the individual's complete level of wellness. Indeed, part of the reason why health professionals promote the idea of wellness is to show people that all the areas of their lives depend on one another.

Motor control

When considering individual differences in the performances of motor skills, scientists are careful to make the distinction between a person's abilities and skills. An ability is a stable, enduring trait that allows a person to perform a task at a certain level of competency. Abilities are thought to be genetic and to stay at about the same level throughout a person's life. Skills, on the other hand, can be developed as a result of practice. A person who becomes skilled at a certain task is capable of performing it consistently at a high level. Many tasks require a mixture of ability and skill. In music, for instance, some individuals may be born with the ability to hear proper pitch and intuitively understand musical structures, but they will still have to develop the skills to play a certain instrument.

Motor development timeline

In early infancy, a child's motor patterns will be confined to basic reflexes, like sucking and grasping. The first motor skills to develop are called the gross motor skills, which include the movements of the head, body, legs, and arms. Most infants will be able to walk by the time they reach ten months of age. Fine motor skills (those accomplished with precise movements, especially of the hands) develop between the ages of one and five. By the time a child reaches the age of six, the child can usually draw basic shapes, button a shirt, tie shoes, and write legibly. More complex manipulative skills (like throwing, catching, and striking) will not be fully developed until about the age of ten. Most of the differences observed between motor skills among children are the result of differences in socialization; that is, children who are given an equal chance to develop Hick's motor skills usually do so at approximately the same rate.

Basic motor pattern development

In general, children learn and develop their basic motor patterns through play. For this reason, children below the age of about seven should have daily activities emphasizing the use of large muscle groups so that they may develop muscular coordination. Simple games involving a soft ball are also a good way to develop a young child's basic motor patterns. Especially during this period, children require careful supervision during play, as they will not have yet refined their sense of force or coordination and may be liable to hurt another child or themselves. Also, children should be encouraged to develop fine motor skills from a very young age. Activities like puzzles are excellent ways to develop both motor skills and spatial intelligence.

Purpose of motor units

When health professionals refer to a motor unit, they are referring to a single motor neuron and all of the muscle fibers it can cause to contract. Every muscle is composed of a number of motor units that are somewhat independent, yet harmonious. There is a distinct hierarchy among motor units: some are used every time a muscle does anything, while others are only called upon for tasks of the most extreme difficulty. Commonly-used motor units are said to be low threshold, while less frequently-used motor units are referred to as high threshold. The amount of stimulus required to activate a motor unit is consistent, meaning that the motor unit will activate and deactivate at about the same level every time.

Sense of effort

As a growing human being develops, he or she will learn how to gauge the degree of effort or force that is required to perform a given task. Anyone who has ever been swatted in the nose by an infant will recognize that children are not always aware of the effort necessary to get someone's attention. As this sense of required effort develops, one will be able to determine whether a given movement requires fast or slow performance, and whether the force behind it must be strong or weak. A slightly more complicated case arises when an individual is somehow constrained. Free movements, in which the only resistance is air and the limitations of the human body, will always require the same scale of effort; constrained motion, however, requires an accurate assessment of the strength of the constraint.

Open-loop motor control theory

The theory of motor control known as open-loop control asserts that movements are made according to a preexisting motor program, a set of muscle commands laid out before the movement is begun. These movements are performed without any adjustment based on feedback, the sensory information transmitted to the brain. Open-loop motor control theory seems to explain many of the common movements that individuals make unconsciously, and there is excellent research evidence to suggest that animals often perform tasks in a way similar to the open-loop model. However, many scientists maintain that open-loop theory is only accurate in situations where the movement is too short for there to be any meaningful feedback.

There are three general criticisms that have been made of the closed-loop theory of motor control. First, some scientists suggest that if a perceptual trace must be developed for every possible movement of which a human is capable, then the volume of these perceptual traces would quickly grow larger than the space available for their storage. Another criticism of the theory is that it has no formula for how movements will be performed for the first time; indeed, closed-loop theory really only applies to movements for which the individual has already developed a perceptual trace. Finally, some scientists insist that many movements are too brief for feedback to play a significant role in their execution, and therefore these would seem to be performed without the assistance of any perceptual trace.

Closed-loop motor control theory

The closed-loop theory of motor control requires that there be two different states of memory in order for a body to be able to correct its mistakes. One of these is a program of movement that is remembered by the body and is called a memory trace. This memory trace is responsible for initiating a particular movement. The state of memory which carries more responsibility for learning and controlling movement is called the perceptual trace. The perceptual trace is basically a standard of correctness: if the feedback resulting from a motion initiated by the memory trace indicates a departure from the perceptual trace, a change in the movement is ordered. In this model, the quality of a movement is only as high as the quality of the perceptual trace.

Individual differences research

A whole field of motor learning research, known as individual differences research, is concerned with charting the various behavioral abilities of different people. In this field, individual differences are defined as stable, enduring differences among people that contribute to permanent differences in performance. Identifying advantages in motor learning requires not only observing repeated superiority in the performance of a task but in determining what particular ability accounts for the disparity in performance. For instance, it is not enough for a scientist to watch one person consistently make more successful free throws than another; in order to conclude that the first person has superior motor skill, the scientist must isolate the particular ability that is superior and collect data in support of the hypothesis.

Other factors affecting motor performance

It is the job of a physical educator to remind students that natural ability is only one of the factors that contribute to motor performance. Some individuals perform well because they have been given more opportunities to learn than an average person. Individuals with an active temperament seek out opportunities and tend to have better motor performance. Body type contributes to motor performance, also, in that healthy, flexible people are more able to take advantage of their natural abilities. A child who is raised in a family or community that supports athletic endeavor is more likely to develop good motor skills. Finally, motivation, competitiveness, and vigor cannot be underestimated as factors affecting motor performance. No individual can be successful at the highest level of competition simply by relying on his or her natural ability.

General motor ability myth

In the early days of motor ability research, it was thought that all the abilities called into play in performing a task were part of the same ability, known as general motor ability. This idea became popular at the same time as the notion of the intelligence quotient, which claimed to be able to give a universal assessment of cognitive ability. Besides being convenient, the idea of a general motor ability seemed to be borne out in most cases. Subsequent research, however, has indicated that the motor abilities of an individual may vary widely between tasks. For instance, individuals with great muscular strength are often inflexible and incapable of performing precise tasks quickly. Indeed, recent tests have shown that there is a great degree of variability even within the category of balance.

Body awareness

In order to successfully develop and implement basic motor patterns, the human body has to have an awareness of its own dimensions and potentials. For instance, the body must be aware of its current orientation: not only its location and position, but also the range of motions that are possible from its current position. For instance, one develops an intuitive understanding that it is difficult to jump from a sitting position. The body, as it matures, will also develop a sense of balance in its various parts, so that wild movements can be made with the limbs without throwing the entire trunk off balance. Similarly the body will develop the ability to automatically transfer weight for the best performance of a given movement.

Relationships with people and objects

The full development of motor skills requires the ability to assess and adjust to the various relationships that affect motion. These can be classified as either relationships with people or with objects. In relationships with people, an individual needs to be able to determine whether his motion is to be matching or contrasting. For example, a child on a see-saw has to determine that he cannot make the same pushing motion at the same time as his partner. One also has to determine whether one is leading or following another and adjust movements accordingly. As for the relationships with objects, it is essential to be able to know the orientation of the object in relation to oneself, as well as to be able to determine whether one will need to go around, through, over, or under the object.

Median plane of movement

Fitness professionals have a few technical terms to describe the various planes of the body in which motions can be made. The median (or midsagittal) plane extends from the top of the head down and divides the body into two symmetrical halves, right and left. Any other plane of the body that runs parallel to the median plane is known as a sagittal plane. Any kind of movement which takes the body forward from its standing position is known as flexion. Raising the leg in front of oneself, for instance, is referred to as flexion of the hip. Any movement that takes the body backwards and occurs in a sagittal plane is known as an extension; tilting the head back, for example, is called extension of the neck.

Motor ability assessments

Figure eight run and balance beam
In the assessment of motor ability known as the figure eight run, subjects are required to run around a small course that demands making several quick turns. This test is timed to determine an individual's degree of speed and agility. In the balance beam test, subjects are required to perform a few different movements (for instance, standing on one foot, raising arms above the head, or standing on the toes) while traversing a beam two inches wide and twelve feet long. Subjects are timed and awarded points based on the number of movements they are able to perform on the balance beam. There are a few other clinical tests designed to measure balance, but most of these require expensive equipment and are unsuitable for the classroom.

Vertical jump and bar snap
It has been difficult for scientists to create tests of motor ability that are general enough to measure something other than the performance of the specific activity of the test. The vertical jump test measures leg power by requiring the subject to jump straight into the air from a stationary position. The individual's score is measured as the difference between the individual's standing reach and the highest point touched during three trial jumps. The bar snap exercise measures agility, power, and coordination. In this exercise, the legs are lifted and swung forward as far as possible while the subject is holding onto an overhead horizontal bar. The bar snap exercise is considered to be quite challenging. It is therefore not appropriate for everyone.

Speed and reaction time
Speed is one of the easier aspects of motor ability to measure. Typically, an individual's speed is tested by timing a fifty- or hundred-yard sprint. Some measures of speed seek to

eliminate differences caused by acceleration and only measure time once the individual has reached top speed. In order to measure reaction time, special equipment must be purchased, allowing the measurement of time to the hundredth of a second. Scientists use a number of different movements as gauges of reaction time, ranging from a simple motion of the hand to a full-body response. There are extensive records of male and female motor skill norms so that physical educators can determine how students compare to the general population.

Speed development

In order to train for running distances of up to two miles, athletes need to train the anaerobic fast-twitch muscle fibers. This is most easily done by interval training, in which distances of between 100 and 400 yards are run as quickly as possible, with a brief period of rest in between. In order to train for sports that require a burst of speed along with cardiovascular endurance, such as soccer or basketball, it is good to run continuously, occasionally breaking into a sprint. Most fitness professionals believe that training at distances slightly greater than those required for competition is the best way to prepare. Also, many athletes report positive benefits from assisted intervals, in which running is done downhill. Theoretically, this will teach the muscles to work more quickly than usual.

Explosive speed

In order to develop explosive running speed, a person must perform exercises that strengthen the quadriceps. Running hills, climbing stairs, and pushing a football sled are all good ways to develop bursts of running speed. It is also a good idea to incorporate short bursts of speed into a running routine. Some athletes will run three miles, sprinting for ten seconds of every minute. Another way to improve running speed is by a series of sprints, with plenty of time to recover in between. If a person is training for a sport like soccer or football, he or she should incorporate a change of direction into the sprints, so that the muscles associated with changing course are also trained.

Speed over long distances

Sports that require maintaining a high speed for longer than two minutes primarily rely on slow-twitch muscle fibers rather than on aerobic capacity. In order to train for running, swimming, or cycling long distances, one should combine over-training (training at distances much longer than those that will be covered in competition) and interval training (in which a number of smaller distances are traversed, with brief rest periods in between). It is important to learn to regulate effort over a long period: distance runners, for instance, must learn to reserve some strength for the important stretch run. Often long-distance runners benefit from running sprints at a pace much faster than they would normally run, in order to condition their muscles to a faster pace.

Locomotor movements

Crawling
One of the first locomotor movements that anyone learns is crawling. The motor pattern associated with crawling is quite simple. First, the individual must be able to support him or herself on hands and knees, which requires a bit of upper-body strength. Then, as the right hand moves forward, momentarily shifting the center of gravity, the left leg also moves

forward to stabilize. Similarly, as the left hand moves forward, the right knee slides forward so that balance is maintained. Using this simple pattern of movement, one is able to propel himself or herself forward. It is interesting to note that crawling, just like walking and running, relies on momentarily falling out of balance and then restoring that balance to propel the individual.

Walking
Walking is one of the most basic motor patterns. Many people are surprised to learn that walking is essentially just a process of losing and regaining balance: the individual shifts his or her center of gravity off the base of support briefly, and then extends a leg to catch himself or herself. This makes more sense, perhaps, when one remembers what a baby's first steps resemble. During walking, one's body should not shift dramatically from one side to the other , or bob up and down violently. The most natural way to walk is with the arms and legs working in opposition. That is, the right arm will swing forward as the left leg strides forth, and the right arm will swing back as the right leg strides.

Running
The locomotor pattern of running takes a few years to fully develop. When it is mature, a running pattern involves the trunk leaning slightly forward, with both arms swinging in wide arcs and in opposition to the motion of the legs (as in walking). The supporting leg makes contact with the ground almost directly under the center of gravity. The knee of the supporting leg bends forward slightly as the foot makes contact, and then the extension of this leg propels the body forward. Meanwhile, the other knee swings forward to create forward momentum. The swinging of the arms creates vertical momentum, which as an individual grows older allows the stride to lengthen.

Leaping
The locomotor pattern for leaping is based on the pattern for running. This is evidenced by the fact that a leap takes off from one foot and lands on the other. The position of the arms is also the same in a leap as they are in a run, that is, the left arm swings forward with the right leg, and vice versa. The swing of the arms is more exaggerated in a leap, in order to generate more momentum and distance. Once the individual touches down, he or she bends the supporting leg in order to absorb the force of the body. The knee of the supporting leg often bends considerably more than it does during the run pattern. During a leap, the trunk of the body is a bit behind the center of gravity, in order to maintain the balance upon landing.

Skipping and jumping
The locomotor pattern for skipping is a combination of a step and a hop, accomplished first with one foot and then the other. Like a gallop, the skip has a somewhat uneven rhythm. There is the same alternation of feet and opposing motion of the arms that accompanies walking, but also a same-sided hop that throws the motion off-kilter. Jumping, on the other hand, is a fairly simple motor pattern in which one propels oneself off the ground for a moment. To jump, one begins with feet parallel and shoulder-width apart. It helps to swing the arms back, and then forward as the knees are bent and extended, lifting the body off the ground. The momentum generated by the upward progress of the arms increases the height of the jump.

Hopping and galloping

A hop is a basic locomotor pattern in which one springs off one foot, in any direction, and lands on the same foot. During a hop, the knee does not straighten all the way. Most of the propulsion of the hop and absorption of the force of landing is achieved by the ankle joint. Galloping is a more complex movement. When galloping, one lifts the lead leg, bends it, and then advances it forward to receive the weight. While this is going on, the back foot will advance to replace the supporting leg, perhaps hopping a bit forward once it has fully taken the place of the supporting leg. The rhythm of a gallop is generally uneven.

Chasing, fleeing, and dodging

The locomotor patterns for chasing, fleeing, and dodging all depend on the presence of some other moving thing. Chasing is the attempt to overtake something or someone that is fleeing. In order to chase effectively, a person needs to be able to quickly reach top speed and make sudden changes in direction. When fleeing, a person is traveling away from someone or something that is pursuing him or her. Again, this pattern of movement requires being able to reach top speed quickly, change directions, and dodge. Dodging is the ability to rapidly move the body in some other direction than the original line of movement. Effective dodging may include faking one move and executing another, twisting the body, or stretching in a certain direction.

Traveling

The National Standard for Physical Education has defined traveling as possessing a basic level of competency in many different movement forms and demonstrating proficiency in a few specific areas. A person who can travel in this sense is able to combine different movement patterns, and use motor patterns in a variety of different environments. He or she should be able to move forward or sideways using a number of different patterns, and be able to change directions quickly when necessary. A person who can travel will also be able to set locomotor patterns to music, develop dance sequences to accompany music, and perform dance and gymnastic movements. Finally, an individual who has achieved this level of competency will have mature patterns of walking and running.

Nonlocomotor movements

Rolling

Rolling is one of the easiest non-locomotor movements, and is usually mastered within the first few months of human life. To roll, one simply lies down with the arms either pressed to the sides or raised above the head. Rolling usually begins by lying on one's back. Then by flexing the abdominal muscles, one is able to shift the trunk off the center of gravity so that the body rolls over. Once a half-turn has been accomplished, it is usually easier to continue a roll. Sometimes a roll is accelerated by bending the knees and swinging the legs in the direction of the roll when one is on one's side or stomach.

Turning

Turning is one of the basic nonlocomotor movements; that is, it does not attempt to change the location of the body, but rather to alter its position. A turn is simply a smaller part of a full rotation, and like a larger rotation is created by a shift in the support base. To turn, one begins by placing one foot in front of the other. The speed of the turn is aided by holding the arms straight out from the shoulders, so that they are parallel to the ground. The body is then rotated to the right or left by a twisting of the hips. The feet should be set slightly apart to widen the base of support, since this twisting motion will cause the weight to be shifted so that it rests primarily on the leg on the side one is turning towards.

Jumping and landing
When it is discussed as a nonlocomotor movement, jumping is merely the transfer of weight from one foot to another. Landing is the motor pattern by which individuals regain their balance and reestablish a standing position. During a jump, the individual's arms will have been flung up, but during landing, the arms should be extended to the sides to aid in maintaining balance. The knees, hips, and ankles should be slightly bent in order to best absorb the shock of landing. Further, it is a good idea to land on the balls of the feet so that compensatory movements can shift one's weight forward to the toes or backward to the heels, as necessary.

Twisting and transferring weight
In the study of nonlocomotor patterns, twisting is considered to be identical to turning, with the only exception being that the feet are set shoulder-width apart, with toes pointing forward, during the entire movement. This tends to increase stability as the upper body rotates. Most individuals are able to twist their bodies a little more than 90 degrees to each side. Transferring weight is a component of many of the locomotor movements, like walking, jumping, or leaping. It simply means leaning in one direction or shifting the pelvis such that more of the body weight is on one of the legs.

Stretching and balancing weight
The nonlocomotor pattern for stretching involves extending (or, in some cases, hyperextending) any of the joints so that they are as long, or as straight, as possible. Although stretching normally entails a bit of discomfort, it should not be performed if it causes serious pain. Any stretching action should be performed slowly and smoothly, without bobbing or jerking. Most of the time, it is best to allow the body to gradually accustom itself to a given stretch. When balancing, the body is attempting to maintain a stationary position or adjust to the force of gravity while performing certain movements. A good practice for balance is to stand on one foot and attempt different motions with the head, arms, trunk, and opposing leg.

Manipulative movements

Throwing
Throwing is a basic motor pattern used by an individual to propel an object away from the body. A sequence of movements allows this action to be carried out. First, grasp the object with one or both hands. The legs should be shoulder-width apart, with one foot positioned slightly in front of the other. In a one-handed throw, the foot that is forward should be opposite the arm that is executing the throw, i.e., when throwing with the right hand, the left foot should be slightly out front. To carry out the throw, slowly bring back the throwing arm, and while taking a small step with the forward foot, begin to move the throwing arm forward. As it swings forward, release the object. Even after the object has been released, continue the follow-through with the throwing arm because maintaining proper form optimizes the trajectory of the object.

Catching
Catching is a basic manipulative skill that involves stopping the momentum of an approaching object and controlling it with the hands. When catching, one should be

standing still, with eyes focused on the incoming object. The arms should be slightly bent in front of the body, and the hands should be the first thing to make contact with the object. Sometimes though, it will be necessary to trap the object against one's body with the hands or arms. Establishing the proper timing for a catch is one of the more difficult motor patterns to learn. Many individuals benefit from starting off by catching a large ball.

Kicking
Kicking is a simple motor pattern in which a foot is used to strike and propel an object in any direction. When kicking, the arms should be held sideways to maintain balance. As one approaches the object, the support foot (the foot that is not striking the object) should be placed next to the object to be kicked. The kicking leg is brought back and then swung forward in an arc from the hip. As the foot makes contact with the object, the knee is fully extended and the body leans slightly backward for balance. After contact, the kicking foot will continue its progress briefly in the same direction as the object before returning to the ground. While kicking, one should keep his or her eyes at all times on the object being kicked

Dribbling a basketball
Dribbling a basketball, or bouncing any other kind of ball off the ground repeatedly, is a simple motor pattern that relies heavily on hand-eye coordination. When dribbling, one's feet should be placed in a slightly off-set, stride position. The knees, hips, and waists should be slightly bent, to improve balance and to make them more capable of quick adjustments. The ball should be pushed against the ground with the fingertips making contact, and the force coming from the extension of the elbow. In basketball, it is always a good idea to maintain the dribble at waist level. The eyes should for the most part be looking straight ahead, although it will be necessary to occasionally look at the ball.

Striking an object
One of the basic manipulative movements used in sports is striking an object with either a paddle or a racket. In this case, one is propelling some object forward with a hand-held implement. In order to do this, one should be holding the racket in the dominant hand, that is, the hand with which one feels most comfortable. When the object is at the height of the shoulder or above, an over-arm motion is used. The racket is drawn back, and rotated forward from the shoulder, with the follow-through drawing the implement away from the body. When striking an object below the shoulder, the racket is brought back behind the hips and then swung forward in an arc from the shoulder. The follow-through on this type of strike is typically more brief. During this movement, the trunk stays still, although it may be bent forward slightly.

Perception and movement

Perception is constantly affected by an individual's level of physical activity and training. Indeed, the information gained through participation in sports can help perception in other areas of life. For instance, baseball players become better at determining the speed with which an object is approaching, and whether it is curving towards or away from their body. One thing that sports do that enhances perception is train the brain to separate important stimuli from the rest, so that reactions may be more rapid and efficient. People in stressful situations often have a tendency to develop a sort of tunnel vision; studies of athletes, however, reveal that the enhanced ability to process information from the visual field make it possible for them to take in a much larger field of vision.

Exteroception

Exteroception is the perception of things in the environment. For humans, visual perception is considered to be the most important form of exteroception affecting motor control. Indeed, many anthropologists have suggested that the survival of the human race depended on the development of an especially keen sense of vision, which could be used to distinguish prey and to hit targets from a long distance. The importance of vision for motor control is indicated by the extensive network of connections between the eye and the brain. Everything from the right side of the visual field is sent to the left side of the brain, and vice versa. The place where the two optic nerves cross is called the optic chiasma.

Perceptual uncertainty

Individuals often have trouble reacting to external stimuli or determining a course of motor activity if they are troubled by perceptual uncertainty. Perceptual uncertainty is any doubt in the validity of one's perceptions; it increases in proportion to the number of stimuli or events in the perceptual field. Many studies have shown that reaction time is increased as distracting stimuli are eliminated. Indeed, in many cases an absence of distraction allows the individual to begin processing a motor response before the stimuli even presents itself. This aspect of motor control is often taken advantage of by sports teams, who seek to slow down opponents by creating distractions in the visual field.

Hearing and sensorimotor coordination

Human beings have developed an excellent sense of hearing, in part because early man needed to be able to hear the approach of potential predators or prey. Human beings are not only able to hear a sound and determine what it is, but they are also able to determine where it is coming from. This is done by comparing the sounds heard by the right and left ear. When a sound comes from straight ahead, it reaches both ears at the same time; if it is off to one side, however, it will be heard first by the ear on that side. The brain is able to take this minute difference in timing and wave quality and determine the location from which the sound has come. This information is then used by the brain to determine how the head is to be moved and how the body should be positioned.

Focal and ambient vision

Human vision can be considered as either focal or ambient. Focal vision is concerned with those objects in the eye's immediate focus, is used to determine the identity of objects in the outside world, and can be easily diminished by low light. Focal vision is dependent on the perceptive ability of the cones within the retina, which are concentrated in the middle and can determine detail because they each have a bipolar cell attached. Ambient vision, on the other hand, incorporates the entire retina, is used to determine the location of objects, and is not terribly affected by poor light. Ambient vision relies on the receptivity of both rods and cones, and so is able to discern both detail and spatial relations.

Proprioception and kinesthesis

Proprioception is an individual's perception of the arrangement of his or her own body parts. It may be applied to individual parts or to the body as a whole and to the body while stationary or while in motion. Kinesthesis is a related term which refers to the sensations of body position, tension, and movement. Although kinesthesis was formerly only concerned with moving body parts, its definition has been broadened to the point where it is almost synonymous with proprioception. An individual's proprioception is mainly achieved by the vestibular system (a complex in the inner ear that controls balance), joints, tendons, and muscles. The varying tension and pressure on the various muscles of the body are transmitted to the brain.

Proprioception and sensorimotor control

The control of muscles is mainly accomplished through the combined efforts of the muscle spindles and Golgi tendon organs. Muscle spindles are tiny receptors in the muscle fiber which send and receive information to and from the central nervous system. These spindles stretch along with the muscle. Golgi tendon organs are located in the tendons that attach to muscles. They are usually concerned with slowing down any violently fast contractions by inhibiting the actions of the motor neurons in the spinal cord. Both the muscle spindles and the Golgi tendon organs work to respond to external stimuli with the appropriate muscular responses, and to keep those reactions from becoming too violent.

Cerebellum, medulla oblongata, and reticulating activating system

The cerebellum is the area of the brain that refines skilled movements. Besides enabling the body to move efficiently and swiftly, this part of the brain coordinates the skeletal muscles for the purposes of maintaining balance. The medulla oblongata mediates the reflexes that result in the raising or lowering of the heart rate, blood pressure, and rate of breathing. The brain also contains a complex network of neurons known as the reticular activating system. This system alerts the brain whenever important sensory information is gathered by the outlying sensory nerves.

Cerebrum, thalamus, and hypothalamus

The motivation, coordination, and direction for physical activity all come from the brain. The cerebrum is the portion of the brain that deals with all conscious functions. This area of the brain directs many things crucial for movement: sensations, voluntary movement, skills, judgment of distance, and the appropriate level of force needed for a particular activity. The thalamus is the area of the brain that receives sensory messages and coordinates reflex movements. The hypothalamus, on the other hand, coordinates the autonomic functions of the body, such as the processes of sweating, shivering, and the dilation or constriction of the blood vessels in response to external stimuli.

Spatial environment

In order to effectively develop, select, or administer a pattern of motor behavior, an individual has to know a few things about his or her spatial environment. Most of these determinations occur unconsciously. First, an individual must have some idea of the space that his or her body is taking up; that is, the location and position of his or her body at the beginning of a movement. The person must also have a reasonable idea of the general space in which the movement is to occur. Once these things are known, the person can determine whether the movement should occur backwards, forwards, diagonally, sideways, up, or down. Finally, the person can make a more long-term assessment of the appropriate path and speed of the motion.

Neurological-reflexive factors

A number of neurological-reflexive factors affect motor control. All of these seem to reduce the number of commands the individual must obey in order to execute a particular motor program. For instance, reciprocal inhibition is a feature of human reflexes that prevents the reflex from being stimulated while the extensors in the joint are activated; thus, the doctor will get no response with his rubber mallet when you hold your leg in certain positions. The body also has what is called a central pattern generator: that is, a sort of kinesthetic memory of common movements. In some experiments, scientists have been able to stimulate the body of an animal to perform a certain movement, even if the connections between the animal's brain and body have been severed.

Gender, conditioning, and the development of motor skill

Research has consistently shown that there are basic differences in the motor performance of men and women. However, these differences have been discovered to be based on differences in conditioning and body structure rather than on innate differences in ability. Girls tend to have far fewer opportunities to develop motor skills than do boys. This phenomenon is blamed on a number of different factors, from sexism in society that discourages girls from playing sports to socialization that encourages girls to engage in more sedentary activities. In any case, female and male athletes who have the same number of motor experiences are found to develop at much the same rate. This information is especially valuable for physical educators who may have to confront the false assumption that girls are not meant to play sports.

Coordinative structures and motor control

The concept of coordinative structures suggests that some motor programs can group together seemingly independent parts of the body for the easier performance of certain tasks. Formerly, theorists assumed that there must be particular commands for each independent muscle group when an action is to be performed. Although this more–recently understood feature of the motor system may relieve the body of some administrative stress, it can be problematic as well, as anyone knows who has tried to improve a bad golf swing. Scientific research has shown, however, that with practice individuals can develop the ability to uncouple their coordinated structures and restore independent control.

Characteristics of skilled movement

Sheridan asserted that four characteristics of skilled movement must be accounted for by any theory that professes to describe motor control. First, a skilled movement will display some flexibility of movement. In other words, there must be the ability to accomplish the same task with a variety of different muscles and bones. Second, a skilled movement must have a degree of uniqueness because it is physically impossible for any two movements to be exactly alike. Third, a skilled movement must display some consistency, i.e., the individual will perform it in a similar way in a variety of situations. Fourth, a skilled movement will have some degree of mutability, i.e., the individual will be able to make small adjustments during its performance.

Gender, body structure, and motor performance

Research into the differences in motor performance between men and women has revealed that most of the advantages claimed by either gender are the result of differences in body structure. Men, for instance, tend to have more muscle mass in their upper body, and so they are likely to develop superior performance in skills like throwing or striking. Women, on the other hand, are noted for having a lower center of gravity and therefore balance, and so they may be better than men in the performance of certain movements. Both genders are limited in motor performance by their flexibility, skeletal size, body composition, and overall level of fitness. It has been frequently observed that the difference in motor performance between the best and the worst man is much greater than the difference between the average man and woman.

Muscular system

The muscles of the body are attached to the skeleton by tendons and other connective tissues. Muscles exert force and move the bones of the body by converting chemical energy into contractions. Every muscular act is the result of some muscle growing shorter. The muscles themselves are composed of millions of tiny proteins. Muscles are stimulated by nerves that link them to the brain and spinal cord. There are three types of muscles: cardiac muscles are found only in the heart and pump the blood through the body; smooth muscles surround or are part of internal organs; skeletal muscles are those a person controls voluntarily. Skeletal muscles are the most common tissue in the body, accounting for between 25 and 40% of body weight.

Somatic system

The portion of the human body's nervous system that is responsible for moving the skeletal muscles is the somatic system. The movements created by the somatic system may be acts of the will or reflex actions. Such movements require an increased blood flow to certain areas, so the somatic nervous system relies on the autonomic system, which controls the involuntary muscles, to provide a proper setting in which to effect action. The motions ordered by the somatic system are the result of information gathered by the nerves. The nerves most closely concerned with the somatic system are those that extend out to the extremities of the body.

Skeletal system

The skeletal system is composed of about 200 bones which, along with the attached ligaments and tendons, create a protective and supportive network for the body's muscles and soft tissues. There are two main components of the skeletal system: the axial skeleton and the appendicular skeleton. The axial skeleton includes the skull, spine, ribs, and sternum; the appendicular skeleton includes the pelvis, shoulders, and the various arm and leg bones attached to these. There are few differences between the male and female skeleton: the bones of a male tend to be a bit larger and heavier than those of the female, who will have a wider pelvic cavity. The skeleton does not move, but it is pulled in various directions by the muscles.

Nervous system

The nervous system collects information for the body and indicates what the body should do to survive in the present conditions. For instance, it is the nervous system that administers a bad feeling when the body is cold, and then sends a more positive message when a person warms up. These important messages are sent by the nerves, which vary in size and cover the entire body. The central nervous system is composed of the brain and spinal cord, and the peripheral nervous system is composed of the rest of the body, including those organs which a person does not voluntarily control. The peripheral nervous system is divided into sympathetic and parasympathetic systems, which counterbalance one another to allow for smooth function.

Lymphatic system

The lymphatic system is connected to the cardiovascular system through a network of capillaries. The lymphatic system filters out organisms that cause disease, controls the production of disease-fighting antibodies, and produces white blood cells. The lymphatic system also prevents body tissues from swelling by draining fluids from them. Two of the most important areas in this system are the right lymphatic duct and the thoracic duct. The right lymphatic duct moves the immunity-bolstering lymph fluid through the top half of the body, while the thoracic duct moves lymph throughout the lower half. The spleen, thymus, and lymph nodes all generate and store the chemicals which form lymph and which are essential to protecting the body from disease.

Digestive system

The digestive system is composed of organs that convert food into energy. This process begins with the teeth, which grind food into small particles that are easy to digest. Food is then carried through the pharynx (throat) and esophagus to the stomach. In the stomach, it is partially digested by strong acids and enzymes. From there, food passes through the small and large intestines, the rectum, and out through the anus. On this journey, it will be mixed with numerous chemicals so that it can be absorbed into the blood and lymph system. Some food will be converted into immediate energy, and some will be stored for future use; whatever cannot be used by the body will be expelled as waste.

Endocrine system

The endocrine system creates and secretes the hormones that accomplish a wide variety of tasks in the body. The endocrine system is made up of glands. These glands produce chemicals that regulate metabolism, growth, and sexual development. Glands release hormones directly into the bloodstream, where they are then directed to the various organs and tissues of the body. The endocrine system is generally considered to include the pituitary, thyroid, parathyroid, and adrenal glands, as well as the pancreas, ovaries, and testes. The endocrine system regulates its level of hormone production by monitoring the activity of hormones; when it senses that a certain hormone is active, it reduces or stops production of that hormone.

Dynamic systems theory

The dynamic systems theory of motor control is also referred to as the ecological theory or action systems theory. It posits that there is a dynamic (constantly changing) relationship between the individual and the environment. Within this relationship, the individual perceives various things and reacts to them either reflexively or voluntarily. Movements are the result of the integrated interaction of many smaller systems of biological, muscular, skeletal, neurological, and cardiorespiratory agents. This integration is known in dynamic systems theory as self-organization. This theory allows for the fact that minute adjustments are made constantly during the performance of a movement.

Reflex theory

The reflex theory of motor control states that movements are the result of rapid, automatic responses to stimuli in the individual's environment. According to this model, once the reflexes in the spinal cord are stimulated by the sensory receptors in the various parts of the body, the reflexes process the information and stimulate a muscular response. Over time, an individual becomes conditioned to respond in a similar way to common stimuli, and the individual's reactions become faster and more precise. This theory of motor control accounts for the consistency of movement, but it does not seem to make room for voluntary control of movement. Also, it does not allow for the minute adjustments that individuals seem to be able to make during the performance of a movement.

Ecological theory

The ecological theory of motor learning is based on the dynamic systems theory of motor control. It asserts that movement is the result of an interaction between the individual and the environment. This interaction is in large part based on the individual's sensory and perceptual skills. According to the ecological theory of motor learning, individuals are constantly scanning their environment, looking for ways to improve their performance of movements. Over time, individuals become better able to isolate the important information in the immediate environment and respond precisely and appropriately to it.

Schema theory

The schema theory was developed in part as a reaction to the closed-loop theory's inability to describe how new actions are performed, how motor programs are stored, and how feedback can be a part of even the shortest movements. As with closed-loop theory, there are two distinct memory states in schemata theory. These are called schemata (the plural of schema), and are abstract versions of commonly-performed movements. According to the schema theory, the body takes common actions and develops a motor program of the general features of common actions. Then, the body is able to use that abstracted program to perform any similar action. Also, the body will call up an appropriate program when it is called upon to perform a new action.

According to schema theory, performance of a given movement enables the body to make an abstract motor program of that movement so that it will be able to perform similar movements in the future. This is known as a generalizable motor program, and is composed of the invariant features of the movement: that is, the aspects of force and timing which do not vary in other performances of the motion. These features are scaled (or, in scientific

- 22 -

terms, parameterized) so that they can be applied to different cases. These specific requirements are covered in the motor program as variant features, such as which muscles are to be used.

In schema theory, the body has four sources from which it can gain information about how best to perform movements. The first source of information is called the initial conditions, and is the current status of the individual: his or her posture, position of limbs, etc. The response specifications identify the unique requirements of the response, for instance which direction it will take, which limbs will be involved, etc. During the performance of this response, the body will receive the sensory consequences, giving it an idea of the status of the movement. Finally, the response outcome will give the individual a sense of the end result of the movement. All of these sources of information are used by the two schemata: the recall schema, which organizes the specific programs needed for a response; and the recognition schema, which evaluates the outcome and makes any adjustments.

Information-processing theory

According to the information-processing theory of motor learning, an individual receives information in the form of stimuli from the outside world, selects a response, and then executes that response. During the reception of information, the individual must determine the nature of the stimulus. This will be more or less difficult depending on the familiarity of the stimulus, the number of competing stimuli, and the individual's personal characteristics. In the next phase, the individual determines what response, if any, is required. Then, the individual organizes the appropriate motor response. The resulting movement is known as the output. One of the criticisms of the information-processing theory is that it fails to account for the role of memory or anticipation in motor performance.

Hierarchical model

One theoretical model that scientists use to explain motor control is the hierarchical model. According to this model, there is a higher level in the motor system that adjusts according to feedback and a lower level that performs the commands of the higher. The lower level, like a low ranking soldier in battle, continues to execute a set of directions until the upper level gives a different order. This model is a hybrid of open-loop and closed-loop theory because it allows for both automatic and modifiable movements. Some studies have indicated that when learning a new task individuals begin by using a closed-loop motor control and gradually move to a more hierarchical style.

Inverted-U principle

Researchers have spent a great deal of time trying to determine how arousal and anxiety affect motor performance. One of the principles that have emerged from this research is known as the inverted–U principle. It asserts that an individual's performance will increase along with arousal level for a while, but if arousal continues to increase, then performance will begin to decline. The principle gets its name from the shape it takes when represented on a graph. The range of arousal in which an individual performs best is known as the zone of optimal functioning. Different individuals have different zones of optimal functioning depending on their trait anxiety: that is, their general disposition to consider situations as dangerous or threatening.

Reaction time

An individual's reaction time (RT) is the time observed between the presentation of a stimulus and the occurrence of the person's response. RT is especially important for the information-processing school of motor learning because it provides a direct measure of the time taken by a complete processing and response event. The number of stimuli presented is one of the common factors that influence RT: the fewer stimuli, the shorter RT is likely to be. RT will also tend to be shorter if there is good compatibility between stimulus and response, i.e., the desired response is appropriate to the situation and uncomplicated. Finally, RT is generally much shorter if the desired response is one that has been practiced and performed many times in the past.

Spatial and temporal anticipation

Researchers into motor performance have classified anticipation as being either spatial or temporal. When a person can predict what is likely to happen in a given situation, it is known as spatial anticipation. For example, if you are driving and the car in front of you brakes in advance of an intersection, you may suspect that the driver is going to turn. This is spatial anticipation. Temporal anticipation, on the other hand, occurs when an individual can predict when something is going to happen or the length of time that something will take to happen. This kind of information is useful in many kinds of settings, from gauging the speed of an oncoming object to anticipating the appearance of a certain stimulus. Most researchers, however, think that motor reaction is more dramatically improved by spatial anticipation than by temporal anticipation.

Hick's Law

Hick's Law was developed during the study of choice reaction time while investigating the amount of time it takes an individual to respond to an unanticipated stimulus. Basically, Hick's Law declares that choice reaction time will increase in proportion to the number of choices made available. This law, which seems a bit obvious on the surface, has become a fundamental principle of the study of motor performance because it has been able to establish such a clear predictive measure for reaction time. In fact, subsequent studies have shown that reaction time seems to increase by the same amount every time the number of choices is doubled. This law has found applications in everything from basketball to military tactics.

Muscles of the body

Head, neck, and shoulder

Some of the more precise and delicate muscles in the human body are found in the head, neck, and shoulders. The human face is covered with muscles that control facial expression. Also, the circular muscle surrounding the eye controls the lifting and shutting of the eyelid. One muscle that, despite its strength, is frequently forgotten is the tongue. The sterno-mastoid muscle turns the head to the side. The trapezius muscle connects the collarbone (clavicle) to the neck and raises the shoulder. Finally, the deltoid muscles are found on the outside of the shoulder and control the raising and lowering of the upper arm.

Upper torso

The human torso contains a number of large muscles that control the movements of the body's trunk and limbs. The pectoral muscles are found in the upper chest and contain both major and minor versions: the major pectoral muscle is responsible for moving the arm across the chest, while the minor pectoral muscle runs at a diagonal from the clavicle to the rib cage and assists the work of the major pectoral muscle. The serratus muscle runs diagonally around the side of the chest, and controls the movement of the scapula, or shoulder blade. The intercostal muscles run along the outside of the ribcage, and control the breathing. There are also a number of small muscles that surround and assist the motion of the scapula.

Arm

The deltoid muscle lies at the outside and top of the human arm, and controls the raising and lowering of the upper arm. The biceps is the muscle running the length of the front of the upper arm: it is responsible for bending the elbow. A large tendon connects the biceps to the arm near the elbow. There are a few muscles in the forearm, known as flexors, which help control the motions of the hands. Running the length of the back of the upper arm is the triceps muscle, which works in congress with the biceps to control the extension of the arm. The back of the forearm contains another set of hand flexors. The hands themselves contain a number of tiny muscles responsible for the precise movements of the fingers.

Lower torso

The muscles of the torso with which many people are most familiar are those that cover the stomach: the abdominal muscles. There are two sets of abdominal muscles: the oblique abdominals extend along a person's side and control the tilting or leaning of the upper torso, while the abdominal rectus muscles cover the front of the stomach and are responsible for flexing the trunk, raising the pelvis, and compressing the abdomen. All of these muscles, also serve to keep the internal organs in place and protected. On the back of the lower torso, the latissimus dorsi extend from the spine around to the side, tapering to a point just under the armpit. These muscles are responsible for moving the arm backwards.

Buttocks and leg muscles

The buttocks are covered by two sets of muscles, the gluteus maximus and gluteus minimus. The gluteus maximus, or "greater" gluteus, are found on the outside and control the extension of the thigh and the lifting of the body from a crouching position. The "lesser" gluteus muscles are found inside the gluteus maximus, and control the rotation of the thigh. The inside of the very upper leg is covered with a set of adductor muscles, which move the legs together; on the outside of the upper leg lie the abductor muscles, which bring the legs apart. The quadriceps extend along the front of the upper leg and extend and raise the leg. The sartorius muscle flexes the lower leg and runs from the hip diagonally to the inside of the knee. A long muscle on the front of the lower leg flexes the ankle and raises the foot: it is called the anterior tibial. The hamstring muscles run along the back of the upper leg and control the extension of the lower leg; the gastrocnemius and soleus muscles make up the calf.

Skeletal

Skeletal muscle is the striated tissue that is attached to the skeleton and, through contractions, causes all of the movements of the body. Muscle tissue is made up of long molecules of protein, mainly actin and myosin. The various strands are combined in dozens of different forms to create the various muscles of the body. Whenever one of these muscle fibers is stimulated by a neuron, it contracts as much as it can. Therefore, muscles that need to perform precise and delicate operations have a much larger ratio of neurons to muscle fibers, because they need to more closely regulate the amount of force created by the contraction. The muscles of the calf, for instance, have far fewer neurons per muscle fiber than do the muscles controlling the fingers.

Bones of the body

Head
The human skull, often thought to be a single unit, is actually composed of a few different bones. The top of the skull, the bone which covers most of the brain, is called the cranium. The part of the skull covering the top of the face, down to the upper jaw, is the maxilla. The lower jaw is called the mandible. On the back of the head, the bottom of the cranium is slightly thicker at the back of the head; this feature is called the occipital ridge and allows more muscles to be attached. Humans also have what is known as the mastoid process, a group of structures at the hinge of the jaw that allow the motions of the jaw to be powerful and controlled. The human cranium has two suture lines, running perpendicular to one another along the back of the head, which indicate where the cranial capacity of humans has adjusted to the increasing size of the brain.

Spine
The spine is perhaps the most complex skeletal structure in the human body. It connects to the cranium at the occipital ridge, and then extends all the way down to the coccyx, a small pointed bone at the base of the pelvis. The top seven vertebrae are called the cervical vertebrae, and are found between the occipital ridge and the top of the rib cage. The next twelve vertebrae are known as the thoracic vertebrae, and extend from the top to the bottom of the rib cage, which they anchor. Below these are the five lumbar vertebrae, which curve inward slightly to support the upper body. The spine connects with the pelvis at the sacroiliac joint, below which lie the sacrum and coccyx in succession.

Upper torso
The bone commonly known as the collarbone is the clavicle; it extends from one shoulder to the other and is connected in the middle to the sternum, a long bone extending down the front of the torso. At the bottom of the sternum lies the xiphoid process, which helps to protect the vital organs beneath the rib cage. The bones frequently referred to as the shoulder blades are clinically known as scapula. These are large, triangular bones that are found behind the shoulders and have a great deal of surface area for the attachment of muscles. The human rib cage is made up of twelve bones on each side, extending from the spine around the sides to the front of the body. There is no truth to the notion that males and females have a different number of ribs.

Hips and legs
The spine connects to the pelvis at the lumbo-sacral joint. The pelvis, which is broader in a woman so that she can bear children, creates a sort of bowl for the visceral organs of the lower torso. At its front and bottom is the pubic arch. The pelvis is connected to the upper bones of the legs, the femurs, by a ball-and-socket hip joint. The femurs extend down to the hinge joint at the knee, which is covered by the patella or kneecap. The lower leg, below the knee, is made up of two bones: the fibula is the narrow bone on the outside of the leg, while the tibia is slightly thicker and runs along the inside. These bones are connected at

the ankle to the foot in a complex joint structure. The bones of the feet and toes are known as the tarsals, metatarsals, and phalanges.

Arms and hands
The upper arm is connected to the clavicle by a large ball-and-socket joint. The bone that extends from this joint to the elbow is called the humerus. At the elbow, the humerus is connected to the radius and ulna by the elbow joint. In an arm extended so that the palm is up, the radius is the bone that runs along the outside or thumb side of the arm and the ulna is the longer bone that runs along the inside. These bones connect to the complex network of bones that make up the wrist; the complicated nature of the wrist joint allows for the amazing dexterity of the hand. The carpal are those small bones at the base of the hand that connect to the wrist joint. Each hand then has five metacarpals that connect the carpals to the fingers. These are the bones that can be felt through the back of the hand. The bones that make up the fingers are known as phalanges.

Long bones
Long bones, such as the femur, are composed of three parts. These sections develop independently but become fused into one as the individual reaches adulthood. The central shaft of a bone is called the diaphysis, and the two knobby ends are the epiphyses. The hollowness of bones makes them lighter and sturdier. The epiphysis contains an alveolar structure, in which fibers are arranged to best handle the stress on the bone. The hollow diaphysis contains bone marrow, where blood cells are produced. On the outside of a bone is a membrane called the periosteum, which carries blood vessels and assists in repairing bones that have fractured.

Body part movements

Trunk
The mobile vertebral column allows a person to move his or her torso in a number of different directions. Anterior flexion is a movement in which the person leans his head forward and thus stretches the back. Leaning back is called posterior extension. Bending to either side is referred to as lateral flexion or side-bending. The trunk can also be twisted on the pelvis, a motion called right or left rotation. The range of movement varies within the back depending on the shape of the vertebrae (lower vertebrae are largest and least mobile), the thickness of the intervertebral discs, and the degree to which the thoracic vertebrae are inhibited by the ribs. The movements of the trunk should not be confused with those in which the back stays straight while the hips move.

Transverse plane
The transverse (or horizontal) plane of movement divides the body into upper and lower halves, known professionally as the superior and inferior halves. Any movement that takes place in the transverse plane and moves the body outward is called a lateral rotation. For example, twisting the leg so that the toes point outwards , would be called a lateral rotation of the hip. A movement that brings a part of the body inward is called a medial rotation. There are a couple of special terms that refer to the rotation of the forearm: pronation, in which the palm of the hand faces backward, and supination, in which the palm is pointed forward .

Frontal plane

The frontal plane, also called the coronal plane, is any plane that runs perpendicular to the median plane, which divides the body into right and left halves. The frontal plane divides the body into a front and back, which is clinically referred to as anterior and posterior. Any movement in a frontal plane that moves a part of the body towards the median plane is called an adduction. Crossing the legs, for instance, can be referred to as an adduction of the hip. A movement that takes any part of the body away from the median plane is referred to as an abduction; extending the arm away from the body, for instance, is an abduction of the shoulder. For the torso and neck, a movement in the lateral plane away from the median plane is called lateral flexion or side-bending. In fingers and toes, the reference is the middle finger or toe, and adduction and abduction refer to this axis rather than to the median plane.

Arm

The excellent mobility of the scapula and the versatility of the arm muscles combine to allow a variety of movements. When the arm is raised so that it is perpendicular to the ground in front of the person, it is called anterior flexion. Raising an arm parallel to the ground on the side is called lateral abduction. Moving the arm back from its position resting at the side is called posterior extension, and has a much smaller range than most arm movements. Bringing the arm from a raised position closer to the body is known as medial adduction. When the arm is then moved behind the body, it is a combination of adduction and extension. The rotation of the humerus on its axis, for instance with the elbow bent and held to the person's side, can be called either medial or lateral rotation, depending on the direction of rotation.

Scapula

The scapula is located just behind the back of the rib cage, although it is not connected to it. Instead, the scapula is suspended by a complex network of ligaments and muscles, and can therefore move in a number of different ways. Raising the scapula (and the shoulder) is called moving superiorly, or elevation. Inferior movement of the scapula, also called depression, occurs when the shoulder moves downward. When the shoulder moves forward, it is called moving laterally. Lateral movement of the shoulder can also be called protraction or abduction. When the shoulder is moved back, it is known as medial movement, retraction, or adduction. The shoulder can also be rotated so that the inferior or bottom side moves toward the midline or away from the midline.

Wrist

The wrist is capable of a variety of movements. When the wrist is bent so that it is closer to the anterior surface of the forearm, the movement is known as flexion of the wrist. The posterior surface of the hand and forearm approach one another in extension of the wrist. The wrist can also tilt the hand from side to side. When the hand is moved so that the thumb approaches the radius, it is known as abduction. When the hand is moved so that the little finger is closer to the ulna, it is called adduction. The range of motion for adduction is greater than that for abduction. Because of the combinations of muscles involved, adduction is usually combined with flexion and abduction with extension.

Elbow

The elbow is capable of four distinct movements. A movement that decreases the angle between the upper arm and forearm is known as flexion. When flexion is active (that is, when the muscles are contracted), the movement is limited by the contact made between the muscles. Passive flexion has a greater range of motion. Extension of the elbow is any movement that increases the angle between the upper arm and forearm. The upper limit of such an angle is 180 degrees. When the lower arm is rotated so that the palm faces down, and the radius crosses over the ulna, it is known as probation. When the radius and ulna are parallel, and the palm faces up or forward, it is known as supination of the elbow.

Hip
When the upper leg is raised in front of the body, it is known as hip flexion. The range of motion for hip flexion is greater if the knee is also bent. Any motion that increases the angle between the anterior surface of the upper leg and trunk is known as extension. The body has a much smaller range of motion for extension than for flexion. The ballet move known as the grande arabesque combines leg extension with lateral rotation of the hip, in which the toes point away from the medial plane. Medial rotation of the hip involves moving the leg so that the toes point inward towards the medial plane. In adduction of the hip, the thigh is brought towards or past the medial plane; in abduction of the hip, the thigh travels away from the medial plane.

Finger
The fingers, because of their multiple joints, are capable of some complex movements. Still, all of these motions can be arranged in a few basic categories. When any part of a finger is raised so that it is above the palm when the palm is facing up, it is known as flexion of the finger. When the finger is stretched back so that the angle between finger and palm is increased, it is known as extension. Of course, the hand is not capable of extending fingers at much more than 180 degrees to the hand. When a finger is extended away from the medial line (in the hand the medial line is considered to be an imaginary line running from the base of the hand through the middle finger) it is known as abduction; movement towards the medial line is known as adduction.

Knee
The movements of which the knee joint is capable are fairly limited. Knee flexion occurs when the angle formed by the posterior thigh and leg decrease. In active flexion the muscles of the leg are contracted, , and the range of motion is considerably smaller than when they are relaxed during passive flexion. Also, the knee's range of motion is greater when the hip joint is flexed. Extension of the knee is simply movement that increases the angle made by the posterior leg and thigh, and hyperextension is any movement that increases this angle above 180 degrees. The knee is capable of a very slight bit of rotation. In medial rotation, the front of the knee moves counter-clockwise, and in lateral rotation it moves clockwise.

Pelvis
The descriptions of the various movements that can be achieved by the pelvis assume that the femur remains in a fixed location. When the pelvis is titled forward, so that the lower back is curved and the abdomen protrudes, it is known as anteversion of the pelvis. The opposite move, in which the pelvis tilts back and the lower back straightens, is called retroversion. The pelvis can also shift so that it channels all of a person's weight to one femur. For example, when a person stands on one leg, movement on the side bearing the weight is called inferolateral, while movement on the other side is called superomedial. Finally, the pelvis is able to perform a limited medial or lateral rotation, a motion incorporated in hula dancing.

Foot

The movements of the foot can be described generally, although often the terms used will refer to movement involving only a particular part. Dorsiflexion is a tilting of the foot upward, so that the angle between the superior surface of the foot and the anterior surface of the leg is decreased. Plantar flexion, also known as extension, is the opposite motion, in which the toes are pointed down. In abduction of the foot, the toes are pointed away from the medial plane; in adduction of the foot, the toes point toward the medial plane. Finally, eversion of the foot occurs when the sole of the foot is directed away from the medial plane, and an inversion of the foot occurs when the sole is directed toward the medial plane.

Muscular movement

When discussing muscular movement, health professionals use a few different terms. An agonist is any muscle that is responsible for the action being discussed. For instance, the agonist responsible for the bending of the elbow is the biceps. An antagonist is any muscle that opposes the movement of the agonist. A fixator is any movement that locks the body in a certain position, thus giving the other muscles a steady foundation on which to work. A prime mover is a muscle or group of muscles that is primarily responsible for the movement of a joint. Finally, a synergist is a muscle that supports, enhances, or guides the actions of the prime mover.

Mechanical factors

Obviously, the human body has certain limitations within which the motor system must work. The forces that the body generates in movement are the result either of the contraction of the muscles or the elasticity of the tendons. These forces are often referred to as being active and passive, respectively. Muscles have the most potential for active force when they are extended; at this point, the muscle fibers are all lined up and capable of contracting. As for the force generated by the elasticity of the tendons, this may be considered in two different ways. The tendons that extend off the ends of the muscles are said to be serial elastic components, while the tendons that run alongside the muscles are referred to as parallel elastic components.

Stability

In order to reach maximum effectiveness in movement, one needs to understand some of the basic principles of body mechanics. One of these basic principles is stability. In general, an individual will be more or less stable depending on the area of his or her supporting base. This is why, for instance, linemen in football prepare for contact by lowering themselves and placing at least one hand on the ground. A very stable stance, however, may inhibit sudden movement. In the case of the lineman, this is not a problem as he knows in which direction he will have to move first; in other sports, however, it may be necessary to sacrifice a bit of stability for mobility. A wrestler, for instance, must stand a bit more upright in order to be prepared for an attack from any side.

Acceleration

Acceleration is the measure of the rate of change in velocity over a certain period of time. Since acceleration is a vector, it can be caused by a change in speed, direction, or both. When acceleration is negative (the object loses velocity) it is often referred to as deceleration. Acceleration is typically calculated by finding the difference between the starting and ending velocities and then dividing by the length of time in which this change was made. Typically, acceleration is measured in meters per second squared (SI) or feet per second squared (English units).

Torque

Torque is the force that causes something to rotate. Torque is calculated as the product of the force applied and the distance of the force from the axis of rotation. In other words, torque will be greater the farther away it is from the axis, if the same amount of force is applied. As an example, consider a door: it will be easier to rotate on its axis (hinge) if it is pushed from the side away from its connection to the door frame. The same principle applies to many other things, among them automobile engines and the human body. Torque is generally measured in either Newton-meters (SI) or foot-pounds (English units).

Force

Force is simply the push or pull that is exerted on an object. Force is reported as a vector; that is, it has both a magnitude and a direction. The effect of force will be, in part, dependent on the point of the application of the force and the line of action of the force. The point of application is the precise location where the force is exerted on the object. The line of action is an imaginary line running from the point where the force is exerted out in the direction of the force. Force is calculated by multiplying mass and acceleration. Force is typically measured in Newtons (SI) or pounds (English).

The amount of force a body can produce is closely related to the stability of that body. The more stable the individual's foundation, the more force he or she will be able to exert. In order to maximize force, one should try to allow the strongest muscles to do the most work; this is one of the reasons health professionals recommend lifting heavy objects with the legs rather than the back. Generally it is recommended that one always channels lines of force along the spinal column and major bones of the body, rather than at an angle to these structures. In other words, one should avoid exerting unnecessary pressure on the spinal column by lifting things at an angle. Heavy objects should be carried as close to the body as possible, and the base of support should always be broad.

Mass

The mass of an object is simply the quantity of matter in it. Every object has a mass, which remains constant even if other masses are added to it. Mass should not be confused with weight, which is dependent on the amount of gravitational pressure that is exerted on the object. An object will have the same mass on earth as it would have on the moon or floating in outer space. The mass of an object will indicate the amount of force needed to move it: the greater the object's mass, the more force will be needed to overcome its stationary inertia. Mass is measured in either kilograms (SI) or slugs (English units).

Center of gravity and stability

The stability of an individual can be greatly improved if he or she simply lowers his or her center of gravity. The center of gravity, otherwise known as the center of mass, should be perpendicular to the ground along the same line as the geometric center of the base if the individual wants to have maximum stability. That is, an individual will be less stable as he or she moves the center of gravity away from the midpoint of his or her stance. In some cases, this is a good idea: runners, for instance, often lean in the direction they will be running in order to gain an advantage. Indeed, the process of walking is nothing more than continuously moving he center of gravity forward and "catching" oneself with an alternate leg.

Friction

Friction is the force created by an object's contact with the ground as it moves. Specifically, friction is the force exerted by the ground which tends to slow down the movement of the object. If there were no friction, objects on which a force has been exerted would move forever at the same speed. The force of the friction depends on the weight of the moving object and the surface of the ground. Very smooth ground surfaces are not likely to create much friction, whereas rough, uneven surfaces will quickly bring an object to a halt.

Centripetal force

Centripetal force is any force exerted on an object that is moving in a circle. A centripetal force creates centripetal acceleration, which is any change in velocity that occurs during circular motion. Velocity is normally calculated as a vector, which has both magnitude and direction, but in the case of circular motion the direction of the object is constantly changing. Contrary to intuition, when an object is in circular motion the centripetal force is towards the center of the circle. This becomes evident if a person remembers what it was like to be swung in a circle as a child: the faster the swing, the more pull (centripetal force) The child feels.

Inertia

Inertia is the term used in physics to describe any object's resistance to a change in velocity. The greater the inertia, the greater is the object's resistance to an increase or decrease in velocity. This simply means that more force is required to change the velocity of an object that has greater inertia. The moment of inertia (also called rotational inertia) is an object's resistance to a change in its velocity of rotation. The particular rotational inertia of an object depends on its mass, shape, and how the mass is distributed through the object. A football, for instance, is much more resistant to rotating end-over-end than it is to spinning laterally.

Weight

Weight should never be confused with mass. Though weight is proportional to mass, it will vary depending on the gravitational force in which the object is located. Therefore, weight can be found by multiplying the mass by the gravitational constant. On the surface of the earth, the gravitational constant is 9.8 meters per second, or 32 feet per second, which is the rate at which objects will accelerate when dropped. Weight is measured in either Newtons (SI) or pounds (English units). Weight is a vector, and so must have both a magnitude and a direction, although the direction will almost always be straight down, towards the center of the earth.

Momentum

Momentum is the tendency of an object in motion to continue moving. Momentum is calculated as a vector, meaning that it has both a magnitude and a direction. Momentum is calculated by multiplying mass and velocity, so two objects traveling at the same speed will have different momentums if they have different masses, and two objects of the same mass will have different momentums if they are traveling at different velocities. The greater the momentum of an object, the greater the force required to stop it.

Velocity

Velocity is simply the measure of the speed and direction of an object. It is calculated by dividing distance by time. A simple equation for velocity indicates that the final distance should be subtracted from the initial distance, and the difference divided by the length of time taken to cover that distance. So, if an individual runs from the ten yard-line to the fifty yard-line on a football field in five seconds, his velocity would be eight yards per second. Velocity is typically measured in either meters per second (SI) or feet per second (English units), although it can be expressed in any units of length and time.

After-contraction phenomenon

The after-contraction phenomenon is the increase in force of movement that seems to occur when the neuromuscular system becomes excited. In other words, the body's tendency to perform a certain movement lingers after that movement has been performed for a long time or with a great deal of effort. One way to experience this phenomenon is to press against a wall with one arm for a minute. After the minute is up, you should feel some tendency within the arm to rise up again. Many scientists believe that the after-contraction phenomenon occurs in many areas of daily life, and that it indicates the body's ability to quickly accustom itself to changes in the outside world and new motor patterns.

Tonic neck response

Over a series of studies, scientists were able to demonstrate a clear link between movement in the neck and seemingly unrelated movement in the limbs. Specifically, when the head is turned to one side, the arm on that side will tend to extend, while the opposite arm will tend to flex. This phenomenon was long observed in infants, but until recently, scientists had not noticed that it continues to occur in a somewhat more infrequent form among adults. Subsequent studies have shown that people are able to produce more force when they turn their head towards the limb that they are using. This runs contrary to the former idea that maximum force could only be generated in another part of the body when the head was facing forward.

Neurons

Neurons may vary considerably in size and speed, but they all operate in a similar manner. Neurons operate on an all-or-nothing basis; that is, they either fire or do not, and will not fire more intensely because of a stronger stimulus. . For this reason, neurons are said to have a threshold, which is a minimum amount of stimulus required for function. The basic reflex exercise conducted during a medical exam is a good example of this function: when the knee is struck with the rubber hammer, the impulse must travel up the leg to the spinal cord, where it crosses from the sensory neurons to the motor neurons through a junction known as a synapse. The amount of time between contact and the resulting action, a slight contraction of the quadriceps, is known as the synaptic delay.

Neurons and muscular movement

In order for the nervous system to determine what movement is appropriate, it must be able to gather accurate information from the neurons, the single cells that make up a nerve. Neurons may be very small and round, or they may extend as fibers for several feet. Sensory neurons are those that carry messages of heat, cold, pressure, smell, and so on, to the brain. The neurons that carry messages from the central nervous system to the various muscle systems are called motor neurons. The major nerves of the body contain both sensory and motor neurons. There is a third type of neuron, the internuncial, which connect and coordinate the various parts of the central nervous system. Glial cells are those that provide structure to the nervous system but do not otherwise assist in its function.

Mechanical strain on bones

There are several kinds of mechanical stress routinely exerted on bones. First, bones must endure the gravitational stress of holding up the rest of the body. The bones of the back, feet, and legs are particularly taxed by this effort. Next, bones are subjected to stress when they move against resistance, as for instance, when a heavy object is lifted. In these cases, the bones are serving as levers and points of attachment for the muscles. There are also cases in which bones receive stress from the effort of holding up a heavy object, , such as when a person holds on to a heavy suitcase. This gravitational pressure from an external object is known as traction.

Anatomical reference terms

There are a few basic reference terms used in discussing anatomy with which every physical educator should be familiar. Lateral means further to the median plane, while medial means closer to the median plane. Anterior means facing forward or found in the front, while posterior means facing towards the back or located there. Superior means facing towards the top or located there, while inferior means facing or located at the bottom. Superficial means external, or close to the outside of the body, while deep refers to things inside the body. Finally, the term proximal means closer to the trunk or to some other major joint, while distal means further from the trunk or from some other major joint.

Joints

In an ellipsoid joint, the oval-shaped section of one bone fits into an elliptical cavity in another. This connection allows for movement in two planes. The wrist is the classic example of an ellipsoid joint. In a pivot joint, a pointed or rounded area in one bone fits into a ring-like structure on another. In a pivot joint such as the joint connecting the base of the spine and pelvis, rotation is the only possible movement. In a saddle joint, both of the connecting surfaces are shaped like saddles, and fit together snugly. In a saddle joint, movement can occur in two planes. The best example of a saddle joint is the connection of the thumb to the hand.

The body has several different types of joint to allow for different kinds of movement. In a ball-and-socket joint, one of the connecting surfaces is rounded and the other concave. As with all joints, a ball-and-socket joint is filled with fluid to allow the smooth movement of the two parts. In a hinge joint, the convex surface of one bone fits against the concave surface of the other, and is arranged so that motion can only occur in one plane. An elbow is an example of a hinge joint. In a gliding joint, both the connecting surfaces are basically flat, and so movement is very limited. The intercarpal joints connecting the mass of bones at the base of the hand is an example of a gliding joint.

Flexibility

A person's flexibility is his or her range of motion around particular joints. An individual's flexibility will vary according to age, gender, and posture. Some individuals may be less flexible because of bone spurs, and some individuals may be less flexible because they are overweight. Typically, an individual's flexibility will increase through childhood until adolescence, at which point joint mobility slows and diminishes for the rest of the individual's life. Muscles and the connective tissue around them (tendons and ligaments) will contract and become tighter if they are not used to their potential. Lack of flexibility can lead to a buildup of tension in the muscles and can increase the risk of injury during exercise.

Joint capsule

A joint capsule is a sort of sleeve that surrounds a joint, preventing any loss of fluid and binding together the ends of the bones in the joint. The outside of this sleeve is made of a tough material, while the inside is more soft and loose so that movement is not impeded. Joint capsules are often especially strong in areas in which movement should be discouraged; for instance, there is a strong joint capsule section on the back of the knee, which in part makes it difficult for the lower leg to bend forward. The fibers of the outer joint capsule are known as ligaments, and the inside of the joint capsule is called the synovial membrane. The synovial membrane secretes a fluid that keeps the joint lubricated and removes debris.

Cartilage

The areas of bones that are close to joints are covered in a shiny connective tissue known as cartilage. Cartilage supports the joint structure and protects the fragile bone tissue underneath. Cartilage is susceptible to injury because it is subject to gravitational pressure as well as pressure born of joint movement itself. Long-term stress to cartilage can result in rheumatoid arthritis and osteoarthritis. There are no blood vessels in cartilage; nutrients are delivered by the synovial fluid, and from nearby blood vessels. Cartilage contains a huge number of spongy fibers because it needs to absorb a great deal of shock. Especially resilient cartilage, known as fibrocartilage, is found between the vertebrae and in the knees, among other places.

Pelvis

The pelvis is a large, roughly cylindrical structure of several bones. The pelvis bears all of the weight of the upper body, and passes this weight on to the femurs through a pair of ball-and-socket joints. The pelvis must also absorb the shocks that come from the lower body during running or jumping. The pelvis is divided into a superior and inferior portion by a horizontal plane across the middle. The pelvis also has three hip bones: the ilium, ischium, and pubis. Once these bones are fully fused in adulthood, they interact with the top of the femur. The shape of the pelvis can vary considerably between individuals, especially in the shape of the pelvic inlet, the cavity separating the inferior and superior regions of the pelvis.

Ligaments

Ligaments are dense bundles of fibers running parallel to one another from one bone in a joint to another. Ligaments are a part of the joint capsule, although they may also connect to other nearby bones that are not part of the joint. Ligaments are not like muscles; they cannot contract. Instead, ligaments passively strengthen and support the joints by absorbing some of the tension of movement. Ligaments do contain nerve cells which are sensitive to position and speed of movement, and so ligaments can hurt. One function of this pain is to alert the person to an unnatural or dangerous movement of the joint. Ligaments may also be strained or rupture if they are placed under unnecessary or violent stress.

Muscle attachment

In most cases, a muscle is attached to two different bones. In a movement of the body, the origin bone is fixed in some way and the other bone, known as the insertion bone, moves because of a muscle contraction. Occasionally, health professionals will refer to the origin bone as the proximal bone. Muscles may be attached to bones by means of tendons or muscle fibers.

Muscle tissue

Muscle tissue is made up of bundles of fibers which are held in position and separated by various partitions. These partitions range from large (deep fascia, epimysium) to small (perimysium, endomysium), and often extend beyond the length of the muscle and form tendons connecting to a bone. Each muscle cell is extremely long and has a large amount of nuclei. Every muscle cell contains a number of smaller units called sarcomeres; these contain thick filaments of the protein myosin and thin filaments of the protein actin. Muscle tissue contracts when a nerve stimulates the muscle and the thin filaments compress within the sarcomere, causing a general muscle contraction.

Good nutrition

In order to aid Americans in eating a healthy diet, the United States Department of Agriculture (USDA) has developed a set of Recommended Daily Allowances that indicate how much of a certain food a person should eat every day. They have also issued a number of guidelines to help with dietary choices. To ensure good nutrition, the USDA encourages people to eat a wide variety of foods, including plenty of fruits, vegetables, and whole grains. Sugar, salt, and alcoholic beverages should be consumed in moderation. A healthy diet will be low in saturated fat and cholesterol because these increase the risk of heart disease and cancer. Maintaining a healthy weight throughout life reduces the risk of high blood pressure, heart disease, and stroke.

Nutrients

Every human body needs the same nutrients to build bones, muscles, and other tissues and to give the body energy. These nutrients are proteins, carbohydrates, fats, vitamins, minerals, and water. Nutrients are converted into whatever the body needs through the process of digestion. During the digestive process, each organ either mechanically or chemically breaks down food into molecular units that are small enough to be absorbed by the cells of the body. There have been thousands of experiments conducted to determine the right amount of nutrients for a particular population. Epidemiological studies are those that focus on the diet of a particular group of people, while metabolic studies are those that consider the processing of a particular nutrient during animal or human metabolism.

Kinds of nutrients

There are six kinds of nutrients: proteins, carbohydrates, fats, vitamins, minerals, and water. Proteins, known as the building blocks of the body, are used to grow, maintain, and replace the cells of the body. Carbohydrates are the organic compounds that supply the body with glucose. Simple carbohydrates are referred to as sugars, and complex carbohydrates are called starches. Fats provide energy to the body and help to transport certain vitamins. Minerals are any naturally occurring inorganic elements that are needed in very small amounts so that the body can perform some function. Water is, perhaps, the most overlooked nutrient. Water is crucial for promoting good digestion and for maintaining body fluids and regulating temperature.

United States Department of Agriculture recommendations

Vegetables
The USDA recommends that individuals have between three and five servings of vegetables every day. Vegetables are low in fat and high in fiber, and they provide essential vitamins and minerals. Numerous studies have shown a link between vegetables and a diminished risk of almost every kind of cancer. A single serving of a vegetable can be as little as one cup of a raw, leafy vegetable (like spinach or kale), a half-cup of any other vegetable, three-quarters of a cup of vegetable juice, or one potato or ear of corn. It is best to eat a wide variety of vegetables. Crucifers (winter squash, carrots, broccoli, cabbage, etc.) are high in fiber and vitamins, whereas dark green vegetables like collards and mustard greens are a good source of calcium and iron.

Breads, cereals, rice and pasta
The USDA recommends that Americans have between six and eleven servings a day of breads, cereal, rice, and pasta. These foods are considered to be fundamental to a healthy diet because they contain plenty of simple and complex carbohydrates, the latter of which contain plenty of vitamins and minerals. Complex carbohydrates ought to represent about half of an individual's daily consumption. A typical serving from this group could be a slice of toast, or a half-cup of pasta or rice. Brown rice and whole grain breads and pasta are considered to be the best way to get all the nutrients from a serving. Increasing the daily fiber intake can be achieved by eating whole grain bread or fiber-enriched white bread.

Meat, poultry, fish, dried beans, eggs, and nuts
The USDA recommends that every person have between two and four servings of meat, poultry, fish, dry beans, eggs, and nuts. All of these foods are excellent sources of protein,

which is required to meet the body's need to build muscle and bone. These foods also have a high supply of phosphorus, zinc, iron, vitamin B-6, and niacin. One serving from this category may consist of as little as two or three ounces of lean meat, fish, poultry, an egg, or a half cup of dry beans. It is a good idea to eat a wide variety of foods from this category because many are high in fat. Fish, in particular, is a healthy alternative to beef or pork, as it is extremely high in protein and loaded with vitamins and minerals.

Fruit
The USDA recommends that every person eat between two and four servings of fruit every day. Fruits, along with whole grains and vegetables, are a good source of vitamins, minerals, and fiber. They have also been proven to be a good safeguard against cancer; in fact, the risk of developing cancer is twice as high among individuals who consume very little produce compare with those who meet the recommended guidelines. A serving of fruit may be as little as a medium apple, banana, or orange, a half-cup of sliced or canned fruit, or three-quarters of a cup of fresh fruit juice. Since fruits require different digestive acids than most foods, they are most easily digested when they are consumed on an empty stomach or before the rest of a meal.

Fats, oils, and sweets
The USDA does not recommend a daily serving amount for fats, oils, and sweets; the guidelines state that these foods should be consumed sparingly. Most items that fall into this category have calories but virtually no nutritional value. These foods may be found as additives to other foods (as in the case of jelly or sweeteners) or as foods in their own right (candy and cookies, for example). Sometimes, processed foods contain high amounts of these foods. Ketchup, "low-fat" yogurt, and soft drinks all have outrageous amounts of either sugar or fat. There is no benefit to consuming these foods, and the body may actually be undermined by excessive consumption of them.

Milk, yogurt, and cheese
The USDA recommends that each individual consumes two or three servings of milk, yogurt, and cheese every day. All milk products are high in calcium, riboflavin, protein, and vitamins A and B-12. Care is necessary when selecting foods from this group, as many dairy products are very high in fat. A serving in this category can be an eight ounce glass of milk, a cup of plain yogurt, one and a half ounces of cheese, or one tablespoon of cheese spread. Obviously, it is healthier to drink a glass of skim milk than to eat a tablespoon of cheese spread to reach the daily ration of dairy. Cottage cheese is an especially healthy way to get the right amount of calcium without eating too much fat.

Personal weight-loss plan

There is no diet that is appropriate for every person, so dieters need to learn how to determine the dietary choices that are right for them. It is important when making dietary decisions to consider what kind of eater you are. For instance, if you are the kind of person who enjoys eating but perhaps does it too much, you should try to catalog all of your consumption and pinpoint some areas where you can make changes. If you eat when you are in a particular emotional state (like depression, loneliness, or anxiety), it is good to treat the causes of this mood in order to treat the eating problem. If you are the kind of person who tends to eat small meals but be constantly eating during the day, you should try to ensure that you snack on fruits and vegetables rather than high-fat and carbohydrate items.

Losing weight

It is extremely difficult to lose much weight and keep it off; in fact, 95% of the approximately eight million individuals who diet every year gain the weight back within five years. Losing a great deal of weight quickly can be just as destructive to health as obesity. For some severely obese individuals, the best way to lose weight may be a medical procedure like gastric bypass surgery or cognitive therapy. Others may need simply to reduce caloric intake and increase their activity level. Many people find it helpful to lose weight in partnership with other people, and many organizations exist to provide social support to dieters. In any case, attempts to lose weight should always be done in consultation with health professionals.

Food preparation and medical hygiene

There are a few basic hygiene habits that every individual should practice when preparing food or performing basic medical procedures. Always clean off the areas where food will be prepared, and wash your hands after touching any uncooked foods. Do not use the same tools to prepare different foods. Always refrigerate foods before and after they are used. Label stored food to indicate when it was produced. Dispose of any uneaten food that cannot be stored. When performing basic medical procedures, always use sterile bandages and any necessary protective clothing, like masks, gloves, or eyewear. Always make sure any medical waste, like used bandages, is disposed of securely.

Food-borne infections

Every year, about 9000 people die in the United States from some kind of food poisoning. These infections usually are manifested in nausea, diarrhea, and vomiting, occurring anywhere from 12 hours to 5 days after the infection. Salmonella is a common form of food infection; it is found in undercooked chicken, eggs, and processed meats. E. coli bacteria, which can come from undercooked or inadequately washed food, can be very dangerous. The FDA has strict regulations on the preparation of meat to prevent these bacteria from reaching the consumer. Another less common but very dangerous form of food-borne infection is botulism. Botulism is generally derived from improper canning practices.

Food additives

Additives are any substances added to a food that alter its color, taste, consistency, or storage time. Additives are extremely common in American food production; in fact, the average citizen consumes about 160 pounds of additives a year, most of them sweeteners. These additives may have benefits: many delay the growth of mold or harmful bacteria. However, some additives may be dangerous to the health of the consumer. Nitrites, which are used in bacon, sausage, and other meats to prevent spoilage, are capable of combining with other substances in the body to create cancer cells. Sulfites, which are used to prevent browning, may cause a severe allergic reaction for some individuals. The Food and Drug Administration has begun strictly regulating the use of food additives.

Food allergies

Every person has heard horror stories of fatal food allergies, but the actual incidence (risk) of these deaths is not high enough to cause particular concern. Whenever a person has a severe allergic reaction to a particular food, it is because the body has decided that that food is harmful and is trying to fight against it. Milk, eggs, seafood, wheat, soybeans, chocolate, and peanuts are all known to cause allergic reactions in many people. The symptoms of a particular food allergy may include sneezing, nausea, hives, dizziness, or headache. Since these symptoms can emerge up to 72 hours after the food is consumed, it is sometimes difficult to determine what food is at fault. If you feel you have a severe allergy, you should seek the advice of a doctor immediately.

Food poisoning

There are a few steps that students should know to decrease their risk of catching a food-borne infection. First, they should always clean their food thoroughly. This includes washing produce and cleaning all cooking equipment with extremely hot water. They should drink only pasteurized milk. They should avoid eating raw eggs, even in salad dressings, as these may contain Salmonella. The most important safeguard to students' health is eating only well-cooked meat. In general, foods should either be heated to a minimum of 140º or stored at temperatures colder than 40º (Fahrenheit scale). Leftover food should be refrigerated as soon as possible and consumed within the next few days.

Smart food buyer

With the constant swirl of competing nutritional products on the market today, the average consumer may find it somewhat overwhelming to make the right purchases. There are a few basic tips that can help any student become a more savvy food buyer. First, students should be ready to seek the advice of a doctor or nutritionist before they make any major alterations to their diet. Any diets that base their results on hair analysis can be immediately dismissed, because analyzing diet this way is impossible. Similarly, any diet that recommends enormous doses of one or two nutrients should be avoided; mega-doses of any one vitamin or mineral can be dangerous. If an advertisement relies solely on the testimonials of nonprofessionals and offers no medical evidence, it should probably be dismissed.

USDA Food Guide Pyramid

In 1992, the USDA introduced the Food Guide Pyramid as a handy illustration of proper dietary guidelines. There are five components to the food pyramid, and the body requires them in varying amounts. The food groups and the daily requirements for each are as follows: bread, cereal, rice and pasta (6-11 servings); vegetables (3-5 servings); fruits (2-4 servings); milk, yogurt, and cheese (2-3); meat, poultry, fish, eggs, dry beans, and nuts (2-3 servings); and fats, oils, and sweets (less than a serving). Foods in one group cannot substitute for those in another. One of the more controversial aspects of the Food Guide Pyramid was its emphasis on minimizing meat consumption; according to the USDA, the maximum daily intake of protein should only be five to seven ounces.

Forms of fat

Fats are divided into two main categories: saturated and unsaturated. Saturated fats are mostly found in meat, lard, butter, coconut, and palm oil. Doctors consider these fats to be the most hazardous to health because they increase the risk of heart disease and certain kinds of cancer. Unsaturated fats include sunflower oil, corn oil, olive oil, and canola oil.

The last two oils are called monounsaturated fats and are particularly good for the body because they lower cholesterol. Recent research has concluded that the most harmful kinds of fats are trans fats, which are formed when liquid vegetable oil is processed to make table spreads and cooking fats. Trans fats have been consistently shown to create buildup in arteries, a process which can impair heart health.

Water

A person should drink 7 to 10 average sized glasses of water daily. Water is probably the most important substance a person can consume. Water carries nutrients throughout the body and regulates body temperature. Water lubricates joints, aids digestion, and helps speed waste matter out of the body. Losing even 5% of the body's water causes immediate physical symptoms, like dizziness, fatigue, and headache; losing 15% of the body's water can be fatal. The normal daily loss is between 64 and 80 ounces of water a day, which is equal to about 9 large glasses of water. Many fruits and vegetables contain helpful water, but people should still consume the recommended amount of water each day. People who are active, live at a high altitude, or travel a great deal should be sure to drink even more water.

Fiber

Whole grains, fruits, and vegetables are all excellent sources of fiber. Fiber can be either insoluble or soluble. Insoluble fibers (cellulose and lignin, for example) speed digestion and can reduce the risk of colon cancer and heart disease. Wheat and corn bran, leafy vegetables, and fruit and vegetable skins are all great sources of insoluble fiber. Soluble fibers (pectins and gums, for example) lower cholesterol levels and help manage the level of blood sugar. They can be found in the pulp of fruits and in vegetables, oats, beans, and barley. Doctors warn that most Americans do not eat nearly enough fiber. However, increasing fiber in your diet should be done gradually, as a sudden increase in fiber can result in bloating, cramps, and diarrhea.

Cholesterol

Many fats can increase cholesterol, a substance in the body which has consistently been linked with heart disease. Cholesterol has many positive uses in the body, like helping the liver operate and helping to form many hormones, but if cholesterol becomes too abundant, it can build up in the arteries and impede the flow of blood. Research has shown that saturated fats cause a more significant buildup of cholesterol than unsaturated fats or other foods that contain cholesterol. In order to minimize cholesterol in the diet, individuals should cut back on fats altogether, but especially limit their intake of saturated fats. Monounsaturated fats, like canola and olive oil, are a good, low-cholesterol source of fat.

Daily values

On a food label, the daily values are the amount of each nutrient that a person should consume every day. Most of the daily values, including those for total fat, saturated fat, carbohydrates, fiber, and protein, are based on the assumption of a 2000-calorie diet. The daily values for cholesterol, sodium, vitamins, and minerals are the same for every adult. The percent daily values, then, indicate what percentage of a particular nutrient is found in the food. Obviously, the ideal diet would include 100% of each nutrient. Individuals who consume considerably less or more than 2000 calories a day should adjust their daily values for total fat, saturated fats, and cholesterol accordingly.

Calories

There is a great deal of information printed on the Nutrition Facts label on every packaged food. Calories describe the amount of energy that can be derived from the food. Specifically, a calorie is defined as the amount of energy needed to raise the temperature of 1 gram of water by 1º Celsius. In the past, serving size was often manipulated by food companies to make their products seem healthier; serving size is now strictly regulated by the government. All of the producers of a certain kind of food are required to use a similar serving size so that it is easier for consumers to compare products. The number of calories for every gram of fat, carbohydrates, and protein is listed at the bottom of every food label.

Vitamins

Vitamins are nutrients that help regulate growth in the body, maintain the quality of tissue, and release the energy from food. Vitamins allow proteins, fats, and carbohydrates to be used by the body. They also aid in the manufacture of blood cells, hormones, and other compounds. Some vitamins do not need to be consumed; vitamin D, for example, is produced by the body after exposure to sunlight and is then changed into an active form in the liver and kidneys. Most vitamins, though, need to be ingested. Some vitamins, like A, D, E, and K, are fat-soluble and are absorbed through the intestinal membrane. Others, like vitamins B and C, are water-soluble and are absorbed directly into the blood stream. Water-soluble vitamins are evacuated through urine and sweat.

Vitamin supplements

Many Americans take daily vitamin supplements to guard against certain health problems, despite doubts from the scientific community as to the effectiveness of these supplements. Most health professionals insist that the best way to get all the necessary nutrients is to eat a wide variety of foods from all levels of the Food Guide Pyramid. Still, some people may be unable to eat all the foods they need, and taking dietary supplements can be beneficial for them. Dietary supplements can be particularly useful for getting obscure nutrients, like capsaicin, which is derived from hot peppers and known to protect DNA from carcinogens. Dietary supplements can be sold as such, as long as they do not make any claims to diagnose, prevent, treat, or cure any disease.

Multivitamin supplements

As long as people don't depend on multivitamins to supply all of their nutrients and justify an unhealthy diet, there is no harm in taking a daily multivitamin. Most of the health dangers associated with vitamin supplements stem from taking huge daily doses of a single vitamin. This is particularly true for fat-soluble vitamins, like A and D, which will build up in the intestinal tract if they are taken in excess. Overconsumption of water-soluble vitamins can cause health problems as well, however. Vitamin C, which many people take in isolation during cold and flu season, can cause stomachaches and nausea. Indeed, most of the health benefits provided by vitamins can only be provided by a combination of vitamins, and not by an increase in any one substance.

Evaluating food

There are certain categories that everyone should check when evaluating a food. You should always determine the percentage of fat calories in a food. You should avoid fatty foods, particularly those high in saturated fats. Cholesterol is only found in animal products, and many high-fat foods may actually not contain any cholesterol at all. Sugars are not listed on food labels because doctors have yet to agree on a reasonable daily limit. A food is considered high in fiber if it contains five or more grams per serving. A high level of calcium is 200 or more milligrams per serving. It is especially important to check the level of sodium because most Americans consume far too much sodium. A food is considered a "good" source of a vitamin if it contains 10% of the daily value and considered a "high" source if it contains 20% or more.

Antioxidants

Antioxidants are those substances that prevent the negative side effects of oxidation within the body. Three of the most commonly discussed antioxidants are vitamin C, vitamin E, and beta carotene. Besides the unique benefits of each of these nutrients, antioxidants are believed to prevent the damage to the body done by free radicals (oxygen molecules), smog, smoke, and radiation. All of these natural or artificial phenomena are capable of preventing the cells of the body from properly performing their functions. People who consume a large number of antioxidants exhibit lower rates of heart disease, some cancers, cataracts, and infectious illness. However, it has not been conclusively shown that consuming antioxidant supplements necessarily provides a safeguard against disease.

Minerals

Minerals are nutrients that help with the growth and maintenance of tissues in the body. They aid in the formation of bones and teeth and in muscle function; they also help the nervous system to transmit information. Minerals required at levels of about 100 milligrams a day are known as major minerals. Sodium, potassium, chloride, calcium, phosphorus, and magnesium are all major minerals. Minerals required at levels of 10 milligrams or less a day are known as trace minerals. Iron, zinc, selenium, molybdenum, iodine, cobalt, copper, manganese, fluoride, and chromium are all examples of trace minerals. Although it is widely acknowledged that the body requires all of these trace minerals, it has not yet been proven that a greater or smaller amount affects the risk of illness.

Folic acid

In the last several years, food manufacturers in the United States have begun adding folic acid (folate, a B vitamin) to their products. The main reason for the addition is that folic acid deficiency has been linked to birth defects like spinal bifida. Thus, it imperative that women who are trying to get pregnant make certain they are getting enough folic acid in their diet. Another function of folic acid is helping to synthesize hemoglobin, a molecule that carries oxygen in the bloodstream. Folic acid has also been credited with reducing the risk of cervical and other cancers. Many elderly individuals have a low amount of folic acid in their bodies, and scientists believe this may be somewhat responsible for coronary artery disease.

Calcium

The most prevalent mineral in the body is calcium. Calcium aids in the operation of the brain and heart and helps build strong bone tissue. It is especially important for pregnant women to have enough calcium because they will need to provide calcium to their unborn babies. Calcium has also been shown to prevent colon cancer and to control high blood pressure. People in their teens and twenties should be sure to get enough calcium because a calcium deficiency in these years has been linked to the occurrence of osteoporosis in later life. An individual should be able to get an adequate supply of calcium from calcium-rich foods, but some individuals may require a calcium supplement. If so, calcium citrate and calcium carbonate are recommended; supplements from bone meal and dolomite are not recommended because they may contain harmful lead.

Vegetarianism

There are a number of different diets that fall under the heading of vegetarianism. Lacto-vegetarians eat dairy products as well as fruits, vegetables, and grains. Ovo-lacto-vegetarians add eggs to this diet. The most extreme vegetarians only consume plant foods; these people are known as vegans. For vegetarians, the biggest challenge in eating properly is getting complete proteins; meat, fish, poultry, and eggs all provide the nine essential amino acids, while other proteins like beans or nuts may have a low amount of one or more of these. For this reason, it is important for vegetarians to consume complementary proteins, like beans served with rice or sesame seeds served with chickpeas. In general, vegetarians have lower levels of cholesterol and are less likely to be overweight.

Metabolism and energy

An individual's metabolism is the sum of all of the vital processes that require the energy and nutrients from food. Most metabolism is devoted to maintaining basic processes like respiration, heart rate, and blood pressure and is known as the resting metabolic rate. Individuals will also use up energy digesting food or engaging in physical activity. Metabolic rate is dependent on both heredity and habits: Although some people may have a naturally higher metabolism than others, exercise has been shown to raise the general metabolic rate. Muscle tends to metabolize (burn) calories more quickly than fat. When individuals lose a great deal of weight quickly, the body will try to protect itself by lowering the metabolism. When weight is gained, on the other hand, metabolism tends to rise.

Low-calorie diets

Although healthy weight loss does entail reducing the number of calories ingested daily, any diet that drastically alters caloric intake should be avoided. Some risky diets suggest consuming less than 800 calories a day, which can be hazardous to health. Losing weight quickly typically means losing muscle weight, and the heart muscle may become so weak that it struggles to support the body. Moreover, low-calorie diets tend to slow down the metabolism, which means that energy will be reduced and the body will struggle to maintain the new weight. If you develop nausea, abdominal pains, sudden hair loss, irregular menstruation, or chronic fatigue, you may have reduced your caloric intake too much; you should immediately resume normal eating habits and see a doctor.

Yo-yo syndrome

Too often, individuals assume that eating foods labeled as fat free, low-calorie, or "light" gives them permission to eat as much as they want. However, many of these so-called diet foods are high in sugar and may be high in calories, despite being low in fat. Too much of any food, no matter how healthy, is counterproductive to a diet plan. In particular, artificial sweeteners and fake fats should be consumed in moderation. Another common dieting problem is the yo-yo syndrome; this term applies to a pattern of repeatedly losing and then regaining weight. Studies have shown that continual weight fluctuation can be hazardous to the health. Exercise, however, has been credited with maintaining a healthy metabolism even while dieting. This enables the person to keep weight off once it has been lost.

Viruses

Viruses are the smallest of the pathogens, but they are also the most difficult to destroy. Viruses consist of a small bit of nucleic acid (either DNA or RNA) inside a coating of protein. Viruses are unable to reproduce by themselves, so they infest the reproductive systems of cells already in the body and command them to make new viral cells. These new cells are then sent to other parts of the body. Some of the most common viruses are influenza, herpes, hepatitis, and papilloma. It is difficult to treat viruses without also damaging the cells that they are using. Antibiotics, for instance, have no effect on viruses. Special antiviral drugs must be taken, and even these do not entirely eliminate the presence of the virus.

Pathogen, host, and vector infections

Contracting and carrying an infection is a complicated process. Infections are caused by pathogens, against which the body must defend itself. In clinical terms, an infection always has a host: either a person or a population that comes into contact with one or more pathogens in the environment. In this context, a vector is the biological or physical vehicle that moves the agent to the host; in other words, the vector is the mode of transmission. There are various kinds of microbes that can cause an infection: viruses, bacteria, fungi, protozoa, and helminths (parasitic worms). With the exception of helminths, all of these pathogens can only be seen with the aid of a microscope.

Fungi

Fungi are either single-celled or multi-celled organisms made up of long, thread-like fibers and reproductive spores. Fungi do not have chlorophyll and therefore have to obtain their food from organic material. On some occasions, this organic material is human tissue. When fungi infect the body, they release enzymes that consume and digest cells. Fungi generally attack the portions of the body that are covered with hair, like the scalp, groin, and external ear canal. Fungi are also blamed for the condition known as athlete's foot. Fungi are not treated with antibiotics but with specifically antifungal medications. Yeast is one of the more common types of fungus.

Bacteria

Bacteria are simple, one-celled organisms and are the most common microorganism and pathogen. Most bacteria do not cause disease; in fact, many bacteria are important to body processes. Bacteria can harm the body when they release enzymes that actually digest other body cells or when they produce toxins. Since bacteria are quite different from the normal body cell, they can usually be effectively treated with antibiotics. However, not just any antibiotic can be used to treat every bacterial infection; a doctor must determine the particular strain of bacteria that is causing the problem before he or she writes a prescription. Over time, bacteria may become resistant to antibiotics, so it is best not to take too much of this effective treatment.

Helminths

Helminths are tiny parasitic worms that attack specific tissues of the body and steal nutrients from the host. One common helminth is the fluke. The fluke burrows through the skin and enters the circulatory system, where it competes with the body cells for the available food. Another common helminth is the tapeworm, which is often contracted by humans who eat undercooked beef, pork, or fish that contain the larvae. There are a number of medications available to treat the various types of helminths. Of all pathogens, helminths are the only ones that are visible with the naked eye. It is not effective to try to defeat a helminth-based infection with antibiotics.

Protozoa

Protozoa are single-celled animals that damage and destroy cells by releasing toxins and enzymes. Effective public health measures have minimized the danger of protozoa infection at present, though it has not always been this way. Even today, many people suffer from malaria, a common protozoa-caused disease. Typically, these diseases are treated with general medical attention to the symptoms, by replacing all lost fluids, and with drugs that specifically target protozoa. The most common protozoa-caused disease in the United States at present is giardia, an intestinal infection that comes from drinking contaminated water. The symptoms of giardia are nausea, fatigue, and abdominal cramps, and it can be life-threatening if it is not treated promptly.

Humoral and cell-mediated immune mechanisms

The mechanisms employed by the immune system to fight disease can be either humoral or cell-mediated. Humoral immunity is the protection provided by antibodies, the proteins that are derived from white blood cells. This kind of immunity is most useful in fighting bacterial and viral infections. Once a certain type of invader, or antigen, enters the body and triggers the creation of a certain antibody, the immune system will be able to fight this antigen every time it appears. This process can also be accomplished through inoculation, in which a small amount of the antigen is purposefully introduced to the body. Cell-mediated immunity is when various T cells protect specific cells against parasites, fungi, and other invaders. These T cells may accomplish a number of different things, from activating other immune cells to helping the antibodies do their work.

Eating disorders

Eating disorders have only been acknowledged and treated in the past few decades. The most common eating disorders are anorexia nervosa and bulimia nervosa. Typically, eating disorders have to do not only with food, but also with a person's overall self-esteem and body image. They are a threat to physical, psychological, and mental health. Some of the medical problems that stem from eating disorders are an increased susceptibility to cold, irregular heartbeat, bloating, constipation, osteoporosis, the growth of fine hair all over the body, depression, severe abdominal pain, and even sudden death. Individuals who have an eating disorder or who suspect that someone they know may have one should immediately see a doctor.

Extreme dieting

Many Americans are causing themselves serious harm by pursuing unhealthy dietary plans, often unnecessarily. Indeed, it has been observed that most people who are dieting should not be, and most people who should be are not succeeding. Few people actually diet for health reasons; most do so to improve their appearance. Extreme dieters are those who lose enough weight quickly to cause physical symptoms, such as vulnerability to cold and weakness. Extreme dieters tend to only consume a narrow range of foods and may focus obsessively on diet as a remedy for all of their problems. Although extreme dieting is not technically anorexic behavior, it is considered dangerous and should be immediately stopped in consultation with a health professional.

Diet pills and liquid diets

Everyone has seen the advertisements for diet pills that promise to reduce weight with minimal effort. As recently as the 1970's, American women were sold so-called diet pills that were nothing but amphetamines. Even today, the diet pill and weight-loss product industry is enormous. However, many of these products pose a risk to health. In addition, diet pills may not even effectively reduce weight because the individuals who take them may feel empowered to eat as much as they like. Liquid diets should also be avoided in most cases. Although today's liquid diets offer a more comprehensive range of proteins, carbohydrates, vitamins, and minerals than those of the past, anyone considering their use should still seek medical advice.

Binge eating

Closely related to compulsive overeating, binge eating is the swift consumption of an abnormally large amount of food. Individuals who have a problem with binge eating often feel they have no control over their eating and typically binge at least twice a week over a period of six months. A particular binge often lasts for more than an hour and may include the consumption of more than 2,000 calories. Binge eaters do not use vomiting or laxatives to control their weight; instead, they gain weight. This can lead to contributing symptoms like depression, anxiety, and low self-esteem. Some five million Americans may be binge eaters, and it is most common in college-age women. People who binge eat should immediately seek medical attention.

Compulsive overeating

If individuals cannot stop themselves from eating, if they eat a great deal or very quickly, then they may be compulsive overeaters. Compulsive overeaters eat even when they are full, and they often eat alone if they believe their consumption of food is shameful. Most doctors agree that compulsive overeating is more common in women, especially those who suffer from low self-esteem or a sense of abandonment. It can be difficult to recover from compulsive overeating because, unlike other abused substances, food is a habit that cannot be completely kicked. A person should seek medical advice if they are constantly eating when depressed, if they get no satisfaction from food, or if they have the fear of not being able to stop eating once they start.

Anorexia nervosa

People who suffer from anorexia nervosa believe that they are overweight and seek to avoid eating to the detriment of their health. Even individuals with below normal body weight may consider themselves unattractively overweight. In the restricting type of anorexia, the individual seeks to lower his or her weight by dieting, fasting, and exercising. In the binging/purging type of anorexia, the individual tries to limit his or her weight by ingesting huge amounts of food and then forcing him or herself to vomit or defecate. There is any number of possible causes of anorexia; it may be genetic, physiological, or social in origin. In any case, it is extremely destructive to the body and must be stopped as soon as possible.

Bulimia nervosa

Individuals who suffer from bulimia nervosa go on extended eating binges and then take drastic steps to reverse their effects. People with purging bulimia make themselves vomit or take massive doses of laxatives to remove food from their system; people with non-purging bulimia either fast or exercise excessively in an effort to lose weight gained during binges. Bulimia often develops after extreme dieting reconfigures the brain to obsess about consumption and weight loss. Breaking the diet leads the individual to feel guilty and overcompensate by purging. Bulimia, like anorexia, poses major risks to health and should be treated as soon as possible. It can cause dehydration, tooth decay, erosion of the esophagus, and eventually death.

Obesity

Obesity is defined by health professionals as the state weighing 20% or more than the ideal body weight. Mild obesity means the person is between 20% and 40% higher; moderate obesity means the person is from 41% to 100% heavier than they should be; and severe obesity indicates a body weight more than 100% higher than the ideal. Every segment of American society has cases of obesity, although it is especially high among African American and Mexican American women. Of particular concern is child obesity, which has increased by about 50% in the last 20 years. Obesity in children increases the risk of heart disease, diabetes, and osteoporosis later in life. Obesity is often the result of slow and steady weight gain over a number of years rather than sudden change in lifestyle, so individuals should be on guard against developing obesity.

Obesity related health risks

There are numerous dangers to health associated with obesity. Obese individuals are almost three times as likely as their fellows to have diabetes or high blood pressure. For women, obesity can lead to heart attacks, chronic chest pain, higher blood pressure, ovarian cancer, and breast cancer. For men, obesity may contribute to heart disease and to cancer of the colon, rectum, and prostate. More generally, obesity is often at the root of psychological problems like depression, guilt, and anxiety. However, many studies have shown that the differences in health between obese and non-obese individuals seem to grow smaller with age, raising the question of whether mild or moderate obesity can be condemned entirely.

Causes of obesity

When obese individuals claim they have no control over their weight, they may be somewhat correct. There is a protein in the brain responsible for limiting food intake and signaling satiety; if this gene is defective, obesity can be the result. Obesity may also be caused by the individual's failure to eat properly or get enough exercise. Impoverished people are more likely to be obese, partly because they are not taught about nutrition and because a diet rich in fruits and vegetables can be expensive. Some individuals may be predisposed to obesity by overfeeding during childhood; their fat cells are large and numerous, and this is more likely to contribute to obesity. People who suffer from psychological disorders like depression and chronic anxiety are also more inclined to obesity.

Exercise and muscles

When the endurance of muscles is increased, a greater capacity for aerobic metabolism develops. In fact, the aerobic enzymes that metabolize carbohydrates, fats, and proteins will double after a few weeks of endurance training. Muscle training that aims at increasing strength or speed also enlarges the individual fibers of muscle. There is some evidence that weight training causes a splitting of muscle fibers, causing new ones to be formed. Finally, regular exercise increases the amount of blood that circulates through muscles, since new capillaries will form around muscle fibers.

Muscles are in a constant state of change. If muscles are not used, they will atrophy and weaken; on the other hand, if they are regularly exercised, they will grow stronger and possibly larger. Muscles are best exercised when they are overloaded or asked to do more than they usually do. When you are training your muscles, you will need to gradually increase the amount of the weight or the number of repetitions to ensure that your muscles are always receiving a challenge. Many fitness professionals contend that a good muscular workout will be somewhat painful because muscles can only be developed by exceeding their normal requirements. However, not every kind of pain is profitable for a muscular workout, and individuals should be careful to distinguish muscular fatigue from injury, particularly when they are lifting heavy loads.

Benefits of exercise to body

Maintaining physical fitness has a number of advantages besides improving personal appearance. It has been shown time and again that habitual exercise is the best way to prevent coronary death. In fact, individuals who don't exercise are twice as likely as active individuals to die of a heart attack. Exercise makes the lungs more efficient, as they are able to take in more oxygen and make better use of it. This provides the body with more available energy. Exercise also benefits the bones. Individuals who do not exercise are more likely to have weak or brittle bones, and they are more prone to osteoporosis, in which bones lose their mineral density and become dangerously soft.

Other benefits of exercise

The benefits of regular exercise are both physical and mental. It is well documented that frequent exercise improves a person's mood, increases energy, focus, and alertness, and reduces anxiety. In fact, long workouts cause the release of mood-elevating chemicals called endorphins into the brain. Exercise also reduces the risk of disease. By aiding in the proper digestion, exercise reduces the risk of colon and rectal cancers. Studies have also indicated that women who exercise are less likely to develop breast cancer. Finally, exercise is beneficial because it helps people lose weight and keep it off. The body's metabolism remains elevated for a prolonged period after exercise, which means food is processed more quickly and efficiently. In addition, regular exercise helps suppress the appetite.

Nutrition and exercise

For most people, the balanced diet depicted in the USDA Food Pyramid will supply all the nutrients the body needs to maintain a program of physical fitness. However, individuals who are seriously testing their endurance by exercising for periods of more than an hour at a time will need to increase their intake of complex carbohydrates, which keep the level of blood sugar stable and increase the amount of available glycogen. Contrary to popular thought, heavy workouts do not require a diet high in protein, and in fact, consuming too much protein can put a severe strain on the kidneys and liver. Similarly, most health experts discourage the use of dietary supplements and body-building foods unless under supervision because these products can easily result in nutritional imbalances.

Vigorous exercise

If an individual wants to receive the health benefits of exercise and achieve a high level of physical fitness, then he or she will need to engage in vigorous exercise. Vigorous exercise is defined as any activity that raises the metabolic rate to six or more times the resting rate and generally means burning 1,500–3,000 calories per week during exercise. The American College of Sports Medicine recommends aerobic exercise be performed for 20 to 60 minutes three to five times per week and that strength training be performed two or three times per week. Studies have consistently shown that individuals who engage in regular vigorous exercise outlive their sedentary peers.

Exercise-related injuries

According to research by the American Physical Therapy Association, most exercise-related injuries occur in the knees, back, shoulders, and feet. These can be acute injuries, like sprains, pulled muscles, or fractures, which are caused by sudden trauma; or they can be overuse injuries, which arise from performing the same activity too many times. Tendinitis, muscle strains, and stress fractures are all example of overuse injuries. To prevent injury, people should always get training from someone with experience and always make sure to stretch thoroughly before and after exercise. Individuals should always wear appropriate protective equipment and never exercise while under the influence of alcohol or drugs.

Water and exercise

Water is the most important thing for a person to consume before, during, and after exercise. On hot days, active people can sweat up to a quart of water. If you become dehydrated, your heart will have a difficult time providing oxygen and nutrients to muscles. Even sports drinks cannot provide the hydrating effect of cool water because the sodium, sugar, and potassium in them delay their absorption into the body. Salt tablets should be avoided as well; they are potentially dangerous and unnecessary. Although people do lose a bit of sodium when they sweat, this is more than offset by the huge amount of salt in the average American diet.

Adjusting to temperature during exercise

If you are exercising outdoors, it is essential to take the appropriate steps to protect yourself against excessive heat and cold. On extremely hot days, it is more important than ever to stay hydrated. Loose-fitting, breathable fabrics are appropriate for hot days. Always remain alert for any signs of heat exhaustion, like dizziness, light-headedness, or headache. In very cold weather, cover as much of your body as possible with layers of clothing. Clothing should be dark and breathable, as waterproof clothing will keep your perspiration from evaporating. Make sure to cover your head and neck, since at least 40% of heat escapes the body from these areas. Clothes should always be loose enough to ensure that circulation is not hindered.

Different strategies of exercise

Individuals who are attempting to build strength will need to use a different training strategy than those who are only seeking to build muscular endurance. In order to build strength, you should be doing a low number of repetitions with a very heavy weight. As your muscles grow stronger, you should gradually increase the amount of weight the muscles are required to move. In order to improve muscular endurance, on the other hand, you should do a large number of repetitions with a considerably lower weight. Sometimes, it is necessary to build up a minimum of strength before you can work on endurance. An example of this is learning to do push-ups before moving on to endurance training with push-ups.

Intensity of exercise

Intensity can be defined as the amount of effort or work that must be invested in a specific exercise workout. A good balance is necessary to ensure that the intensity is hard enough to overload the body but not so difficult that it results in overtraining, injury or burnout.

Frequency of exercise

Frequency refers to how often a person exercises. After any form of exercise is performed the body completes a process of rebuilding and repairing. So, determining the frequency of exercise is important in order to find a balance that provides just enough stress for the body to adapt and also allows enough rest time for healing.

Time/duration

Time or duration is the length of time an individual session of exercise should last. The duration will vary according to the intensity and type of the exercise.

Male and female muscular endurance

Most studies have determined that there is very little difference in muscular endurance and body composition between fit males and females. Certainly, the range of difference is much wider within each sex than it is between comparable members of different sexes. Still, there are some general biological differences that create disparities in physical performance. For one thing, since girls tend to undergo the changes of adolescence before boys, they out-perform boys for the first few teenage years. After adolescence, males tend to be taller, heavier, stronger, and faster. Increasingly, though, fitness researchers are suspecting that male advantages in fitness may stem in large part from prejudicial treatment in society. Indeed, many studies have shown that males at every age tend to receive more encouragement and training in athletic endeavor than do females.

Ballistic stretching

Not all stretching is good for the body. Ballistic stretching, in which one bounces or jerks muscles around, is capable of overstretching muscle fibers, which can result in muscle contraction rather than expansion. Ballistic stretching can also tear ligaments and weaken or break tendons, the connections between muscle and bone. The best way to stretch a muscle is to gently ease it into a stretching position, and then hold that position for a prolonged period. A stretch should never be painful, although it may feel a bit uncomfortable. Rather than immediately trying to achieve the desired level of flexibility, it is better to hold the greatest stretch the body is capable of holding comfortably. Frequent and controlled stretching is the best way to pursue flexibility goals.

Static stretching

The health benefits of proper stretching are numerous. Proper stretching before and after a workout lengthens the muscles and prevents strain. Stiff muscles can often cause an individual to move awkwardly and be susceptible to injury. Most physiologists recommend that people engage in static (or passive) stretching for several minutes before and after vigorous exercise, and at least four or five times a week. Static stretching means gradually moving into a stretched position, which is then held from between six to sixty seconds. Static stretching after a workout helps move lactic acid out of the muscles, increases the range of motion, and speeds blood, oxygen, and nutrients to the muscle tissue.

Isometric, isotonic, and isokinetic exercises

Muscle exercises can be either isometric, isotonic, or isokinetic. Isometric exercises are those in which the muscle tries to move an immovable object. The muscle contractions usually last five to eight seconds and are repeated five or ten times a day. Isometric exercise may raise blood pressure and is not generally recommended for building strength. In isotonic exercise, the muscle moves a moderately heavy load several times. Isotonic exercise befits strength when it is done a small number of times with a high weight load, and benefits flexibility and endurance when it is performed many times with a low weight. Isokinetic exercises are performed on a machine that is specially designed to overload muscles at every point in their range of motion. These machines are highly effective in developing muscles, but are typically very expensive.

Building muscles safely

In order to properly train muscles, a person should always ensure that he works each muscle group until it is very tired. He should always allow his breathing to slow down to close to normal before continuing weight training. It is considered proper to breathe in when the muscles are relaxed, and exhale as they are contracted to perform the exercise.

One should never hold one's breath while muscle training. Muscles need adequate time to recover after an intense training session, usually between two and four days. Muscles can actually be harmed if they are worked on consecutive days. Still, muscles will begin to atrophy after five days of rest, so a person should try and perform muscle exercises at least twice a week.

Developing a personalized muscle workout

In order to effectively exercise the muscles, a person needs to exercise every major muscle group. This includes the deltoids (shoulders), pectorals (chest), triceps and biceps (back and front of the arm above the elbow), quadriceps and hamstrings (front and back of the leg above the knee), gluteus maximus (buttocks), and abdomen (torso below the chest). As long as all of these muscle groups are treated, exercise programs can vary widely from person to person, with the only important stipulation being that each muscle is worked until it is very tired. Weight training programs are composed of repetitions or reps , the number of times each motion is performed and sets, the number of groups of reps to be performed.

Weight lifting and repetition

An excellent way to increase muscular endurance is high-repetition, low-resistance weight training. Using small barbells and performing four to six sets of about twenty repetitions each is a great way to increase endurance in the upper body. Weights for endurance-building activities should be between 60 and 70% of maximum resistance. In order to increase muscular endurance for a particular sport, one can simply practice that activity for a long period of time. This method of improving endurance is not as quick as weight training, but it allows one to practice sport-specific skills at the same time. It should be noted that muscular endurance is confined to the muscle group that is being worked; that is, for instance, long periods of running will do little for upper body endurance.

Isometric exercise

Isometric exercise, in which the muscle does not contract but exerts itself against a stationary object, can cause immediate gains in strength, although these advances will diminish in time. In fact, almost all of the strength gain from an isometric exercise program will come in the first six weeks. The greatest benefits are from the maximum effort held for several seconds and performed several times a day. Because isometric exercise does not involve the contraction of the muscle, it does not improve strength throughout the range of motion. For this reason, it is most commonly used by athletes who want to improve strength at one particular joint angle. Oftentimes, isometric exercises are recommended for injured individuals whose muscles have been immobilized by a cast.

Dynamic resistance

Strength improvement is most often accomplished through isotonic or isokinetic exercise. Isokinetic exercise is exercise in which resistance remains the same throughout the entire range of motion. When muscles are forced to perform repetitive resistance exercises, they are encouraged to synthesize more contractile protein, which increases strength. Exercising at close to the maximum level of resistance creates the most strength. An appropriate weight is one which can be moved between 4 and 8 times for four sets. Most individuals find that a good place to start is at 20% of body weight for upper-body exercises, and 50% of body weight for lower body exercises. Strength can develop within a few weeks of regular training.

Speed workouts

Muscle speed can be substantially increased through regular training. Workouts designed to improve speed are usually very strenuous, so they should never be performed without adequate stretching and warm-up. In order to increase muscle speed, one can simply perform a regular exercise as quickly as possible. Speed training should not be confused with interval training, however: one should fully recover from each repetition before starting again. In order to develop running speed over a short distance, one should repeatedly sprint for ten to fifty yards. Any distance of a thousand yards or greater will rely on endurance and strength rather than speed, so interval training is more appropriate.

Assisted speed and weight training

Many athletes try to improve their muscle speed by working out under circumstances in which their muscles will have to work harder than normal, and so will become used to more rapid exertion. For instance, sprinters may train by running down a moderate hill, and swimmers may train their arms to work more quickly by swimming with flippers on their feet. Serious athletes will also aim to improve muscle speed through weight training. Sprinters spend a great deal of time trying to develop strong and flexible quadricep muscles, so that they can explode from the starting line and have a longer stride. Lifting a weight quickly tends to improve muscle speed.

Over training

Many people who are inspired to pursue physical fitness quickly burn out because they over-train. That is, they force themselves to exercise too intensely and too often, so that they put their bodies through a great deal of strain. Some of the signs of overtraining are continual muscle soreness, frequent injury, unintended weight loss, nervousness, and the inability to relax. People who are overtraining may have a hard time completing their workout, and will definitely have a hard time recovering. If one feels as if he may be guilty of overtraining, he should ease off his exercise program for a while, giving himself 24-48 hours between workouts. It is also a good idea to confer with a fitness professional.

Muscle strength and endurance

Developing healthy muscles is not simply a matter of lifting the heaviest possible object. The ability to use your muscles over and over without getting tired is also an important part of physical fitness. Developing muscular strength and endurance will help make body tissue firmer and more resilient. Well-maintained muscles tend to work more efficiently, and they can withstand more strain. Furthermore, muscular development aids in circulation, with the result that the whole body absorbs and makes use of nutrients in the blood more quickly. Strength and endurance training has also been shown to be one of the most effective ways to lose weight, as developed muscles burn more calories than does fat.

Extending endurance

In research studies, scientists have determined that it requires 2 hours of continuous exercise to create the maximum number of new blood vessels and aerobic enzymes. Of course, most athletes will have to lengthen their work-out period gradually to reach this goal. It is not necessary to perform the entire 2 hours at the same time to gain some benefit. Running, cycling, and cross-country skiing are considered to be the best ways to increase leg endurance. Swimming is excellent for working the shoulder and chest muscles, while rowing is good for testing the endurance of the arms and back. Most athletes who are trying to increase their muscular endurance will exercise for 2 or more hours, three times a week.

Different kinds of strength

There are a few different kinds of strength. A movement in which several different muscles are involved in a series of continuous contractions is considered dynamic strength. Lifting a heavy object above one's head is an example of dynamic strength. The muscle contractions involved in such a maneuver are called isotonic, meaning that while the length of the muscle changes, the amount of tension in the muscle stays approximately the same. Static strength is exhibited when force is exerted on an object without any movement of the object occurring. Trying to push a parked truck is an example of an activity involving static strength. In such a case, the activity of the muscles is known as isometric because the length of the muscles does not actually change.

Assessing muscle strength

Strength, put simply, is the ability of the muscles to exert force. In order to determine how much stronger one person is than another, maximal strength must be measured. Unfortunately, maximal strength can only be ascertained by determining the most amount of force a person can exert for a brief instant and, for obvious reasons, this is a difficult thing to ascertain. Also, it should be noted that strength can really only be accurately attributed to a particular muscle or group of muscles; an individual may have a strong upper body and at the same time be very weak below the waist. Indeed, the strength of one muscle group is unrelated to the strength of any other group.

Muscular power

When fitness experts refer to muscular power, they mean the degree of explosiveness with which a muscle can exert force. Muscular power is defined as the muscle's ability to exert force over a brief period of time. Mathematically, power is calculated as the force multiplied by the distance, divided by the time. If the distance covered by a particular action is constant (say, the distance from a box on the floor to a shelf overhead), then it should be possible to increase power simply by increasing the force used to accomplish the act or decreasing the amount of time taken to perform the act. Most athletic endeavors require a great deal of muscular power, whether for jumping, running, throwing, etc.

Muscular endurance

Muscular endurance is closely related to strength, though it is also somewhat distinct. Muscular endurance is the ability to continue performing any muscle activity despite fatigue in that particular muscle (as opposed to general cardiovascular fatigue). Dynamic (isotonic) endurance is a measure of the number of repetitions of a given exercise that a muscle can perform. Static (isometric) endurance, on the other hand, is a measure of the length of time that a given muscle can hold a contraction. Unsurprisingly, the force required to hold a contraction is inversely proportional to the length of time that contraction can be held. The body seems to be able to adjust naturally when it knows that a particular contraction will have to be held for a long period of time.

Muscular endurance training

In order to build muscular endurance effectively, a person needs to perform sustained exercise at a low level. Developing the best possible muscular endurance entails exercising for two consecutive hours; at that point, the glycogen in muscles is almost fully depleted, new blood vessels are being formed, and there is the greatest amount of aerobic enzyme development. Of course, shorter periods of more-intense exercise can also deplete the stores of glycogen. It should be noted that developing endurance for a particular form of exercise requires performing that exercise for a long period of time; one cannot effectively build endurance for swimming, for instance, by running for a long period.

Principles of strength training

Developing strong muscles not only will improve performance in most sports, it will also reduce the risk of injury. The overload principle of weight training asserts that the best way to build muscle strength is to train at the maximum level of resistance, so that muscles will become accustomed to more difficult labor. The progression principle of weight training asserts that the best way to build muscle strength is to gradually increase resistance as strength increases, so that muscles can slowly become capable of handling a bigger load. Every theory of strength training insists that weight exercises should be performed throughout the entire range of motion, so that flexibility is not compromised in the interest of strength.

Cardiovascular fitness

An individual's cardiovascular fitness is the ability of his or her heart to pump blood through the body at the necessary rate. Proper cardiovascular fitness can be achieved through aerobic exercise: that is, any activity during which the amount of oxygen taken into the body is equal to or more than the amount the body is using. Jogging, walking, or riding a bike are all examples of aerobic activity. The heart also gets an excellent workout during anaerobic exercise, in which the body takes in less oxygen than it needs to maintain the activity. Sprinting or swimming fast can be anaerobic exercises, if they leave the person breathless. Nonaerobic exercise, like bowling or golf, does not challenge the heart and lungs and therefore will not improve cardiovascular fitness.

Cardiovascular system during exercise

Exercise stimulates the release of adrenaline and lactic acid into the bloodstream, increasing the heart rate. The blood pressure also increases, to ensure that enough blood is delivered to the brain. Generally, the distribution of blood changes during exercise: less blood is delivered to organs, and more is directed to the working muscles. In particular, less blood flows to the kidneys and intestines, which means that much less urine is produced during exercise. While a normal resting lung capacity is about 5 liters of air per minute,

- 56 -

during vigorous exercise the lungs may be able to hold close to 200 liters of air every minute. Indeed, the lungs are able to process enough oxygen to accommodate any level of exercise; the maximum level of exertion is actually determined by the output of the heart.

Regular exercise strengthens the muscles associated with respiration. Although the number of alveoli (places where carbon dioxide and oxygen are exchanged) remains constant, the improved strength of the intercostals muscles between the ribs allow the lungs to hold more air. Exercise also increases the overall blood supply, making it more difficult for individuals to become dehydrated during vigorous work. Training increases the number of red blood cells, which makes it easier for blood to supply oxygen to the body. Interestingly, regular exercise not only improves the function of existing blood vessels but creates new blood vessels in working muscles. Within the muscles, individual fibers are enlarged by exercise and there is an increase in the aerobic enzymes that process oxygen.

Exercise and the heart

Exercise improves the ability of the heart to pump blood throughout the body, increasing the volume of blood distributed with each beat by 20 to 30%. This increase in volume allows the heart to slow down so that it only beats between 40 and 60 times a minute. There is no change to the maximum heart rate, however; an individual's maximum heart rate is determined at birth and decreases only with age. It is true that exercise increases the length of time one can exercise at a high percentage of maximum heart rate. As is well known, blood pressure is decreased by regular exercise, even during exercise itself. Finally, the overall cardiac output is improved by exercise; in other words, healthy muscles receive more blood.

Target heart rate

In order to get the most from a cardiovascular workout, you must be working at about 60% to 85% of your maximum heart rate. For men, the maximum heart rate is calculated as the age in years subtracted from 220. So, the maximum heart rate of a twenty-year-old man is 200. The formula for women is similar, except age is subtracted from 225. The threshold of the target heart rate during exercise, then, will be found by multiplying the maximum heart rate by .60. So, for that twenty-year-old man, the target heart rate begins at 120. A person shouldn't try to achieve their maximum heart rate, especially when just beginning an exercise program. However, unless you exercise within your target heart rate range, you will not really improve the condition of your heart and lungs.

Determining resting heart rate

Health professionals recommend keeping track of your heart rate during exercise to make sure that you are conditioning your heart and lungs without overexerting. Most people are able to easily gauge their pulse by pressing on the carotid artery on the side of their neck. To do this, tilt your head back slightly and use either your middle finger, index finger, or both to find the pulse. In order to determine your resting heart rate, take your pulse at a time when you have not been engaged in any physical activity. Count the number of pulses in a minute (it may be easier to count the pulses in ten seconds and multiply by six). This is your resting heart rate. If you are in good physical condition, your heart rate should not vary too much from this number even after three minutes of heavy exercise.

Male biological advantages

After adolescence, there are a few biological advantages held by males that enable them to outperform women of similar fitness levels. For one thing males usually have larger hearts and lungs than females, and so they also have a greater aerobic capacity and cardiac output. Males also have, on average, a higher proportion of hemoglobin in the blood, which enables them to speed oxygen to needy muscles more quickly. The heart rate of a male is typically stronger and slower than that of a female. Males generally have more muscle mass and less fat, so the cardiorespiratory system can spend more of its energy nourishing muscle. Finally, the shoulders of a male are typically broader and the arms and legs are longer, which gives the average male a longer stride and reach than the average female.

Women and contact sports

There persists a popular assumption that contact sports are more dangerous to women than to men. This is untrue: repeated studies have shown that the rate of injury among females who participate in such sports as soccer, rugby, and basketball is roughly the same as for males. Furthermore, the kinds of injuries most commonly suffered by females are by and large the same suffered by men: sprained ankles and knee injuries. Assuming that women are given the same level of training, supervision, and protective equipment as males, there is no reason to suspect that they are any more vulnerable to injury.

Iron deficiency among women

There is a persistent myth that vigorous exercise can deplete the iron resources of a woman. The life of this fallacy is in part due to the fact that women have slightly lower levels of hemoglobin than do men; this substance is necessary for carrying oxygen to cells, and requires iron for its formation. Women are at no risk of developing anemia or any iron-deficiency as long as they make sure to eat a diet rich in leafy vegetables, whole grains, beans, fish, and meat. If a woman does not eat enough iron, however, or loses a great deal of blood, the iron reserves may become depleted. This can seriously inhibit a fitness plan by making it difficult for oxygen to be transported to the needy cells

Pregnancy and exercise

There is no evidence that women should not continue to exercise during pregnancy. It is impossible for exercise to deprive a fetus of nourishment, and vigorous activity will not harm a fetus, which is safely guarded by the amniotic fluid. Moreover, pregnant women can receive many health benefits from exercise. A fitness plan that emphasizes body composition can help offset the weight gain associated with pregnancy. Exercises that develop strength in the abdomen, lower back, and pelvic floor can be helpful for minimizing back pain and the discomfort of carrying a child. Exercises that aim at increasing flexibility can help reduce muscle soreness during the last trimester. Finally, regular exercise can reduce the insomnia, fatigue, and constipation that often affect pregnant women.

Exercise and menstruation

There is no danger in exercising vigorously while menstruating. Though some women may feel hindered by the cramping and soreness they feel during this period, these symptoms are in no way an indication that the body needs to rest. Moreover, many women find that vigorous exercise actually eases the symptoms of menstruation. There is no reason for women not to exercise for whatever length of time and at whatever level of intensity they prefer. Specifically, there is no truth to the notion that women should avoid swimming during menstruation. Studies have shown that there is no danger to health posed by the physical exertion of swimming, nor is there any risk in being submerged in hot or cold water.

Exercising after giving birth

Though women are likely to receive major health benefits from resuming an exercise program soon after giving birth, they should delay resuming vigorous or contact sports for at least four weeks. Often women can benefit from immediately resuming a program designed to strengthen the abdominal muscles, which may have been distended during pregnancy. Women should gradually increase the intensity of their exercise programs as they recover from labor. Most women find that after six months they are back at their peak level of performance. In a related note, there is no reason to suspect that exercise can interfere with lactation, so women who are breastfeeding may participate in any vigorous activity for which their body is otherwise ready.

Stress and muscles

Over time, stress can begin to cause serious damage to an individual's muscles and skin. The most common kind of headache associated with stress is the tension headache, which is caused by an involuntary flexing of the muscles around the scalp, head, and neck. A migraine headache, in which blood vessels in the brain are constricted and then widened, can also result from stress. Many people also experience acne, eczema, herpes, or hives because of stress. Many doctors now prescribe relaxation techniques to their patients along with medication or medical procedures when they feel that stress may be the reason for the headache, muscular tension, or skin condition.

Muscle shapes

The muscles of the human body come in a variety of shapes, depending on their function. In the trapezius, the muscle fibers are arranged in a broad, flat pattern, and attach at a large number of points along the scapula. The biceps, on the other hand, is a long, narrow muscle. The muscles of the deep back are very short, and appear as knotty bundles along the spinal column. Longer muscles are generally capable of producing highly visible external movements, for instance the transporting of heavy objects, while small, deep muscles are more often responsible for precise, balancing adjustments. Muscles that only cross over one joint are called monoarticular, while those that extend across and move more than one joint are called polyarticular.

Cooperative games

Many teachers find that cooperative games are a positive way to build teamwork among students while still developing motor skills and strategy concepts. There are five basic components that are emphasized by a cooperative game: fun, cooperation, equality, participation, and trust. A good cooperative game must be enjoyable, or else students will not want to continue. It must also require students to have faith in one another. and the active participation of all students. The goal of a cooperative game is to generate enthusiasm for physical activity, even among students who are normally reticent about joining in.

Competitive games

A competitive game is any one in which players or teams vie to defeat one another. Competitive games can be a great motivator in physical education class, as long as the competition is seen as a chance for everyone to test their skills and improve, rather than as a chance for superior athletes to embarrass others. In order to keep the games fun for all students, teachers should make a point of assessing student abilities and ensuring that no unfair matchups arise. Also, teachers should stress that competition is a way to find the areas in which each person needs to improve

Invasion games

Basics of invasion games
Invasion games are any team games in which players have to penetrate the territory of an opponent, and either enter a goal themselves or put a ball of some kind into a goal. Invasion games are a good way for students to get an appreciation for different strategies of attack and defense, to develop teamwork skills, and to improve whatever particular skills are required by the game. Some examples of invasion games are soccer, football, basketball, hockey, lacrosse, and Ultimate Frisbee. Invasion games force students to use both their mind and body in order to outwit and outmaneuver their opponents. For this reason, invasion games have been cited as beneficial to coordination, reflexes, and problem-solving skills.

Tactics
When teaching students to participate in invasion-style games, it is important to ensure that they understand the basic rules, strategies, and tactics of the given game. To this end, students should be taught when to pass and when to maintain control of the ball (passing, of course, should be done when one is defended). Also, students should begin to consider which places on the field are the easiest from which to score, and which places are the easiest from which an opponent can score. In most games that have a small goal at one end of the field, it is easiest to score from the middle of the field at that end. Students should also learn about different attack and defense formations, and the various merits of each. Finally, students should learn about the different roles of the members of the team; for example, the midfielders' responsibility to distribute the ball.

Developmental of technical skills
One of the objectives of teaching an invasion game is to improve certain skills, like passing, receiving, or shooting a ball. In order to accomplish this objective, teachers should give direct instruction to students on the techniques used in the game in question (for instance, teaching the bounce and chest passes in basketball), including the demonstration of how to position the body to best advantage. Students should also learn how to shield the ball from defenders, and how to quickly change speed or direction while maintaining control of a ball. In the end, students will have successfully met the skills objective if they can perform with accuracy, understand the basic skills for each game, and know how to keep score in each game.

<u>Evaluation of a student's progress</u>
When students have learned and understand the basic strategies of an invasion game, they should be capable of playing the game in a number of different formations and with teams of various sizes. They should also be able to determine the appropriate strategy for a given game situation; for example, they should know when to pursue a risky attack towards the end of a losing game). Students should also demonstrate the basic principles of defense, by marking opponents closely and keeping the ball away from dangerous areas. Advanced students will be able to look at a game and determine which areas need improvement, and what strategies might be more effective. These students will be able to describe the particular advantages of good players and will know the best tactics to take advantage of their team's talents.

Basketball

Basketball is an excellent activity for physical education classes because it is a team sport incorporating skills that can easily be practiced individually. There are a number of basic games that will improve basketball skills, and by the time they are in high school, students should be able to work on strategy and teamwork concepts. Basketball is also a good choice for physical education classes because very little equipment is required. To play basketball, all a class really needs is a ball and a basket. One consideration is that students should have appropriate footwear; running shoes may not provide adequate ankle support and can mark up a gymnasium floor. There is infinite room for improvement in basketball skills, so students should not ever get bored.

Basketball skills

<u>Passing</u>
In order to pass a basketball, the student should hold it with the fingertips rather than the palms of the hands. When receiving a pass, the elbows should be bent in to "give" with the ball and absorb the force. When passing the ball, the elbows should be straightened quickly and the wrists snapped. A chest pass is typical for long passes: the ball is held at chest level and thrown through the air to another player. One foot should be placed in front of the other in a striding position. A bounce pass is thrown with a similar form, except that it is designed to hit the floor and go to the other player's chest. This pass is good for connecting with closely-guarded teammates. A two-handed overhead pass is made with a short striding motion, and is particularly effective against shorter opponents.

<u>Shooting</u>
In every type of basketball shot, the body should be lined up squarely with the basket if possible. The elbow of the shooting arm should be directly behind the ball. The eyes should be fixed on the rim of the basket, and the arm should be fully extended when the shot is released. A good shot will have a bit of backspin. When shooting a lay-up, the shooter should approach the basket at about a forty-five degree angle, with the dominant hand on the outside (that is, the right hand if approaching from the right side). The body should be lifted by the left leg. In a jump shot, the ball should be placed just above the front of the head, with the elbow of the shooting arm just behind the ball. The ball should be released with a snap of the wrist when the shooter is at the peak if his or her jump.

Catching and dribbling

The most important thing a person should do when catching a basketball is to keep his eyes on the ball, and make sure he has caught it before he moves. To catch a pass, the person advances towards the ball with hands extended: if the pass is at waist level or higher, the thumbs should be kept in and the fingers up. The hands should move towards the body as they receive the ball, so that they cushion the impact. In order to dribble a ball successfully, the person should keep his knees bent and move in a slight crouch. The forearm of the hand that is dribbling should be parallel to the ground, and the ball should be pushed with the fingertips rather than slapped with the palm. Most of the force in a dribble should be from the wrist.

Soccer

Soccer has long been the most popular sport in the world, and it is rapidly gaining in popularity in the United States. One of its advantages for physical education is that it is a sport that emphasizes foot-eye rather than hand-eye coordination, as do most other sports. Soccer also combines skills that can be practiced individually with team goals and strategy. It demands a great deal of body control and provides an excellent cardiovascular workout. Although regulation soccer matches are played with eleven on a team, any number of games can be played with a smaller group. All that is really required for soccer is a ball, although students may benefit from having special footwear, shin guards, and goalie gloves.

Soccer skills

Tackling and goalkeeping

In soccer, tackling is primarily concerned with taking the ball away from an opposing player, rather than bringing that player to the ground. A single-leg tackle may be used when approaching a player from behind, the side, or from straight ahead. The defender uses one leg to reach for the ball, while the other supports the body. The goal keeper on a soccer team is the only player allowed to use his or her hands. Because goal keepers may be required to dive for a ball, they often wear some protective padding. If a goalie is not close enough to a ball to catch it, he or she may want to punch it away. Once the goalie has controlled the ball, he or she may roll it, throw it, or kick it away.

Dribbling and kicking

In soccer, dribbling is simply controlling the ball while advancing it in a certain direction. The ball is moved by gently touching it with the inside or outside of the foot. Effective dribbling entails keeping the ball close to the body, rather than kicking and running after it. Students should get practice moving in different directions while dribbling. To try a shot or pass in soccer, the player needs to kick the ball. A proper pass is hit off the inside of the foot, with the opposite foot planted next to the ball and pointing in the direction of the pass. Sometimes a player may want to pass with the outside of the foot, although it is more difficult to pass the ball a great distance with this method. A shot is executed in the same way as a pass, with the ball making contact with the instep and the lower leg following through after the ball is struck.

Trapping and heading

Trapping the ball in soccer is the process of bringing a moving ball under control. Because the ball is often moving quite fast in a soccer match, it is a valuable skill to be able to slow it down. This can be done with any part of the body except for the hands or arms, although most trapping is done with the instep. In order to effectively trap the ball, the player must give way slightly when the ball makes contact, to prevent it from rebounding violently. Heading the ball is an effective way of moving an airborne ball. It is important for the player to strike the ball, rather than letting the ball strike him, since this makes the ball easier to control and the strike less painful. The head should lean back before the ball arrives, and then forcefully redirect the ball, following through in the desired direction.

Softball

Softball is a controversial game among physical educators; while some say that it is not active enough for young students, others argue that it is a good game to learn because it can be played throughout life. Softball is unlikely to be fun unless the participants have a decent skill level; therefore, activities should focus on basic skills until a sufficient level is reached. A softball field is easy to construct anywhere, but players will probably need to have gloves and helmets. Also, bats and balls will obviously be required. If students are going to require some time working on individual skills, they should each have a glove and ball. For inexperienced players, it is better to use a ball that is softer than normal.

Softball skills

Catching and throwing
If possible, a person trying to catch a ball should always move his body into the path of the ball. When catching a ball above the waist, both arms should be extended with the fingers up and the thumbs on the inside. Although the ball should be caught with the gloved hand, the other hand should be close by to catch the ball if it should pop out. When catching a ball on the ground, the player should advance towards it while crouching forward. The eyes should always be fixed on the ball, following it as it falls into the glove. After catching the ball, the player may need to throw it: this is typically done by holding the ball with three or four fingertips. The player should always step with the foot opposite to the throwing arm while throwing the ball.. Because throwing a softball is a difficult skill, students may benefit from slowing down the process to determine what feels natural.

Pitching and batting
In softball, a pitcher must start the throwing motion with both feet on the rubber rectangle on the mound. The ball is held in front of the body at first, and then the pitcher brings it back behind him, cocking the wrist. The pitcher then swings his throwing arm towards the plate while stepping forward with the opposite foot. The ball is released as the wrist snaps, with the arm continuing on its follow-through. The batter should be waiting with both hands gripping the bat, the dominant hand on top. As the ball arrives, the batter steps towards it with the foot closest to the pitcher. As the batter swings, he should keep his eye on the ball and try to swivel the hips as contact is made. After contact, the bat should continue with its follow-through.

Volleyball

Volleyball has long been a popular sport in physical education, because it offers a good workout, keeps an entire class involved, and improves a number of different skills. Volleyball is also a sport that is very popular with girls, so it is a nice alternative to male-dominated sports like football and baseball. A volleyball court can be set up just about anywhere, although many schools will have gymnasiums that can be converted into excellent volleyball courts. The height of the net may be adjusted in accordance with the skill level of the players. Any athletic shoe is appropriate for volleyball, although students should be sure to wear shoes with non-marking soles if the game is being played in a gym. Volleyballs are inexpensive and can be purchased in varying weights and degrees of softness, the choice depending on the location of the court and the skill level of the players.

Volleyball skills

Passing and setting
In volleyball, the ball can be passed twice on one side of the net before it must be struck onto the other side. Forearm passes are typically used to receive a serve or spike from the opposition, because they are effective at controlling a fast ball. In order to execute a forearm pass, the player stands with feet shoulder-width apart, one foot slightly ahead of the other. The forearms should be rolled outward to create a flat surface for the ball to hit. Depending on the speed of the ball, the player may want to slightly swing his arms forward, with elbows locked, during contact with the ball. An overhand (or set) pass is executed by positioning the body just under the ball. The hands should be cupped so that the ball makes contact with the fingers and thumbs of both hands at the same time. The legs should bend slightly during a set pass, so that the ball can be more easily controlled.

Serving
In order for students to enjoy a game of volleyball, they need to acquire a basic repertoire of skills. It may be necessary to spend a bit of time practicing serving before playing a regular game. An underhand serve begins with the left leg slightly forward, and both knees slightly bent. The ball is held in the left hand as the right hand swings back and then forward, striking the ball with an open or closed fist just above the waistline. Contact should be made with the heel of the hand. An overhand serve should put no spin on the ball. The left leg will also be slightly forward at the beginning of this serve. The ball should be tossed 2 or 3 feet above the right shoulder, after which the right arm should swing back and strike the ball while fully extended. Again, contact should be made with the heel of the hand.

Spiking and blocking
In volleyball, spiking is striking the ball from above the net into the opponent's territory, usually at a downward trajectory and with great force. Before spiking, a player may want to get a bit of a running start in order to maximize his jump. With the feet together, the player jumps straight up with both arms raised. The left arm should swing slightly in advance of the right, which strikes the ball with an open palm. A spike can be blocked by any of the three players on the front line of the opposing side. Blockers should jump a moment after the spiker, and raise both arms with fingers spread. The arms should be no farther apart than the width of the ball, as the point of the block is to forbid the passage of the ball.

Tennis

Tennis is very popular in physical education because it provides an excellent workout, yet can be played for a lifetime. Tennis is also a wonderful social game; men and women can play together in mixed doubles, and there are many breaks in the action that allow for conversation. The equipment requirements for tennis are a bit higher than for other sports; in order to play, every student will need a racket and a few balls. Tennis courts can be made of a variety of different surfaces, from concrete to grass. Students should have shoes that provide plenty of ankle support, as tennis requires stopping and starting frequently. A tennis net is usually about three feet high in the middle of the court.

Tennis skills

Lob, overhead shot, and serve

A lob shot in tennis is exactly like a ground stoke, except the angle of the racket is changed so that the ball will soar. Lob shots are typically made in an effort to send the ball over an opponent who has come close to the net. The overhead shot, or smash, is similar to a serve, and is struck when an opponent's lob has not gone high enough. An effective overhead shot sends the ball onto the opponent's side so quickly that he or she has no chance to return. Serving is probably the most difficult shot to master in tennis; a serve is struck from behind the baseline. When serving with the right arm the left leg is placed slightly forward and the knees are bent slightly. As the player rises, he throws the ball 2 or 3 feet above his head and strikes it with the right arm fully extended. The right leg will typically stride forward during a serve.

Volleying and ground strokes

Many people do not understand that tennis is a game primarily played with the legs; the player who can consistently put his or her body in the best position to hit a shot will probably win. The volley is the simplest shot in tennis, and is usually the first to be learned. A volleys is any shot that is hit before it bounces on you're the player's side of the court; a volley requires no backswing and is therefore not unlike "catching" the ball in the center of the racket. Ground strokes can be either forehand or backhand, and are considered to be the foundation of tennis skill. The backhand, which is hit with the non-dominant hand, is typically a bit harder to learn, and is usually a weaker shot than the forehand.

Boxing

Boxing is perhaps a bit too violent for most physical education programs, but it does provide a tremendous workout for the entire body. Besides boxing itself, most boxers spend a great deal of time jumping rope, running, and sparring. Punching a light bag is excellent for developing hand-eye coordination, muscular endurance, and cardiovascular endurance. Punching a heavy bag is excellent for developing the muscles of the arms and back, as well as those muscles of the legs that provide a firm foundation for punching. Many individuals can gain major health benefits by incorporating some of the training used by boxers into their workouts: shadow-boxing, for instance, is excellent for cardio-vascular health and muscular endurance.

Badminton

Badminton is a popular sport in physical education classes because it requires a fairly low level of skill (much less than tennis, for instance) and can provide a good cardiovascular workout. Badminton can be played both indoors and out, singles or doubles, and the basic equipment is relatively inexpensive. The rules are similar to those of volleyball: points can only be scored by the one who is serving, a basic game is played to fifteen points, etc. Instead of a ball, badminton is played with a shuttlecock, the most basic version of which consists of a piece of cork with feathers attached. Though badminton can be very strenuous when it is played at a high level, it can be enjoyed by individuals of any fitness level.

Aquatics

Aquatic exercises, also known as water calisthenics, are particularly effective for older individuals or those at a low level of fitness. They provide a low-impact workout for the entire body. The buoyant effect provided by being submerged in water is a major benefit for those plagued by muscle or joint pain. Exercises which involve moving against or through the water are isokinetic and are good for building muscular strength and endurance. Most water calisthenics program are not vigorous enough to provide a high level of cardiovascular exercise. Interestingly, though, it is easier to stretch in water, and so flexibility can be greatly improved by aquatic exercises.

Canoeing and kayaking

Canoeing and kayaking are extremely enjoyable activities that can also enhance both cardiovascular health and muscular endurance in the arms and trunk. In particular, the latissimus dorsi, deltoids, triceps, and biceps are exercised by paddling. In canoeing, an open, rounded, hollow craft is propelled across the water with a single, one-sided paddle. A kayak, on the other hand, entirely covers the lower body of the rower and is smaller and lighter. A kayaker uses a single paddle that has flat blades on both ends. If taken at a leisurely pace, canoeing and kayaking provide only a moderate workout, although they require a bit of upper-body endurance. Paddling at a rate of 4 miles per hour for longer than thirty minutes, however, is likely to bring an individual well into his or her target heart rate.

Diving

Competitive diving requires that the entire body be flexible, and that the legs be strong. While diving does not deliver much of a cardio-vascular workout, if it is done for a long period of time it can provide a fine test of muscular endurance. Many divers strive to improve their overall fitness by incorporating long periods of swimming into their workout. Also, some diving instructors recommend that during practice, divers should try to make a number of dives in rapid succession, as this will test the endurance of the leg muscles. Diving itself is excellent for flexibility, but most divers will be unable to complete more advanced maneuvers unless they undertake a determined stretching program away from the water.

Cross-country skiing

Cross-country skiing is one of the most comprehensive and arduous workouts available. It delivers an excellent cardiovascular workout, as well as a tremendous challenge to muscular strength and endurance. Moreover, the long strides and reach required for cross-country skiing enhance flexibility. Research has consistently shown that cross-country skiing causes the human body to consume a larger amount of oxygen than almost any other activity. Because cross-country skiing is so arduous, however, it is really only appropriate for individuals who are already in decent shape. For a long time, cross-country skiing was only an option in places that receive a large amount of snow; in recent years, stationary cross-country machines have enabled individuals to get the advantages of this activity indoors.

Track and field

Athletics, also known as track and field or track and field athletics, is a collection of sport events. The word is derived from the Greek word "athlos" meaning "contest". It is a collection of sport events, which can roughly be divided into running, throwing, and jumping.

Cross-training

Many fitness experts recommend cross-training as the most effective way to develop and maintain a high level of physical fitness. In cross-training, the individual alternates between two or more different kinds of physical activity. Triatheletes, who enter competitions in which they must run, swim, and ride a bicycle, are perhaps the best known example of cross-trainers. Cross-training is so effective because the different activities work different muscle groups, and therefore gives a more balanced workout. Cross-training also minimizes the strain on any one particular part of the body, which helps one avoid injury. Moreover, cross-training gives the individual some variety in his or her workout, which is likely to make it more enjoyable

Ultimate Frisbee

There are a number of vigorous games that can be played with a Frisbee, none of them more popular than Ultimate. When it is played at a high level, Ultimate provides an excellent cardiovascular workout as well as a stern test of muscular endurance. A game of Ultimate is a bit like rugby: teams try to advance the Frisbee into an opponent's end zone by passing it. Individuals may run only when they are not throwing the Frisbee, which cannot be dropped if a goal is to be scored. The agility and coordination required of a successful Ultimate player make it a popular choice among physical educators. Since there is a certain level of throwing and catching skill that must be acquired before a game of Ultimate can be undertaken, it may be a good idea to have students practice basic skills first.

Ropes course

Ropes course background
Over the past couple of decades, many physical education classes have incorporated adventure skills training because of the excitement they provide and the teamwork they necessitate. Ropes courses consist of a series of obstacles that students will need to overcome individually or as a team. Because many of these activities contain an element of risk, they should only be performed under close supervision and with the appropriate training. One of the wonderful things about ropes courses is that the different obstacles require different sets of skills, so students may have varying areas of expertise. Some activities may require strength and muscular endurance, whereas others may require balance and coordination.

Kitten crawl and two-rope bridge
In the ropes course activity known as the kitten crawl, students crawl across two parallel, incline ropes that begin at about five feet high and descend to a height of about two feet. In order to perform this task, students should be on all fours and slowly crawl down the rope. Spotters should be aware that students can fall between the ropes as well as off to either side. In the two-rope bridge activity, two ropes about five feet apart are attached to two

trees or posts. Students walk along the lower rope while holding onto the other with their hands above their head. The bottom rope should not be more than four feet off the ground, unless some sort of safety equipment is being used.

Commando crawl and tire swing
In the ropes course activity known as the commando crawl, students crawl a distance of four or five feet across the top of a 2-inch rope. This is done by lying on top of the rope and hooking one foot beneath it while the other leg hangs down for balance. The student then crawls across using his or her arms and leg. To prevent injuries from falls. the rope should not be set very high above the ground. In the tire swing obstacle, students have to move across a series of tires connected with ropes to a horizontal beam. The lengths of the ropes vary, so it will be difficult for students to move from high to low tires and vice versa. The tires should be set three or four feet apart, and none should be higher than four feet above the ground.

Balance beam, inclined log, and swinging log
In a balance beam activity, a log is attached between two trees or posts at a height of about five feet, and students are required to walk across it. If the beam is set higher than five feet, a safety rope should be tied to the student; if the beam is lower than five feet, then a spotter is all that is necessary. In the inclined log activity, a balance beam is placed at an angle. For beginners, it is typically easier to move up an inclined beam. Depending on the comfort level of the student, he or she may want to walk or crawl along the beam. In the swinging log activity, students have to traverse a log that is suspended by ropes from two trees, and is, therefore, moving. Falls are frequent in this activity, so the beam should not be set very high.

Three-rope bridge and tension traverse
In the ropes course activity known as the tension traverse, three ropes are tied horizontally between two trees. Two of the ropes are set at waist height, and the third is to be walked upon. This sort of bridge is often used for traversing a river or canyon, but it should never be set very high unless appropriate safety measures are taken. For instance, many times a rope will be tied around the student's waist and attached to one of the waist-high ropes. In a tension traverse, the student has to balance and move across a tightrope suspended very low between two trees. A rope may be tied at the top of one of the trees for the student to hang onto in an effort to control balance.

Electric fence and boardwalk
In the ropes course activity known as the electric fence, a group of students have to get over a piece of rope extended above the ground at a height of about five feet. In order to do this, they have to rely on teamwork and a small piece of wood, large enough for one person to stand on, so that the others can pass him or her across. There are a number of successful strategies for completing this task. In the group activity known as the boardwalk, four long boards are attached in such a way that a group of students can put their feet on the bottom boards and hold the top boards with their hands. In order to move the boards forward, the group has to coordinate the lifting of their arms and legs.

Cargo net jump and giant's ladder
In the ropes course activity known as the cargo net jump, students move up an inclined log to a jumping platform, from which they jump into the center of a cargo net. The net should be dense enough that there is no danger of falling through, and it should not be set more

than fifteen feet above the ground. A rope ladder may be the most convenient way for students to exit the net. In the activity known as the giant's ladder, students will have to balance, jump, and swing up an enormous ladder made of logs. The rungs of the ladder should be a few feet apart, so students should have some kind of safety rope in case they fall through. Once the student reaches the top of the ladder, he or she can be lowered to the ground with the safety rope.

Faith fall and stream crossing
A common group activity on a ropes course is a faith fall, in which one person falls backward into the arms of the rest of the group. In order to perform this exercise in trust and teamwork, the individual should stand on some elevated platform slightly above the outstretched arms of his fellows. The people who are going to do the catching should not grasp each other's hands, as this may result in heads smashing together when the person lands. In the activity called stream crossing, students have to move from one area to another without touching the ground. They are given squares of some material to walk on, but there are not as many squares as people, so the students have to devise some strategy to get all group members across.

Gymnastics

Artistic gymnastics
In artistic gymnastics, individuals perform various short routines in a number of different areas. The events that comprise artistic gymnastics are the vault, uneven bars, balance beam, floor exercises, pommel horse, still rings, parallel bars, and high bar. Most of the time, a routine on each apparatus lasts for about a minute. Although gymnastics at the highest level requires incredible coordination, flexibility, and strength, any person can benefit from learning to do some basic gymnastic maneuvers. The events typically performed by men and women are slightly different: men perform more activities designed to test strength, while the events in women's artistic gymnastics showcase artistry, balance, and agility.

Rhythmic gymnastics
In rhythmic gymnastics, participants develop routines in which they deftly manipulate one of five types of apparatus: balls, clubs, hoops, ribbons, or ropes. Performances in rhythmic gymnastics are made either individually or in five-person groups. In competitive rhythmic gymnastics, judges award points to the participants based on leaping ability, balance, pivot, flexibility, handling of the apparatus, and artistic merit. There is a bit of tumbling skill involved in advanced rhythmic gymnastics, although the main skills incorporated are hand-eye coordination and flexibility. Rhythmic gymnastics is considered to be an excellent way to develop body control, achieve good cardiovascular health, and improve flexibility.

Tumbling movements
Tumbling is any individual gymnastic maneuver in which the hips are at some point above the head. Tumbling maneuvers are used not only in gymnastics but also in cheerleading and dance. In tumbling, a handstand is executed when the entire body weight is supported with the hands and the body is perpendicular to the ground. A cartwheel is a movement in which the body is rotated laterally with the hips as an axis. The hands support the weight briefly until the feet come back around to provide support. A round off is a fast cartwheel in which the feet are brought together as the hands touch the ground. Then, the body is pushed up into the air, and the person lands on his or her feet.

Gymnastics, cheerleading, and dance often involve some of the self-propelled acrobatic maneuvers known as tumbling movements. In tumbling, an aerial is a cartwheel executed without the hands touching the ground. In some cases, a round off that does not involve the hands will be known as an aerial. A handspring is a movement in which a person springs from the feet forward so that he or she is supported by the hands, and then bounces back onto the feet. A back handspring, is simply a handspring executed by flipping backwards onto the hands and then onto the feet. Novice gymnasts should definitely be supervised as they learn to execute aerials, handsprings, and back handsprings.

Vaulting horse
The vaulting horse is an apparatus used in artistic gymnastics. In competition, the vaulting horse is used by both male and female gymnasts. Though the material used in vaulting horses has changed over the years, the basic vaulting horse is upholstered and measures about four feet long and sixteen inches across. Gymnasts get a running start, hit a trampoline, and then use the upholstered surface of the vaulting horse to propel themselves into the air. Then, they execute a series of saltos, or somersaults, and twists, rotations around an imaginary axis drawn from the top of the head to between the feet. Gymnasts will try to perform the trick as gracefully as possible while still being able to land safely and firmly.

Balance beam
The balance beam is an apparatus used in artistic gymnastics. In competition it is used exclusively by females. The balance beam is a metal or steel frame supporting a wooden beam on which a leather cover is placed. It is typically about 125 cm high, 5 meters long, and 10 cm wide. When performing on the balance beam, gymnasts attempt to execute a number of cartwheels, somersaults, and dance maneuvers while maintaining balance, demonstrating ease and confidence, and moving smoothly between maneuvers. Obviously, it is important to avoid wobbling on the beam, losing balance, or hesitating. At the end of a balance beam routine, gymnasts have to make a leap off the beam, attempting to keep the feet together and landing without stumbling.

Uneven bars
The uneven bars are an apparatus used in gymnastics, especially by females. It consists of two bars set beside one another at different heights; in competition, the upper bar will be set at a height of 246 cm and the lower at a height of 166 cm. The bars are usually made of either wood or plastic. When performing routines on the uneven bars, gymnasts try to keep their bodies as straight as possible, and move easily between the bars. During a routine, a gymnast is required to move from each bar to the other, and perform a move in which the center of gravity is brought close to the bar while spinning around it. It is also important to land cleanly and safely when finishing an uneven bars routine by letting go of the bar and sailing onto the mat.

Parallel bars
The parallel bars are a gymnastics apparatus used exclusively by male gymnasts. They are composed of two wooden or plastic bars suspended at the same height, usually about 200 cm, and set about 50 cm apart. Gymnasts grasp the two bars with their hands and perform a series of flips and holds. A routine on the parallel bars usually lasts about a minute, and is required to contain certain elements, for instance a handstand-type hold. At the end of a routine on the parallel bars, the gymnast thrusts himself upward off the bars, executes a

sequence of flips and twists, and attempts to land with his feet together and without stumbling or falling.

Pommel horse
The pommel horse is an apparatus used in artistic gymnastics. A typical pommel horse is a wooden beam atop a metal frame, with a leather cover on top. Exercises on top of the pommel horse will be designed both a single leg and both legs. Moves performed with single legs usually involve scissoring the legs apart and spinning. For the most part, a pommel horse routine consists of spinning the legs in a circular motion and turning around. These turns, executed with the elbows locked and the arms supporting the entire body weight, are called moores and spindles. At the end of a pommel horse routine, the gymnast dismounts by swinging his body onto the mat, or going into a handstand and pushing off.

Floor exercises
Floor exercises are performed by both male and female gymnasts during an artistic gymnastics program. The floor is typically about 12 meters across and twelve meters long. Most floors contain some sort of spring or foam underneath to aid the jumps and tumbling maneuvers that make up a routine. Floor exercises typically consist of a combination of gymnastic, dance, and acrobatic elements, including somersaults, cartwheels, and splits. At high levels of competition, gymnasts are required to complete a jump of at least two saltos (somersaults). A successful tumble in floor exercises will include a "stuck" landing, in which both feet touch the mat simultaneously and there is no sliding or stumbling.

Horizontal bar
The horizontal bar, otherwise known as the high bar, is a gymnastics apparatus used exclusively in competition by male gymnasts. Typically, the bar is suspended 280 cm above the ground. A routine on the horizontal bar involves a number of flips and reversals of hand position. In fact, in upper levels of competition it is mandatory for the gymnast to perform a maneuver in which he brings his center of gravity close to the bar while swinging around it, and another maneuver in which he throws himself high into the air above the bar and then catches back onto it on the way down. The climax of a horizontal bar routine occurs when the gymnast spins around the bar several times, then lets go and executes a series of somersaults, landing firmly with feet together.

Rings
The rings are an apparatus used in artistic gymnastics. In competition, the rings are used exclusively by men. Rings are usually made of wood or metal, covered with leather, and are suspended at the same height by ropes. In competition, rings are suspended 280 cm above the ground and about 50 cm apart. Rings are usually 18 cm in diameter. A routine on the rings must have components that test the swing, strength, and hold of the gymnast. One famous move associated with the rings is "iron cross," in which the gymnast suspends himself so that his or her arms are parallel to the ground. At the end of a routine on the rings, the gymnast attempts to perform a combination of saltos and land with his or her feet together and without stumbling or falling.

Teaching flow and continuity of movement
One of the most important things that students can acquire from training in gymnastics is a sense of measured, continuous movement. In order to encourage this, teachers should help students to work on their timing and on economizing movement. One way to help students develop a sense of flow is to break maneuvers down into small parts and allow students to

see the components of a complex movement. As students advance, it is proper to show how various gymnastic movements can be linked together so that transitions appear natural. Finally, students should be able to create a basic routine that incorporates a number of disparate elements into one seamless movement.

Introductions to body space and time
When teaching gymnastics, teachers should begin by introducing students to some basic concepts relating to the body, space, and time. First, students should be encouraged to focus on basic locomotor movements (walking, for instance), weight transference, and alert stillness. Students should also spend some time thinking about the body's potential for movement, and developing an awareness of the movements that are possible from any given position. Finally, the teacher should give students some basic instruction on timing, so that they can begin to consider the rhythmic elements of gymnastics. Many professionals suggest the gymnastics teachers should spend some time developing timing by leading simple activities that involve the regulation and synchronization of movement.

Relationship to others' rhythm
As part of an effective study of gymnastics, students should be encouraged to consider their movements in relation to the movements of other students. To this end, teachers should have students develop basic gymnastic routines for pairs and small groups. These groups should have a defined leader to whom the others look for guidance, though this leader may change throughout the routine. Many of these routines will be set to music, so it is important that students also work to develop a sense of rhythm. Teachers should start by having students perform very basic movements to a regular beat and allow the routines to become more complex as the students' sense of rhythm dictates. Also, students should be guided to a basic understanding of how movement can respond to and interpret music.

Dance

Direction
When dance instructors direct the movements of their dancers, they can do so either in relation to body position or in relation to the room. When instructors give directions in relation to the room, they are said to be giving directions of progressive movement. Directions can indicate that a dancer should move along the line of dance, which is a large circle extending around the room; against the line of dance; to the center. or to one of the walls. Directions may also be given with respect to body position, either by using the points of the compass or of the clock (as in, "take a step to five o'clock"). Dance instructors may also indicate turns by specifying right or left, clockwise or counter-clockwise, or inside or outside.

Backleading and center point of balance
In partner dance, the term backleading refers to a situation in which the follower is independent of the leader, or even contrary to the leader. Essentially, backleading occurs when the follower anticipates the next move of the leader but executes it too soon. Sometimes, though backleading can be helpful if it allows the couple to avoid collision with another couple. In any form of dance, the center point of balance is the area around the solar plexus. Dance instructors focus on this area when teaching various forms of dance because it need only shift two or three inches from the area of support before a person loses his or her balance. For this reason, a dancer needs to be conscious of his or her center point of balance at all times.

Open position

In partner dancing, open position means that the two people are connected only by the hands, rather than by other body parts as in closed position. The open position is used in swing dancing and Latin dancing. In these dances, much of the direction for movement is expressed in the tension and compression of the partners' arms. In order to successfully dance in open position, the leader must be able to guide the follower using only a basic frame. Only with a great deal of practice can communication between partners become so easy as to allow for fluidity on the dance floor. For most beginning dancers, open position dancers will look rigid and forced.

Spotting, supporting foot, and sway

Spotting is a techniques used in dance turns. When spotting, a dancer picks a stationary reference point and trains his or her eyes on it; when the motion of the turn makes it impossible for him or her to maintain eye contact with the spot, he or she swiftly rotates his or her head and regains eye contact with the spot. This tends to prevent dizziness and makes turns more fluid. When dance instructions refer to a supporting foot, they mean the foot that bears the full weight or most of the weight at the beginning of the step. Oftentimes, this term will be used when the other foot is doing some special move. In ballroom dancing, a sway occurs when the upper body gracefully moves away from the vertical and tilts to the right or left. In advanced ballroom dancing, sways are used to elegantly lead into some moves, as well as to give dancers better control.

Heel lead, no foot rise, replace, and side lead

In dance, a heel lead is a move in which the moving foot touches the ground heel-first, as if the person were walking. When the instructions for a particular dance refer to no foot rise, this means that the heel of the support foot remains in contact with the floor until the weight is transferred onto the other foot. A replace, on the other hand, occurs when the weight is put back on the previous support foot while maintaining its position. This occurs in dances where the weight is rocked forward onto another foot and then brought back to the original foot. In a side lead, the body swivels as a step is taken. In this sort of lead, the swivel is made to the side that feels more natural; for instance, the body swivels right as the left foot steps forward.

Toe lead, traveling dance, visual connection, and round dance

In dance, a toe lead occurs when the ball of the foot is the first thing to touch the ground. A traveling dance is one in which partners cover a significant distance on the dance floor. Waltzes, polkas, sambas, and foxtrots are all traveling dances. The visual connection between partners is essential for coordinated movement. Though many dance experts contend that physical connection is the best way to maintain communication during a dance, visual connection is necessary during periods in which dancers are apart, and can be especially helpful during turns. A round dance is a folk dance in which couples are either arranged in a giant circle, or in which couples proceed in a general circle around the room.

Ballet

A la seconde, avant, arriere, assemble, arabesque

In ballet, the phrase al la seconde indicates that a particular move is to be done to the side. The term avant means that a step is to be taken forward. The word arriere indicates that a step is to be taken backwards. The term assemble means that the first foot will swing out, and then the second foot will swing under the first, sending the dancer into a leap. This leap will conclude with feet together and landing at the same time. In an arabesque, the body is supported on one leg while the opposite leg is extended behind the body with the knee kept straight. The back is arched during an arabesque, and the back leg may either touch the ground or be raised in the air.

Fouette, grand jeté, pas, and port de bras
In ballet, a fouette (meaning "to whip") is a movement on one leg that forces the dancer to change the direction of the hip and torso without changing the direction or position of the weight-bearing leg. A grand jete is a long, horizontal jump, taking off from one leg and landing on the other. A grand jete usually involves doing a split in mid-air. A pas is simply a step. There are numerous variations on this term. Examples include pas de basque, a cross between a step and a leap; pas de chat, a sideways jump in which both legs are bent back to touch the buttocks; and a pas de bouree, in which the dancer takes small steps on his or her toes. Port de bras refers to the movement of the arms around the body during various ballet movements.

Attitude, battement, chaines, first position, and fourth position
In ballet, the attitude is the pose in which the dancer stands on one leg, with the other leg raised either in front (en avant) or behind (derriere). While holding an attitude, the leg bearing the weight is held with the knee bent at an angle of about 120 degrees. A battement is a kicking of the leg. There are various kinds of battement, for instance battement glisse (a rapid, short kick) and a battement lent (a slow, long kick). A chaines is a series of rapid turns made while moving along an imaginary line or circle. First position, in ballet, is when the dancer stands with heels pressed together so that the feet make a straight line. Fourth position is when the feet are parallel to one another and set slightly apart.

Third position, fifth position, and tours en l'air
In third position both feet are perpendicular to the body with the right foot in front of the left and positioned so that the heel of the right foot is directly in front of the arch of the left foot. Fifth position is similar to third position, except the feet are positioned so that the toes of each foot are next to the heel of the other. Tours en l'air are jumps in which the dancer performs either a single or double rotation while in the air. This is a difficult movement generally performed by male dancers; it can finish with the dancer either in an attitude or arabesque.

Plie, pirouette, rond de jambe, second position and saute
In ballet, a plie occurs when the knees are bent, sometimes all the way until the buttocks touch the feet. A pirouette is one of the more well-known moves in ballet, and occurs when the dancer spins on one leg with the other foot resting on the knee of the supporting leg. Rond de jambe are circles made with the legs; they can be accomplished in the air, or along the ground. A dancer is said to be in second position when his or her legs are more than shoulder width apart, with toes turned out. The French word for jump is sauté, and there are a number of sautés used in ballet. Petits sauté are small jumps in which the feet maintain their position; in changements (in which the feet exchange locations);, and echappes sautés, in which the feet split apart mid-jump and land in second position.

Aerobic dance

A basic session of aerobic dance lasts from thirty to sixty minutes and involves running, hopping, jumping, skipping, bending, stretching, and sliding. These sessions are typically led by an instructor, who guides participants through periods of warm-up, vigorous, and cool-down exercises. Aerobic dance provides an excellent cardiovascular workout, and is very good for burning fat, building muscular endurance, and increasing flexibility. Perhaps best of all, aerobic dance provides a total-body workout. It can also be performed just about anywhere. Individuals with a low level of fitness or with health concerns can begin at a low level of movement and gradually make their workout more difficult.

Considered aerobic fitness

A minimum of aerobic fitness has been achieved when you are able to exercise three times a week at 65% of your maximum heart rate. The easiest means of achieving this level of fitness is by running for 30 minutes three or four times a week. Moderate aerobic fitness is achieved by exercising four or more times a week for at least 30 minutes at a heart rate that is 75% or more of maximum. This level of aerobic fitness is appropriate for athletes who are seeking to play vigorous sports like football or tennis. Maximum aerobic fitness can only be achieved by working close to maximum heart rate several times a week and by exercising vigorously almost every day. In order to achieve this level of fitness, you must consistently work beyond your anaerobic threshold. A good way to do this is having interval training or brief, high-intensity workouts.

Aerobic circuit training

Fitness professionals consistently recommend aerobic circuit training as an extremely effective way to promote and maintain general health. In aerobic circuit training, aerobic and strength exercises are combined so that both cardiovascular and muscular fitness are developed. Aerobic circuit training can be done alone, but it is probably most commonly associated with gyms and health clubs, because it usually requires a variety of fitness equipment. An aerobic circuit workout might combine cardiovascular activities like jogging, stair-climbing, or cross-country skiing with weight-training exercises like lifting weights. Those who practice aerobic circuit training report positive gains in muscular definition and cardiovascular fitness.

Closed position dancing

Closed position is a form of partner dancing in which two dancers hold and face one another. Closed positions of dance require that partners contact one another with more than just the hands; typically, partners either touch with their legs, hips, or shoulders, and one partner may be at times supported by the other. In the most common type of closed position, derived from the waltz, the right hand of the leader is on the back of the follower, while the left hand of the follower rests on the right shoulder of the leader. The other hands of each dancer are clasped together. Many kinds of folk dance involve different forms of closed position; for instance, the Scandinavian dances in which the leader holds the waist of the follower.

Body contact style of dance

One of the forms of closed position (a form of dance in which partners face one another) used in partner dance is called body contact. In this form, the direction given by the lead partner to the other is made through more extensive contact than just the arms. Different dances may entail contact with the thighs, hips, chest, cheek, or forehead. In ballroom dance, couples often touch at the thighs and hips. In many forms of body contact dancing, couples connect at the thigh and then are standing slightly to the side of one another. Most of the more provocative forms of dancing, including the tango and the lambada, make extensive use of the body contact style.

Folk dance

A folk dance is any primitive, tribal, or ethnic form of dance. Many folk dances originated as a component of some ritual or ceremony. Folk dances may entail some sort of special costume, though many , such as the square dance, are performed in a variety of settings. Folk dances are a great way for children to learn about foreign cultures while improving their coordination, timing, and cardiovascular health. Some of the more common folk dances include English Morris dancing, the Spanish fandango, the Irish jig, The Hawaiian hula, the Maypole dance, and the Bohemian polka. These dances are generally associated with a certain song or style of music.

Square dancing

A square dance is a basic folk dance in which four couples are arranged in a square formation, and execute a series of commands given by a caller. In a square dance, the caller does not actually participate in the dance. Most of the steps used in square dance are based on the traditional dances of American immigrants. Dances from which the American square dance has borrowed include the quadrille, Morris dance, and English country dance. At present, there are two common types of square dance: traditional square dance and modern Western square dance.

Contra body movement

Contra body movement (sometimes abbreviated as CBM) is a term used to describe a certain way of coordinating the movements of two dancers. Specifically, during a dance step, the dancer turns his or her body towards whichever foot is moving. For example, if the left foot is moving forward, the torso should swivel to the left; when the left foot moves back, the torso swivels to the right. Contra body movement is a common feature of ballroom dances like the waltz, foxtrot, and tango. The point of contra body movement is to make a smooth transition from movement that is straight ahead or behind to movement to one of the sides.

Connection in dance

Any kind of partner dance relies on connection between two people. Although partners may have to rely on other forms of communication, such as hand signals, the most graceful dance is led using entirely physical connection. In a partner dance, one person leads the other by gently guiding him or her. The physical connection through which the leader guides the follower is called the frame. In tension or leverage connection, dancers pull apart from one another with an equal but opposite force that is generated by the trunk or by momentum rather than by the arms. In compression connection, the dancers are pressed together. Although tension and compression may be sustained in swing dancing, in most dances they are used to indicate upcoming movements.

Judo

In Japanese, the word judo means "gentle way." This is perhaps because judo is one of the more non-combative and graceful of the martial arts. When properly practiced, judo also entails a large amount of training and supervision, so injuries are infrequent. Judo is typically practiced with a partner and under the supervision of a master. Judo borrows many of the moves of jiu-jitsu, especially those in which the weight of one's opponent is used against him or her. However, not only is judo a weaponless form of combat, it also eschews any of the jiu-jitsu moves which could be dangerous in a friendly competition. After the ceremonial bow, a judo match begins with the combatants grasping one another by the jacket collar and sleeve.

Karate

Karate is a Japanese art of unarmed self-defense. In karate, the individual assumes a special stance and delivers specially targeted blows with his or her hands and feet while shouting. Karate is successful because it trains the individual to use a minimum of movement and violence to achieve his or her ends. As a workout, karate is exceptional: it trains all of the major muscle groups, and provides a fantastic cardiovascular workout. In order to practice karate effectively, an individual must have excellent balance and flexibility. Though karate is related to judo, its emphasis on blows rather than throws distinguishes it. Karate is the most globally popular of all the martial arts.

Jujitsu

The Japanese word jujitsu is derived from two characters meaning flexibility or suppleness and art. However, this name should not fool any would-be participants into assuming that jujitsu is a non-violent activity. Rather, jujitsu gets its name because it relies on using passivity to guide one's opponent astray using his or her own force. The techniques of jujitsu allow a master to physically manipulate even a much larger and stronger opponent. Jujitsu is considered to be one of the most comprehensive martial arts in existence. Many of the techniques found in jujitsu rely on joint locks, chokes, and throws, all of which incorporate an advanced knowledge of movement and the human body.

Kung Fu

Kung Fu is a Chinese martial art that is based on assuming low, strong stances and making powerful blocks. Because Kung Fu relies on positively resisting aggression, it requires a great deal of patience as well as muscular strength. Kung Fu has existed for many years, and a number of different offshoots have developed, many based on the movements of animals like the crane or snake. Even today, a variety of Kung Fu styles are passed down within families and communities. The styles that developed in the north emphasize kicking and punching, while the Kung Fu styles of the South are more akin to boxing. Some of the blocks in Kung Fu are powerful enough to break the arm of one's opponent.

Kendo

Kendo is a form of fencing that was developed in Japan during the nineteenth century. Though kendo was originally created in the service of samurai warriors, today it is more commonly practiced with bamboo sticks and protective equipment. The sword used in kendo is typically about four feet long, and is grasped with both hands. In kendo competition, one must strike one's opponent with a particular side of the outer third of one's sword. In order to facilitate movement, a participant usually wears a long skirt slit in the middle. It is also typical for a face mask, breastplate, gloves, and protective apron to be worn.

T'ai Chi Chuan

There are a number of different forms of the ancient Chinese art of exercise, personal growth, and meditation known as T'ai Chi Chuan. T'ai Chi can be practiced both to promote health and as a means of self-defense. Successful practice will increase awareness of the body, foster a mood of tranquility, and exercise all the major muscles. In order to practice T'ai Chi, the individual must stand such that his or her center of gravity is in his or her trunk or abdomen. This allows breathing to become deep and steady, and the various systems of organs to become more balanced and harmonious. T'ai Chi aims to bring the individual into harmony with nature and reduce conflict with environmental stressors.

Aikido

Aikido is a martial art hailing from Japan. It was developed using elements from jujitsu and kenjitsu, and like these arts, attempts to use the opponent's own fight against him or her. Aikido also places emphasis on grace and economy of movement. Aikido incorporates some of the skills used in spear and sword combat, especially the body movements that have been developed in support of these forms of combat. One of the hallmarks of aikido is the use of joint locks, in which an opponent is immobilized by the application of pressure to a specific body part, and the throw, in which an opponent is made to fly forward by redirecting his or her momentum.

Tae Kwon Do

Though Karate may be the best-known martial art in the United States, Tae Kwon Do is the martial art which is most commonly practiced world-wide. Tae Kwon Do is a Korean martial art, though it bears a close similarity in appearance to Karate. Tae Kwon Do is not only a system of self-defense, it is also an art form and a way of life. The movements taught in Tae Kwon Do are meant to be performed smoothly and swiftly, and with the economy of motion that maximizes power. Part of training in Tae Kwon Do is striving to improve the artistic form of every maneuver. Over time, the regular practice of Tae Kwon Do will improve posture, coordination, and body control.

Capoeira

Capoeira is a Brazilian art of self-defense that has become very popular in the United States in recent years. A session of capoeira training provides both an excellent cardiovascular workout and dance training. It aspires to be a mixture of the participants' body and soul, requiring both mental and physical awareness and agility. Capoeira is performed with a group of people standing in a circle around two combatants, who perform a stylized sequence of fake punches, blocks, and dodges. In a recreational session of capoeira no blows are actually landed. Capoeira is always accompanied by music, mostly percussive, and chanting, which gives a rhythm to the mock-fight.

Sumo wrestling

Sumo derives from the Japanese word meaning "struggle." Sumo was not always a sport for over-sized men in strange diapers. In fact, for a long time it was practiced in order to train soldiers for battle. In fact, all of the ceremony and ritual that accompanies modern sumo wrestling is derived from its military origins. Over time, specific rules, rankings, and the size of the ring have standardized sumo competition. In a sumo match, a combatant loses if he is forced out of the ring or touches any part of his body higher than his knee to the ground. In order to defeat an opponent, sumo wrestlers use a variety of slaps, holds, and tackles.

Family and Emotional Health

Friendship

There is no documented society in human history that has not demonstrated admiration for the institution of friendship. In fact, friendship, with its bonds of loyalty, affection, and respect, is one of the great joys of life. Unfortunately, friendship is not available to people who are not ready to work for it. It requires constant cultivation in order to prosper: individuals must be willing to listen, to express themselves honestly, to tolerate the faults of their friends, and to value trust and loyalty. Most people find that the friendships formed during childhood and adolescence are the deepest and most enduring, perhaps because the formation of strong friendships during this period helped the individual to develop an identity outside the family domain.

Nuclear and extended family

A nuclear family is a family group consisting of one adult couple (one male and one female) and their children. The strong bond among the members of a nuclear family is a consistent feature of almost every society, with one notable exception being the Israeli kibbutz, in which children are raised by the entire community without any particular parents. An extended family consists of more than one adult couple, often the parents, brothers and sisters of a particular heterosexual couple. In many human societies, people live among their extended families, rather than just in a nuclear family unit. This is especially typical in societies where people do not have to move particularly quickly (that is, in agrarian or industrial rather than hunting and gathering societies).

Raising children

At the most basic level, young children have needs for food, shelter, and protection that have to be met. Children also have psychological and emotional needs, and sometimes these are more difficult for a new parent to understand. In order to have strong and meaningful relationships later in life, a child must have a model. In order to enter a certain social role later in life, children need to be socialized effectively, and this happens first in the family unit. Parents are the first to set rules and social norms, and so children get their idea of what constitutes acceptable behavior from their parents. As children grow older, there will begin to be a tension between their need for independence and their ties to the family; parents should be sensitive to their children's needs regarding dependence/independence.

Diverse American families

Although many people may still consider the stereotypical American family as middle-class and white, variety is really the norm when it comes to family arrangement. All of the different cultures that combine in American society bring their own ideas of the family. In African-American households, for instance, women are often seen as the head of the household. In Chinese-American families, both husband and wife may be expected to work even if the wife does not get to make as many decisions. In Latino families, wives are seen as the keepers of wisdom, even if they defer to their husbands on practical matters.

Furthermore, many American families now have a single parent or two parents of the same sex. According to most studies, the most important factor in the development of children is the stability and love in the family, not its particular composition.

Psychosocial development

Every individual has a set of values, i.e., criteria by which they understand and judge the world. Sometimes, individuals claim to have one set of values even though outwardly they are acting according to another. In order to clarify your values, it is a good idea to consider carefully the consequences of your choices and ensure that they are moral and positive. Health professionals define individual values as being either instrumental or terminal: instrumental values are ways of thinking that a person holds important, for instance, being loyal or loving; terminal values are goals or ideals that a person works towards, for instance, happiness. Individuals should be sensitive to the values they are promoting with their choices, given the rapid changes that can occur in individual and societal values.

Self-actualization

In order to reach your highest potential, you have to satisfy a number of basic needs. To illustrate this, health professionals have set up a pyramid of psychological health so that individuals can see the conditions that must be met at each level in order to advance psychologically. Before anything else is accomplished, your physiological needs for food, water, shelter, and sleep must be met. Then, if these needs are satisfied, you can work on achieving safety for yourself and your loved ones. When this is accomplished, you are free to develop loving relationships and fit into a society. These relationships are a necessary foundation for self-esteem and a healthy respect for other people. The person who has satisfied all of these needs is said to be ready for self-actualization, the fulfillment of the individual's unique potential.

Emotional intelligence

In recent years, health professionals have determined that what is known as emotional intelligence may be just as important as an individual's intelligence quotient (IQ). According to the psychologist Daniel Goleman, there are five areas of emotional intelligence: self-awareness, altruism, personal motivation, empathy, and the ability to love and be loved. Studies have shown that individuals with a high level of emotional intelligence will succeed at work and in developing positive personal relationships. An individual's emotional intelligence is not necessarily the same throughout the person's life. Many businesses have begun taking active steps to develop the emotional intelligence of their employees. Essentially, developing one's emotional intelligence requires understanding one's feelings and learning how to express them.

Self-esteem

Self-esteem is the way that you think about yourself. Every person wants to feel important and valued in society and optimistic about the future. Having healthy self-esteem is not only derived from these feelings, but it makes it possible for you to do the things necessary to make yourself happy and content. Most health professionals agree that an individual's self-esteem is largely determined during childhood. Low self-esteem often haunts those who have been abused in the past, and these experiences can unfortunately lead people to seek out relationships in which they are treated poorly. One technique that many health professionals recommend for boosting self-esteem is positive thinking and talking. Even if it feels forced, studies have shown that encouraging yourself to take an optimistic viewpoint can eventually make good self-esteem a habit.

Communicating emotions

The majority of communications taking place in academic and business settings involve factual information. Unfortunately, individuals who are adept at communicating facts may struggle when attempting to communicate personal feelings in a relationship. Personal relationships, which are basic to happiness, can develop only when feelings are openly and honestly shared. In order to do this, people should work on asking straight-forward questions and honestly answering questions about themselves. Being a good listener, asking the right questions, and respecting the other person's answers are necessary parts of establishing good emotional communication. Sometimes, though, this may mean putting aside your own opinions so that you can fully engage with another person and come to understand the other's point of view.

Refusal skills

Students should be equipped with skills in saying "no" to any request they prefer to decline. Techniques for saying "no" are known as refusal skills. First, students should not let the person pressuring them continue talking for a long time; it is always best to quickly decline and change the subject. Refusal skills are especially useful when teens are trying to say "no" to sex. If another person pressures a student to have sex and threatens to break off the relationship, the student should acknowledge the superficiality of the other person's love and be unmoved. It is always best to avoid engaging in a debate with any person who is trying to pressure you into a negative health behavior; simply repeating your refusal until the conversation stops is a very effective way to be assertive without being aggressive.

Nonverbal communication

Even though we normally think of communication as something we do through spoken or written language, we are constantly sending messages to one another with our bodies and tone of voice. Often, physical messages are sent and interpreted without either party being aware. Some of the signals that are used are consistent across cultures, whereas others are unique to a particular culture. For instance, slumped shoulders generally mean passivity and submission in every society. Alternatively, some cultures interpret eye contact as a sign of respect, and others see it as a sign of hostility. One should try to be aware of the messages one is sending with one's posture and gestures to avoid sending messages that are insulting or self-defeating.

Male and female communication

Extensive research has indicated that there are distinct, but not universal, differences between the ways that men and women express themselves. There are various hypotheses for why this is so: some suggest that men need to disclose facts and assert their status with language more often, while women are more schooled in intimate conversations between friends and kin. Many studies have shown that women are more adept at reading body language and in discerning the underlying meaning in verbal communication, while men are better at extracting the factual content. Women seem to be better able to determine the emotional state of the speaker, and often may respond to this rather than the particular words that are spoken. These differences do not hold true for every man or woman, but acknowledging their existence might help to defuse potential conflicts between the sexes.

"I" message

When health educators refer to "I" messages, they mean the process wherein a person acknowledges his or her own feelings and accepts responsibility for them. An "I" message generally consists of the way you feel and the conditions under which you feel that way. An example is "I feel sad because you are ignoring my feelings." The philosophy behind the "I" message is that you control your response to a given situation, even if it seems as if external influences are causing you to feel a certain way. Forcing yourself to acknowledge the way you feel is a good way to take control of your behavior and to prevent others from exerting control. Moreover, most individuals report that they actually feel better when they are open about their feelings.

Gender differences

Science has documented that men and women not only have differences in appearance but actually think and sense in different ways. In most cases, women have stronger senses of hearing, smell, and taste, while men tend to have better vision. Men tend to be stronger, though women often have better fine motor skills. Brain scans have displayed significant differences in the areas of the brain that are more active in men and women. Science has not yet determined whether these differences are entirely physiological or whether upbringing and environment contribute. Most scientists believe that a combination of nature and nurture create the differences between the genders.

Dating

Although the word dating has come to assume a romantic connotation in American society, dating is really any time that is set aside to spend exclusively with another person. Friends are dating if they make a point to see one another. Unfortunately, the tendency to confuse dating with casual sex and drinking has led to a decrease in the amount of casual dating in the United States. Many people assume that dating is strictly for finding a mate, whereas dating has a host of other benefits. These benefits vary from teaching one to make good conversation to getting to know various kinds of people and ways of life. Dating, in its ideal form, is a great way to explore oneself by getting to know a wide variety of people.

Biochemical view of love

A great deal of research has been conducted to isolate and study the chemicals that act in the brain during the experience of romantic love. Scientists have taken a close look at neurotransmitters (the chemicals that send messages throughout the brain) and determined that dopamine, norepinephrine, and phenylethylamine all contribute to the physical feelings of love: sweaty palms, racing heart, deep and rapid breathing. These brain chemicals all have a marked similarity to amphetamines, and the brain can eventually become desensitized to them. On the other hand, partners who develop long-term, stable relationships may gradually increase the brain's release of endorphins, which produce a feeling of well-being and peace.

Anthropological view of love

Romantic love is defined as an intense attraction in which partners idealize each other and relationships are long lasting. Almost every society has some form of romantic love. Many anthropologists speculate that romantic love evolved as a means to induce men and women to form the partnerships in which children can thrive. That is, they view romantic love as a way to propagate the human species. Indeed, many studies have shown that romantic love tends to wane after about four years, about the length of time required to raise a child through infancy. Anthropological studies of many different societies have confirmed that couples tend to break up and desire new partners after about four years together.

Cognitive development

Jean Piaget noted four stages of cognitive development in children. Sensorimotor stage is the period from birth until approximately age 2, during which the infant develops sense organs and learns that objects still exist even when they are out of sight. The preoperational stage extends from age 2 to age 7 and is marked by the child's increasing ability to imagine the mental lives of others (to develop sympathy). The concrete operational stage lasts from age 7 to 12, and the child develops a number of cognitive structures, including the rule of conservation (the understanding that an object's volume does not decrease if its shape is changed). The final stage is known as the formal operational stage and takes place after age 12. In this stage, which not every human undergoes, the capacity for abstract thought (the ability to theorize rather than to rely on direct observation for knowledge) is developed.

Infancy, toddlerhood, and early and middle school age

Infancy extends from birth until age 2. During this period, individuals develop social attachments, basic motor skills, and notions of cause and effect. Toddlerhood extends from age 2 to 4 and is marked by the development of language, the exploration of life through fantasy and play, and an improvement in self-control. Between ages 5 and 12, sometimes called early and middle school age, the individual learns the value of cooperation, basic morals, gender roles, and some basic skills. This is also the period in which individuals typically begin to honestly appraise themselves and consider their place in the world.

Adolescence and early adulthood

Adolescence generally extends from age 13 to 22. During this period, individuals undergo a rapid physical maturation. They will typically begin to have sexual relationships, will seek to develop a personal identity, and may emphasize a peer group over the family. During this period, individuals begin to consider possible careers and should be establishing an internal set of moral values. Early adulthood is thought to extend from age 23 to 30 and to involve a movement toward marriage or longer-lasting romantic relationships. Early adulthood is often focused on the establishment of a career, though individuals will often have children during this period.

Middle and later adulthood

Middle adulthood extends from ages 31 to 50. During this period, individuals occupy themselves with household maintenance and child rearing. Many individuals also devote a great deal of their middle adulthood to advancing their career. Later adulthood begins at 51 and lasts until death. It is inaccurate to suggest that all personal growth has been accomplished by this point. On the contrary, most individuals in later adulthood gradually accept the events of their life, develop a healthy perspective on life and death, and begin to redirect their personal energies to new roles and responsibilities.

Managing moods

Moods are emotional states lasting for a few hours or days. Though every individual will have bad moods from time to time, some are better at managing their moods than others. Researchers have demonstrated that the most effective ways to solve a problem, and hence emerge from a bad mood, are to take immediate action, think about other successes, resolve to try harder, or reward oneself. Individuals who try to distract themselves, perhaps through socializing, will find that this only partly improves their mood. The worst things to do when you are in a bad mood are to vent at another person, isolate yourself, or give up. Using alcohol or drugs to escape a bad mood is also an ineffective way to feel better.

Self-image

One of the most important determinants of how an individual forms relationships with others may be how that individual perceives him or herself. If an individual feels unlovable, it may be impossible for him or her to seek affection from others. If a person has confidence in him or herself, he or she should be able to develop honest and open relationships with others. Though the phrase is a bit clichéd, it is nevertheless true that a person cannot love another without loving him or herself. Sadly, studies have shown that individuals who have a negative opinion of themselves tend to establish relationships with people who treat them poorly and thus reinforce their negative self-image.

Assertiveness

Although assertiveness is often confused with pushiness, it simply means acknowledging one's own feelings and making one's desires known to other people. Being assertive does not ensure that one will always get what one wants. Often, though, the simple act of expressing one's opinion is enough to destroy any feelings of frustration or impotence. Many individuals remain passive for most of their lives and then occasionally explode out of frustration; this is generally a result of not being consistently and politely assertive. Studies have consistently shown that assertive individuals have less stress in their lives, probably because they feel they are in control.

Conflict resolution

It is inevitable in life that everyone will come into conflict with some difficult individuals. Many people persistently spar with others because they have a personality disorder based on low self-esteem or illness. For the most part, you will not be close enough to an individual to try and change them in any permanent way. Therefore, in most cases of conflict, health professionals recommend acknowledging the other person's viewpoint and then finding a way to either avoid or circumvent that person. If confrontation is necessary, you should state your feelings honestly and politely. If possible, try to avoid making confrontations personal. Sometimes it helps to have a third party mediate an especially contentious dispute.

Sexual attraction

Sexual attraction is just one of the many factors that contribute to the formation and maintenance of long-term relationships. In most studies, individuals are found to be most sexually attracted to people who share their age, race, ethnicity, and socioeconomic background. Many sociologists speculate that this is because individuals have more access to people who are similar to themselves and because they intuitively understand that they are more likely to be approved by similar people. In general, men put more emphasis on looks in determining sexual partners, whereas women may value other qualities like dependability and affluence. This may be due in part to the historical need for men to find women who can reproduce easily, while women have sought men who can provide for them during their period of pregnancy and child rearing.

Single life

It is becoming increasingly common in American society for men and women to go their entire lives without marrying. Single people are no longer looked down upon as somehow defective by the rest of society, and so more and more people feel comfortable remaining single for their entire lives. The most commonly given reason for staying single is not being able to find the right person. Most studies show that few people intend to remain single forever, but they are willing to wait until their expectations are met. Some singles still claim that they are discriminated against by insurance companies, credit organizations, and medical care providers. Despite the claims of some that giving equal rights in these areas will erode the institution of marriage, there is growing support for singles' rights.

Failed love relationship

Although people traditionally assume that being abandoned by a romantic partner is worse than leaving a partner, many studies have discovered that the partner who ends a relationship is often more subject to psychological traumas like guilt, uncertainty, and awkwardness. The only real help for the pain of a breakup is time, but the process can be eased if both parties treat one another with respect and kindness. During a breakup, it is important to remind oneself of one's own value as an individual and not to take the other person's decision as a definitive statement about one's worth. Also, it is important to remain engaged with other people despite any feelings of fear one may experience; it is easy to allow feelings of insecurity caused by a breakup to contaminate other relationships in one's life.

Marriage partner

For the most part, people marry someone from the same geographical area and culture as themselves. However, interracial and intercultural marriages are becoming more common and socially accepted. Most studies have revealed that individuals desire a partner with whom they share values and can communicate effectively and for whom they are willing to make adjustments and tolerate flaws. Many couples undergo premarital assessments to determine if they are truly right for one another. These assessments typically try to measure how compatible the interests, values, and behavior of the two people are. Most couples benefit from some form of counseling before marriage.

Marriage

Despite claims that the institution of marriage has been eroding in recent years, more than 90% of Americans will marry in their lifetime. In the past, marriage was as much a business deal as a romantic union; parents often arranged the marriages of their children for social advancement. Though this is still common in some countries, in the United States, people are more likely to wed because of a romantic affection for one another. Yet even today, many couples marry because the woman is pregnant or as a way to escape the authority of their parents. Typically, males are slightly older than females at the age of marriage.

Marital difficulty

Many marriages or committed relationships go askew because the individuals disagree about money. Interestingly, fights about money are rarely about how much money the couple has; instead, couples tend to fight about how the money will be spent and who will keep track of their collective finances. Another subject about which partners often fight is sex. As a relationship matures, one party may lose interest in sex, to the frustration of the other. Married couples often fight if one party feels they always have to initiate sex or if one party feels hurt by the other's indifference. The sex life of a couple will likely change many times throughout the course of a long relationship; the best way to ensure mutual satisfaction is to always be compassionate and communicative.

Sociological types of marriage

According to sociologists, there are two kinds of marriage: traditional and companion-oriented. In a traditional marriage, the two people conform to the prescribed marital roles of their society; for instance, the man becomes the provider and the woman the child-rearer. In a companion-oriented marriage, the partnership and the rewards of romantic love are more important than marital roles. Some sociologists also distinguish different categories for romantic marriages, in which the sexual passion that originally sparked the union remains present for an abnormally long time, and rescue marriages, in which one partner sees marriage as a way to escape some traumatic event in his or her past.

Benefits of marriage

Even though many people claim that the institution of marriage is under assault these days, there are still plenty of documented reasons to suggest that married people lead better lives than singles. Strong, healthy marriages seem to make people healthy and happy. In general, married people have been shown to have more money, better health, and better sex lives than singles. In particular, marriage seems to benefit men. Married men exhibit lower rates of alcohol and drug abuse, depression, and self-destructive behavior than single men. Married men have sex twice as often as singles and are more likely to be satisfied with their sex lives. Married women, on the other hand, see their average wages go down, though this may be explained by the large proportion of married women who work less in order to raise children.

Extramarital affairs

Extramarital affairs are about the most devastating thing that can happen to a marriage. If one partner is discovered to be cheating, the other partner is likely to feel abandoned, inadequate, unloved, and angry. When extramarital affairs are a problem, the parties need to ask themselves whether they really love one another and feel any commitment.

In a different sort of way, marriages in which both members work can be difficult. It may be necessary for one party to move for work or for one to stay home and raise children. When one person's career seems to be more important than the other's, conflicts can often develop. In order to avoid the problems caused by dual-career marriages, individuals should understand their partner's ambitions before deciding whether that person is right for them.

Divorce

Although divorce is becoming more popular all over the world, the United States still perennially has one of the highest rates. Divorce, which is seen by some as a way out of a bad marriage, is not without profound consequences itself. Individuals who have been divorced frequently report depression, anxiety, and feelings of hopelessness as a result. Interestingly, divorced individuals are much more likely to marry again than singles who have never been married. Moreover, with each successive divorce, an individual becomes more and more likely to remarry. This suggests that marriage creates a pattern of companionate living that is very hard to break.

The breakup of a marriage has enormous, indeed incalculable, effects on the children of that marriage. If children are very young when the marriage dissolves, they often remain babyish and emotionally immature for abnormally long periods. Young children may blame themselves for the end of a marriage. Slightly older children may also exhibit these effects and may have a hard time forming relationships outside the family. Teenagers from divorced families tend to have a hard time establishing independence. Interestingly, though, divorce has not been shown to adversely affect a child's performance in school. The negative consequences seem to be exclusively psychological and social.

Couples therapy

It is increasingly common for couples to seek counseling when they have problems. About two-thirds of those who receive counseling report improvements in their relationship. Counseling works best when both parties enter with a willingness to hear constructive criticism and to express their own views respectfully. A good counselor is able to provide an objective and impartial perspective to problems. In order to get the most out of counseling, individuals should try and catalog all of their complaints, as well as the ways both parties could change to improve the relationship. Counselors have observed that every relationship in which both parties want to continue can be saved.

Siblings

Siblings (brothers and sisters) can be almost as important as parents in helping children develop models for their future relationships. Sibling rivalry, for example, can have damaging consequences in other relationships if it is taken too far. Likewise, children who feel they were appreciated by their parents less than their brothers or sisters may go through life expecting to be taken for granted. Typically, people grow more distant from their siblings during adolescence, as each tries to assert his or her own independence. Later in life, though, people report much stronger relationships with their brothers and sisters.

- 88 -

Siblings may not be as close as friends for some, but they nevertheless occupy a unique and prized place in people's lives.

Becoming a parent

Before having a child, every individual should consider the awesome responsibility and massive effect it will have on his or her life. Many people idealize childbirth and don't acknowledge that many parents may feel a bit resentful of the changes they are forced to make. A man may feel jealous of the attention his wife gives to the new baby, and then he may feel guilty for having this jealousy. A new mother may feel overwhelmed by her role, especially given her weakened physical condition. Indeed, studies have consistently shown that marital satisfaction generally declines after the birth of a child. The number of separations and divorces tends to rise after a child enters the family.

Working parents

More and more, mothers are taking jobs after they have children and are contributing increased amounts to the household income. As a result, more parenting responsibilities are falling to men, who now take care of their children about a third of the time, on average. Sociologists studying this phenomenon note that men and women spend time with their children in different ways. Mothers are typically responsible for day-to-day maintenance activities, like bathing, feeding, and teaching, while fathers are more likely to take their children on special outings. Moreover, women are more likely to feel the primary responsibility for the child, regardless of the man's contribution. The happiest couples seem to be those who share parenting duties equally.

Dysfunctional relationships

Dysfunctional relationships are those in which the behavior of the participants does not lead to positive communication or honesty. As one would expect, people who have substance abuse problems or addictive behaviors are more likely to be in a dysfunctional relationship. Sometimes, one party may have an inaccurate idea of healthy relationships and will make unfair demands on the other. If there is not trust in a relationship, sometimes jealousy will cause a person to become paranoid and overly dependent on the other. These kinds of unhealthy relationships exist in every section of society because they spring from personal psychological problems that are universal. Unfortunately, dysfunctional relationships can be very difficult to leave.

One-parent and blended families

More and more families are composed of children and one parent. Though single-parent families are stereotyped as poor and uneducated, many are headed by wealthy and highly educated professionals. Studies have shown that single parents typically spend the same amount of time with their children as do parents in a traditional family. Some of these single parents will eventually remarry, creating what is known as a blended family. Extensive studies have been performed on these complicated and often problematic relationships. One recommendation many doctors make is that children from single-parent or blended families spend time with members of the extended family or community so that they can acquire other models for behavior.

Codependency

There are a few warning signs that your behavior in a relationship may be codependent. If you are constantly making excuses for your partner, or if you spend a great deal of time discussing and worrying about the other person, you may be codependent. If you find yourself monitoring the other person's behavior or taking an inordinate amount of responsibility, then you may be codependent. If you are afraid to get angry or express yourself because you fear being abandoned or if you feel responsible for keeping the other person happy, then you may have become codependent. If you find that you are ignoring other relationships because of your focus on your partner, and your self-esteem depends on his or her opinion of you, then you may be codependent.

A codependent individual is one who allows someone with an addiction to use them to achieve satisfaction. Codependency causes a person to ignore his or her own needs in order to serve someone else's. Codependent individuals will change their identity, undergo unpleasant experiences, and even give up their friends and family in order to serve their partner. People with low self-esteem and their own set of addictions are more likely to become codependent. In order to escape from a codependent relationship, an individual must realize the worth of his or her own life as well as his or her inability to change the other person. Codependent behavior has at its heart a simple desire for love, though this desire is poorly expressed.

Physiological gender differences

There are only a few basic physiological differences between males and females. Males have the ability to make sperm and to contribute the Y chromosome that enables a female to give birth to a male. Only females are born with sex cells, menstruate, give birth, and are capable of breastfeeding. In the embryonic stage, males and females have similar sex organs. After a few weeks of development, though, the gonads differentiate into either testes or ovaries. This differentiation depends on the genetic instructions given by the sex chromosomes. If a Y chromosome is present in the embryo, it will develop into a male; if there is no Y chromosome, the embryo will develop as a female. All future differentiation will be motivated by the gonads, not the chromosomes.

Enabling

Enabling is any behavior performed by a codependent individual that allows the partner to satisfy an addiction. Enabling comes in a few different forms. Shielding is when codependent people keep their partners safe from the negative consequences of their actions by making excuses or covering for them. Controlling is when one person tries to bribe the other with sexual favors in exchange for reducing an addictive behavior. Sometimes a codependent may enable a partner by assuming an unfair share of household responsibilities. Other times, a codependent may rationalize the addictive behavior of the other and therefore not see it clearly. Some enablers become intimately involved in the self-destructive behavior of the other, placing bets or procuring drugs for them. Finally, a codependent may facilitate the safe use of an addictive substance by allowing the user to do it at home.

Puberty

At the onset of puberty, the pituitary gland begins to release the hormones that further differentiate between the sexes. Specifically, the pituitary gland releases gonadotropins, which stimulate the gonads to generate sex hormones. As these gonadotropins do their work, the secondary sex characteristics are developed. In females, larger amounts of estrogen cause the breasts to enlarge, the hips to widen, and fat to be deposited on the hips and buttocks. It also causes her external genitals to enlarge, and initiates the processes of ovulation and menstruation. For males, large amounts of testosterone cause the voice to deepen, the penis to become thicker and longer, muscles to grow stronger, and hair to develop in new places.

Hormone system

Hormones are the chemicals that motivate the body to do certain things. They are produced in the organs that make up the endocrine system. With the exception of the sex organs, males and females have identical endocrine systems. The actions of the hormones are determined by the hypothalamus, an area of the brain about the size of a pea. The hypothalamus sends messages to the pituitary gland, which is directly beneath it. The pituitary gland turns on and off the various glands that produce hormones. Hormones, once released, are carried to their targets by the bloodstream, at which point they motivate cells and organs to action. Hormones can influence the way a person looks, feels, behaves, or matures.

Sexual stereotypes

Although there are clear physiological reasons underlying the various sexual stereotypes, more and more men and women are affirming their personal ability to decide how their sex determines their station in life. Many people are opting for careers that were formerly reserved for the opposite sex; for instance, more men are becoming nurses and secretaries, and more women feel comfortable becoming truck drivers, engineers, and pilots. Many people are adopting androgyny, or the combination of male and female characteristics, as their ideal. They insist that it is more appropriate to let the specifics of particular situation or role determine one's behavior, rather than relying on stale ideas of what it means to be masculine or feminine.

Premenstrual syndrome

Women who suffer from premenstrual syndrome may endure physical and emotional unrest for a period of up to two weeks, or from the period of ovulation to the beginning of menstruation. These ailments are thought to be caused by hormone imbalances created by the menstrual cycle. Most commonly, PMS is manifested as anxiety, mood changes, hot flashes, dizziness, heart palpitations, changes in appetite, irritability, fatigue, and insomnia. The treatment for PMS depends on the particular symptoms exhibited by the woman. Relaxation therapy has been effective in combating many of the anxiety issues associated with PMS. Some women benefit from treatments that adjust their sleep cycle. Other, more severe cases may call for the use of antidepressants.

Menstrual cycle

The hormones released by the female body trigger the ovaries to grow a few immature eggs. Typically, only one ovum is developed during each monthly cycle. The growth of this hormone signals the body to produce more estrogen, which in turn produces more of the hormones responsible for menstruation. In the middle of the cycle, the egg cells are released. This is called ovulation. At this point, the body goes through many of the changes that would support a fertilized egg: the endometrium thickens and becomes richer in nourishing blood, and more estrogen and progesterone are produced. Assuming the egg remains unfertilized, the hormone levels will eventually drop, and the uterine lining will be shed, resulting in some bleeding.

Minimizing menstrual problems

Although some menstrual problems may be inevitable because of the hormone imbalances created, women can still take a few easy steps to minimize discomfort during this process. For one thing, women should continue to exercise; research has shown that physically active women have fewer problems during menstruation. Women can also help themselves by eating regularly and nutritiously, as the body may not be as good at regulating glucose levels during this period. Salt tends to exaggerate bloating problems and should be avoided, along with caffeine. A woman's sensitivity to alcohol may increase during this period, so it is best not to drink too much. Smoking and sweets can also lead to greater menstrual problems.

Premenstrual dysphoric disorder

Premenstrual dysphoric disorder is not related to PMS. It occurs during the last week of menstruation and typically involves depression and anxiety. Menstrual cramps (referred to as dysmenorrhea in the medical community) occur in approximately half of all menstruating women. These may be caused by uterine muscles that contract too frequently or violently, depriving the uterus of necessary oxygen. Exercise has been shown to reduce cramps. Amenorrhea, the condition in which a woman stops menstruating, can occur if a woman exercises too much, undergoes a rapid weight change, or has a hormonal disorder. If it is prolonged, amenorrhea can lead to loss of bone density and the inability to bear children.

Circumcision

When male children are born, they have a bit of skin covering the end of the penis. For over half of the boys in the United States, this foreskin will be cut off in a process known as circumcision. Circumcision is prescribed by both the Jewish and Muslim religions, though many others opt for it as well. Medical proponents of circumcision claim that it reduces the dangers posed by a buildup of oils or secretions under the foreskin. Indeed, studies have shown that uncircumcised males are more likely to develop urinary tract infections. However, those who oppose circumcision claim it is unnecessary and painful and that the procedure creates a risk of infection. There is no clear consensus on the impact of circumcision on sexual performance and satisfaction.

Toxic shock syndrome

Toxic shock syndrome is a rare but potentially deadly infection that affects women under the age of 30 who use tampons. The symptoms of TSS are a high fever, a rash (especially on the fingers and toes), dizziness, extremely low blood sugar, and abnormalities in several organ systems. In order to reduce the risk of TSS, women may want to opt for sanitary napkins instead of tampons. Super-absorbent brands of tampons are particularly hazardous, so women should exercise caution when choosing a tampon. When tampons are being used, they should be changed three or four times a day. It is a good idea to use sanitary napkins at night or for at least part of every day during menstruation. When TSS is diagnosed, doctors usually treat it with antibiotics and intensive supportive care.

Midlife changes in male sexuality

Men do not undergo the same major hormonal turmoil that women do in middle age, but men will still experience a heavy reduction in their level of testosterone. A drop in testosterone can lead to decreased muscle mass, more body fat, low energy, and problems with sexual function. Although some doctors prescribe testosterone supplements to counteract the natural decline, it is thought that this may increase the risk of prostate cancer. Most men will simply have to accept longer periods of arousal before intercourse, that it may take longer to reach orgasm, that orgasm will be shorter, and that they will need a longer period of rest before they can perform sexually again.

Prostate

For young men, the most common problem is prostatitis, or infection of the prostate, which can cause fever. Infrequent or erratic sexual activity is generally the cause of prostatitis. More serious problems start to become possible at around age 40, when the prostate enlarges. This process, known as benign prostate hypertrophy, may cause the prostate to pinch the urethra and create problems urinating or ejaculating. Some men require surgery or medication to alleviate this problem. As a man gets older, he is also more likely to develop prostate cancer. Prostate cancer is more common in African Americans, but all males should get regular prostate exams to safeguard themselves against this common killer.

Abstinence

Abstinence can either mean totally refraining from sexual intercourse or refraining from exchanging bodily fluids altogether. Those who make a point of remaining abstinent throughout their lives are said to be celibate. Abstinence is the only way to entirely avoid the risks of sexual activity, and many high school students have begun making the commitment to refrain from sex until they are older or in a more committed relationship. Before deciding to engage in sexual activity, students should ask themselves whether it would be in line with their values and moral beliefs. Many people will rush into sex without fully considering the physical, mental, and emotional consequences.

Sexual decision-making

Part of the job of a health teacher is equipping students with the skills they will need to lead healthy, safe sexual lives. The first thing they must have in order to make good decisions is accurate and comprehensive information on the subject. Health textbooks are a good place to start, but students should also be directed to whatever books and authorities are qualified to give them well-researched and thoughtful information. Students should be especially well informed about birth control, pregnancy, and sexually transmitted diseases before they have any sexual contact. Part of keeping students informed is making sure that they feel comfortable asking questions and discussing their feelings. This can be with a teacher, a parent, or another community leader.

Homosexuality

Almost every culture in human history has contained elements of homosexuality, the social, physical, and emotional attraction to members of the same sex. In the United States, both male and female homosexuals can be referred to as "gay," while women may also be known as "lesbians." Homosexuality is an extremely controversial subject. Some studies have indicated structural differences in the brains of homosexuals, which may support the idea of a physiological reason for homosexuality. Interestingly, the corpus callosum, a band of fibers that connects the two halves of the brain, is actually wider and more effective in homosexual men than in heterosexual men and women.

Homosexual lifestyle

Although the problems associated with "coming out" (acknowledging one's homosexuality) are well documented, only a small percentage of homosexuals experience major trauma in admitting their orientation. Non-white homosexuals typically have a harder time asserting their sexual identity, often because they fear being ostracized from their family or community.

Bisexuality

Bisexuality, or the sexual attraction to both males and females, can develop at any stage of life. In many cultures, bisexuality is considered the norm. The number of bisexual people is twice the number of people who are exclusively homosexual. Interestingly, the largest proportion of bisexuals are married males who have secret sexual affairs with other men. There has been a storm of controversy around bisexuality, as many heterosexual women have worried about becoming involved with a bisexual man who might expose them to diseases more commonly found in the gay community. These fears are legitimate: between 20 and 30% of women with AIDS were infected by a bisexual partner.

Masturbation

Despite what they may claim in public, research has consistently shown that most people masturbate. The reasons are simple enough: masturbation feels good and is a way to release sexual tension. However, there is still a persistent social stigma associated with masturbation, and many adolescents may still believe that it will give them hairy palms or warts or cause them to go blind. Some doctors now say that masturbation can be a healthy alternative to risky sexual encounters and a good way to avoid being drawn by desire into dangerous relationships. For many women, masturbation is a way to discover what gives them sexual pleasure. Statistically, caucasians masturbate more than other ethnic groups, and people with a high level of education are more likely to masturbate than others.

Male sexual anatomy

The external parts of the male sexual anatomy are the penis and scrotum, the scrotum being the sac that holds the testes. The testes manufacture sperm and testosterone. Sperm are the male reproductive cells. All of the sperm that are not yet mature are stored in the epididymis, a series of tubes next to each testis. The penis itself holds three hollow cylinders: the two corpora cavernosa and the corpora spongiosum. The corpora spongiosum surrounds the urethra, which is the canal through which semen and urine travel. Semen is made up of several substances, mainly water, and is the liquid in which sperm cells are carried out of the body during ejaculation.

The production of seminal fluid requires the work of several different structures. The two tubes that carry the sperm from the epididymis into the urethra are called the vas deferens. The fluid will also pass through the seminal vesicles on its travels, so doctors refer to the seminal vesicles and the vas deferens as the ejaculatory ducts. Some of the seminal fluid will be produced by the prostate gland and secreted into the urethra during ejaculation. The Cowper's glands, also, link up with the urethra and are activated during arousal and ejaculation. The Cowper's glands secret a small amount of fluid at the beginning of arousal; this fluid is not semen itself, though it may contain sperm.

Female sexual anatomy

On a woman, the mons pubis is the round, meaty area located above the pubic bone. The outer lips surrounding the vagina are known as the labia majora. These cover the softer inner lips known as the labia minora. At the upper intersection of the labia minora is a small flap of skin covering the clitoris, which is a small, extremely sensitive erectile organ. Directly below the clitoris is the urethral opening, where urine exits the body. Below the urethral opening is a larger orifice, the vagina. The vagina is the canal leading to all the major reproductive organs in the female body. Below the vagina lies the perineum, which is the area between the vagina and the anus. The anus is the opening that leads to the rectum and large intestine.

Female reproductive organs

All of the major reproductive organs in the female body are accessed through the vagina. At the very back end of the vagina lies the cervix, which is the gateway to the uterus (or womb). The walls of the uterus are composed of a layer of tissue known as the endometrium. On either side of the uterus are the ovaries. Ovaries are about the size of an almond and are composed of egg cells called ova. These eggs are moved from the ovaries to the uterus through the fallopian tubes, canals that extend out and back from the upper uterus. Fallopian tubes have ends that resemble waving fingers. When an egg is released by an ovary, these fingers catch it and direct it into the mouth of the fallopian tube.

Perimenopause and menopause

As a woman gets older, her menstrual cycle becomes more erratic and eventually stops altogether. The period from the first irregular cycle to the last menstruation is known as perimenopause. Once a woman has not menstruated for a full year, she is said to have entered menopause. Although many women make this transition with ease, others are seriously affected. The main cause of menopausal troubles is the decline in estrogen level, which can lead to mouth and gum problems, dry or sensitive skin, hot flashes, fatigue, acne, and even hair loss. Shriveling of the clitoris, vulva, and vaginal lining may make intercourse painful. Some doctors have had success in lessening the symptoms of menopause by giving women replacement hormones.

Female orgasm

Sadly, many women may experience some pain during intercourse. This condition is clinically known as dyspaurenia. In the extreme form of this condition, known as vaginismus, involuntary contractions of the vagina are so severe that penetration becomes impossible. This problem is often caused by sexual anxiety and can be solved through relaxation. More generally, many women who otherwise function normally have a difficult time reaching orgasm consistently. Sometimes, this is simply because they are involved with partners who do not effectively stimulate their clitoris. As with all sexual problems, this is often solved by communication between partners.

Male orgasm

Many men have suffered at some time from premature ejaculation, which is clinically defined as ejaculating somewhere between 30 and 90 seconds after penetration. Other doctors define premature ejaculation as the inability to satisfy a partner at least half of the time. Men use many strategies to try and delay orgasm, from distracting themselves to masturbating before intercourse. There are even anesthetics available that numb the penis to minimize sensation. The best way to control ejaculation, however, is to concentrate on your sexual response and communicate with your partner. With some practice, men should be able to recognize the point beyond which orgasm is inevitable and wait to reach this point until their partner is ready.

Childhood sexuality

It seems odd and even perverse to refer to sexuality in childhood, but many of the foundations for later sexual experience are laid in the early years of an individual's life. For infants, the mouth is the main area for sensual pleasure. By the age of 3 or 4, most children become interested in the differences between men and women, and they may start to develop vaguely romantic feelings towards another person. It is very important for parents to discuss these topics with their children so that the children will have a framework of understanding for their complex and often confusing emotions. Children are likely to have lots of questions, some of which may be uncomfortably direct; parents should do their best to answer honestly and with a minimum of embarrassment.

Adolescent sexuality

As boys and girls enter adolescence, their interest in sex typically intensifies and seeks expression. This makes it essential that health providers give adolescents the necessary knowledge and skills to adjust to the changes in their lives. For teenage boys, it is typical to experience frequent erections and to begin having nocturnal emissions (wet dreams). Masturbation is the most common form of sexual expression for adolescents, especially males. Adolescents may also experiment with kissing and petting, oral sex, and even sexual intercourse. During adolescence, as many as one out of every four teenagers will experience a same-sex attraction, though this does not predict any future homosexuality. Though

American teens are not known to be any more sexually active than teens elsewhere in the world, they do have a higher rate of pregnancy, indicating that adequate birth control information and supplies are not being provided to all those who might benefit.

Stages of sexual response

First stage
Researchers into sexual response have determined that there are four distinct stages of sexual response: excitement, plateau, orgasm, and resolution. Excitement is always the first stage in the process of sexual response. It can be initiated by any sort of sexual stimulus: a thought, a picture, or any direct stimulation of the senses. For men, sexual arousal triggers a rush of blood to the genitals, causing the testicles to lift and the penis to become erect. For women, sexual stimulation starts to enlarge the clitoris and the vaginal lips. The breasts may also become more sensitive. At this point, the vagina increases in length and width. The uterus also lifts, which creates even more space in the vagina.

Plateau and orgasm
During the plateau period of sexual response, the physiological changes that were begun in the excitement stage intensify. The penis continues to expand, and the vagina swells and becomes more sensitive. When orgasm arrives, it is actually quite similar for both males and females. Orgasms typically involve between 3 and 12 pelvic muscle contractions, each lasting about a second. For males, ejaculation begins when the vas deferens, seminal vesicles, and upper urethra contract. Then muscle contractions force semen out of the penis. The female orgasm is more varied: it may either be felt as a series of small orgasms or as a prolonged orgasm after extensive excitement and plateau. The clitoris is almost always involved in the female orgasm; once it has been adequately stimulated, the vagina will undergo a series of contractions.

Final stage
In the final, post-orgasmic state of sexual response, the male and female sexual organs return to their normal and non-excited state. For men, the period after orgasm is typically a refractory period in which they are incapable of reaching another orgasm. If resolution begins without one partner having had an orgasm, resolution may be slower and a bit uncomfortable. In order to improve a sexual relationship, the participants need to maintain good communication. It may be a good idea for couples to set aside a specific time to discuss their sex life so that neither partner feels inhibited from speaking his or her mind. It is always a good idea to make any complaints or requests gently because most people are sensitive on the subject of their sexual performance.

Intercourse

When someone refers to sexual intercourse, they are typically referring to vaginal intercourse or coitus, in which the penis is inserted into the vagina. This is the most common expression of sexuality for heterosexual couples. Vaginal intercourse can be performed in a number of different positions. Human beings are unusual among species in that women can have intercourse at any time during their menstrual cycle, though some women prefer to refrain from intercourse during menstruation. Vaginal intercourse always carries the risk of transmitting bodily fluids, which can cause pregnancy or sexually transmitted disease. In many countries, vaginal intercourse is the most common culprit for the spread of the HIV virus.

Sexual side effects of drugs

Despite the common association in the public mind of drugs and alcohol with wanton sexuality, most controlled substances actually prevent the body from fully realizing its sexual potential. Alcohol, if consumed in great volume, can cause permanent damage to the circulatory and nervous system and can cause alterations in hormones that motivate sexual excitement. Marijuana is known to reduce testosterone levels in men. Tobacco has been shown to damage the small blood vessels in the penis and thereby make erections more infrequent and weaker. Cocaine is particularly bad for sexual performance; it inhibits orgasm and may prevent a man from getting an erection at all. Amphetamines also inhibit orgasm and may decrease lubrication in females. Barbiturates tend to diminish sexual desire, make it difficult to get an erection, and prevent orgasm.

Safe sex

The only way to completely eliminate the health risks associated with sex is by being celibate. However, sexually active people can greatly reduce their risks of illness by participating in monogamous relationships with a partner who has been tested for sexually transmitted diseases. Although AIDS garners most of the attention, there are a number of other diseases that are only partially treatable with modern medicine and can be painful and/or debilitating. Although it is nice to be reassured that one's partner has not been exposed to any harmful virus, the only way to confirm it is through laboratory testing. It is not disrespectful at all to refrain from sexual activity with another person until that person has been evaluated.

Erectile disorders

Every man has occasional trouble establishing or maintaining an erection. Most of the time this is due to fatigue, stress, alcohol, or drug use, but it is also just an inevitable part of growing older. Impotence is clinically defined as the failure to get an erection more than once out of every four attempts. Sometimes psychological factors may be at work in impotence, as men with erection problems put increasing pressure on themselves and make it more difficult to succeed. There are now quite a few prescription medicines designed to treat this condition.

Impotence is often caused by stress, diabetes, adverse drug reactions, and tobacco. Medications for impotence may either treat the part of the brain that controls arousal or work to get more blood to the sex organs.

Sexual anxiety

Many people feel an unhealthy amount of pressure to perform well sexually. There is no such thing as a born lover; most people see their skills improve when they are in a healthy, loving relationship in which communication on sexual issues is strong. Another problem that many people have is trouble becoming initially aroused. Sometimes perfectly healthy couples may for no apparent reason become uninterested in sex, even when they still are attracted to one another. Oftentimes, stress is the culprit in this scenario, and many couples experience a resurgence of sexual desire after they make an effort to reduce the stress in their lives. Drinking to relive stress, however, is likely to only exaggerate poor sex drive.

Sexual deviations

There are a number of sexual behaviors that are considered deviant by the American Psychiatric Association. Fetishism is the practice of getting sexual pleasure from an inanimate object, or an asexual part of the body (the foot, for instance). Pedophilia is any sex involving an adult and a child. Transvestitism is the practice of becoming sexually aroused by putting on clothing appropriate to members of the opposite sex. Exhibitionism is the practice of exposing one's genitals to some unwilling observer. Voyeurism is obtaining sexual satisfaction from looking at other people naked or involved in sexual activity. Sadism is when a person is aroused by inflicting physical or psychological pain on another. Masochism is when a person becomes aroused by having physical or psychological pain inflicted on them.

Sexual addiction

Sometimes people may come to rely so heavily on sex for relief from restlessness or low self-esteem that it becomes a physical addiction. Most health professionals consider a person to be addicted to sex when his or her desire to engage in sexual activity crowds out or damages other areas of his or her life. Sex addiction is not limited to any class, gender, or sexual orientation. Oftentimes, individuals with a sexual compulsion have been physically or sexually abused and seek love in repeated sexual encounters. Individuals with this trouble will often spend a great deal of time trying to procure sex and will use sex to hide from larger problems in their life. A person who feels he or she may be addicted to sex should consult a health professional.

Rape

Rape is sexual intercourse that occurs when one of the partners is nonconsenting, unwilling, and possibly forcibly restrained. There is also what is known as statutory rape, which is sex between a person over the age of 16 and a person below the age of consent (which varies from state to state). Often, rapists are individuals who have a difficult time establishing relationships with other people, have been sexually abused themselves, or have histories of alcohol and drug abuse. Although many rapists blame their victims for provoking their heinous acts, studies have shown that women are raped because they encounter sexually aggressive men, not because of any particular quality in their dress or behavior.

Types of rape

There are a few different categories of rape, depending on the intent of the rapist. An anger rape is an unplanned, random attack, usually motivated by some personal crisis in the rapist's life. A power rape is premeditated and is committed in order to exert total control over some other person. Power rapists are often beset by a feeling of powerlessness in their own lives. Sadistic rape is usually premeditated and involves bondage, humiliation, and torture. The people who commit this kind of rape are aroused by their own anger and the fear of their victim. In a gang rape, two or more men participate in a sexual assault on a single victim. The motive for this kind of rape may be more about camaraderie among the males than sexual gratification for each person.

Rape recovery

Sadly, only a small percentage of the young women who are raped report the crime to the police. This is especially unfortunate, as studies have shown that women recover from being raped more quickly when they know their assailant has been caught and punished. Rape can have both physical and psychological side effects. A woman should seek immediate medical attention after the crime. Also a rape victim should not wash or change clothes before reporting the crime, as there may be valuable evidence there that the police can use to catch the rapist. The most important thing many rape victims should remember is that they are not to blame for what has happened to them.

Sexual harassment on the job

The issue of sexual harassment in the workplace has been explicitly treated by the Equal Opportunity Employment Commission. According to the EOEC, sexual harassment may take one of two forms. In quid pro quo harassment, an individual in a position of authority makes unwanted advances on an employee and indicates that these are a condition of receiving a promotion or a raise or of simply retaining employment. The other type of abuse is harassment by a hostile or offensive environment, in which those in positions of authority are persistently inappropriate or offensive in their dealings with employees. Sexual harassment can range from uncomfortable remarks to unwanted physical contact. Employees who feel they are being sexually harassed on the job should make detailed notes of the situation and seek help elsewhere.

Developmental causes of violence

Children of abusive parents are much more likely to engage in violent behavior as they grow older. Scientists believe that this is, in part, because such children fail to learn other coping mechanisms. Children who live in a violent community are more likely to become overly aggressive, even if they have grown up in a non-abusive home. Children who perform poorly at school or are ostracized by their peers are also more likely to become violent. Individuals who display violent behavior at a young age are often rejected by their community, which only exaggerates the problem. Although the environmental effects are undisputed, there is also speculation that aggressive tendencies may be inherited.

There is a great deal of research to suggest that the portrayal of violence in television, films, and music can incite impressionable individuals to commit similar violent acts. According to some statistics, the average American child will be exposed to about 40,000 deaths and countless more acts of violence during childhood and adolescence. Looking beyond the media, it is well known that poverty, unemployment, and gang involvement often lead to violent acts. The risk of committing a violent act seems to be inversely proportional to the individual's chance for success in society. It should be noted that violence seems to be tied to economics, not race; no racial or ethnic group has been shown to have a greater predisposition to violence than others.

Child abuse

Statistics have shown that impoverished parents are more likely to abuse their children than are other parents. Nevertheless, child abuse remains a problem among every socioeconomic group. Child abuse can be physical, psychological, or sexual. Sexual abuse includes virtually any sexual contact between an adult and child, whether it is kissing, fondling, oral sex, sexual intercourse, or just suggestive conversation. Pedophilia is the clinical term for any sexual abuse of a child that is perpetrated by an individual other than the child's parents. Incest, on the other hand, refers to sexual contact among members of the same family. Oftentimes, children who are psychologically or sexually abused develop physical symptoms or act out against society.

Sexual violence

Although sexual violence must ultimately be blamed on the offending individual, there are a few social factors that contribute to its prevalence. First, there is an unhealthy tendency for individuals to accept male aggression as natural and to envision women as being passive. It is also a myth that the male sex drive is somehow unstoppable. Too often, our society seems to blame the victims of violence as if they had somehow provoked the actions of others. Similarly, many aggressive actions are condoned if they are part of a "joke" or "prank." This only serves to trivialize behavior that can be very painful to the victim. Finally, the condoning and even glorification of sexual violence that is done by the media sends the wrong message to would-be offenders.

Blood tests

Doctors often recommend that patients have blood tests as part of routine examinations. A blood sample will be taken and sent to a laboratory for analysis, which generally consists of a basic blood cell count. Having a high number of white blood cells is considered an indication of infection or possibly leukemia. If there are too few red blood cells, the patient may be suffering from anemia. The various components of blood will also be measured. A high level of glucose indicates diabetes, while excessive amounts of uric acid may mean gout or kidney stones. If there is a high level of cholesterol found in the blood, this may indicate some risk of heart disease.

Depression

A major depression is an overwhelming feeling of sadness that extends over a long period of time. Although about one in ten Americans will experience a major depression in any given year, only about one in every three of these will seek treatment. Most cases of depression can be helped with psychotherapy, medication, or both. An individual may be depressed of he or she feels sad or discouraged for a long period, lacks energy, has difficulty concentrating, continually thinks of death or suicide, withdraws from social activities, has no interest in sex, or has a major change in eating or sleeping habits. Some individuals who do not respond to therapy or medication may consider receiving electroconvulsive therapy, which attempts to change the established (and maladaptive) patterns in the patient's brain by the administration of electrical current through electrodes on the scalp.

Phobias

The most common kind of anxiety disorder is a phobia, an irrational and intense fear of some object or situation. About one in ten adults will develop a phobia at some point in life. The individual may recognize that the fear is excessive and irrational but is unable to function because of the fear. Although many prescription medications have been used to treat phobias, none seem to be very effective unless they are accompanied by behavioral therapy. One effective behavioral therapy technique is gradually increasing the level of the feared object or situation to the patient while demonstrating coping strategies. Medical hypnosis therapy has also proved effective in combating phobias.

Obsessive-compulsive disorder

One extreme kind of anxiety disorder is obsessive-compulsive disorder, in which the individual is plagued by a recurring thought he or she cannot escape and may display repetitive, rigidly formalized behavior. Individuals who suffer from OCD are most often plagued by thoughts of violence, contamination (for instance, being concerned that they are infected), or doubt. The most common compulsions among individuals with OCD are hand washing, cleaning, counting, or checking locks. Individuals suffering from OCD probably recognize that their behavior is irrational but feel powerless to stop it. OCD will eventually get in the way of the person's functioning in other areas of life and will require treatment. Though OCD is thought to have biological origins, it can be treated with a combination of medication and behavioral therapy.

Attention deficit hyperactivity disorder

Attention deficit hyperactivity disorder is the diagnosis given to a range of conditions in which the individual has a hard time controlling motion or sustaining attention. Although ADHD is typically thought of as a disorder that affects children, new research suggests that it is not outgrown and that adults may be just as likely to suffer from it. Individuals suffering from ADHD are impulsive, constantly in motion, and easily distracted. They may feel perpetually restless, may be unusually forgetful, and are likely to be socially immature. Although there is no specific test to determine whether someone has ADHD, most doctors are trained to recognize the condition. Most of those who suffer from ADHD are benefited by behavioral therapy and medication.

Schizophrenia

Schizophrenia, one of the most crippling forms of mental illness, exists when an individual loses the unity of his or her mind and suffers impaired function in almost every mental area. An individual suffering from schizophrenia may see or hear things that do not exist, may believe that an external force is putting thoughts into their head or controlling their behavior, or may suffer delusions about their identity. Many schizophrenics will develop severe anxieties and will become obsessive about protecting themselves. For most individuals, antipsychotic drugs can help to restore mental control and minimize delusional episodes. However, these drugs can cause a person to become apathetic, and many impoverished individuals will lack the resources to receive treatment at all.

Psychotherapy

Psychotherapy refers to a broad spectrum of counseling techniques based on conversation between a trained professional and an individual seeking help. Most mental health professionals are trained in a few different psychotherapeutic styles and can tailor their approach to the patient's needs. Progress in psychotherapy can at times be difficult to measure, and insurance companies have grown increasingly unwilling to pay for long treatments. For this reason, many individuals seek psychotherapy for a specific problem or to correct a specific feeling or behavior. Most people find that the process of talking and listening is therapeutic in itself and allows them to discover solutions to their problems that were unavailable through reflection

Interpersonal therapy

Interpersonal therapy (IPT) was originally developed by doctors performing research on the treatment of major depression. They discovered that many patients were aided by developing an empathetic relationship with a therapist. IPT does not attempt to treat the origins of a psychological disorder; rather, it helps the individual to improve his or her ability to get along with others. This treatment has been most effective for individuals suffering from major depression, difficulties forming lasting relationships, dysthymia (mild depression), or bulimia. Most IPT treatments last from 12 to 16 weeks. During these sessions, the therapist usually talks a great deal more than a therapist practicing psychodynamic psychotherapy.

Psychiatric drug therapy

Psychiatric drugs are those that affect the chemistry of the brain and relieve the symptoms of mental disorder and illness. In recent years, research has produced a generation of extremely safe and effective psychiatric drugs that can help individuals with problems ranging from minor depression to schizophrenia. One of the most common types of drugs is a serotonin boosting medication that is used to treat obsessive compulsive disorder, attention deficit disorder, and depression. Patients should know, however, that it often takes several weeks for psychiatric medications to begin showing results. Also, they should be made aware that these drugs have side effects, some of which are very serious. Psychiatric drugs may continue to be operative after the individual stops taking them.

Suicide

A number of factors can contribute to an individual's decision to take his or her own life. About 95% of individuals who commit suicide have some form of mental illness, most commonly major depression or alcoholism. Individuals who for whatever reason have lost hope that their lives will ever improve are at high risk for suicide. There appears to be a hereditary influence as well: about one of four individuals who try suicide have a family member who committed suicide. Autopsies have shown that suicidal individuals often have a low level of the neurotransmitter serotonin. Finally, it is well documented that individuals who have easy access to firearms are far more likely to commit suicide.

Preparing for death

Many individuals prepare a document that contains their choice of medical treatment for serious injury or illness and provide it to family members in advance of when it would be needed. This is known as an advance directive. Sometimes, an individual will specify a health-care proxy, someone who is authorized to make medical decisions for them if they are unconscious or unable to act in their own behalf. Other individuals may compose what is known as a do-not-resuscitate order, in which they state that they do not want to be revived and kept alive by artificial means. An elderly or ill individual may also grant power of attorney to another person, thus giving that person the authority to make financial decisions on behalf of the ill individual.

Safety and Prevention

Classifications of disease

There are a few different classifications for disease: acute, chronic, genetic, and congential. An acute disease is one that arrives quickly, lasts only a short time, and has distinct, identifiable symptoms. Chronic diseases, such as arthritis, cardiovascular disease, and diabetes, persist for a long time, are often caused by poor nutrition or drug use, and tend to become more common with age. A genetic disorder is one that is caused by an absent or defective gene or by some abnormality with the chromosomes. A congenital disease, on the other hand, is one that is present with an individual from birth and may be the result either of heredity or environmental influences. Heart disease and syphilis can both be congenital.

Infectious and non-infectious diseases

Infectious diseases are those that are caused by a virus, bacterium, or parasite. Infectious diseases are distinguished from non-infectious diseases in that they stem from biological causes, rather than from physical or chemical causes (as in the case of burns or poisoning). An infectious disease will always have an agent (something that has the disease and spreads it to others) and a vector (a way of transmitting the disease). In the case of malaria, for instance, a parasite contains the disease, and it is introduced to the body when a mosquito carrying it places it in the bloodstream. The vector of an infectious disease does not need to be biological; many diseases are transmitted through water, for example.

Recurrence of infectious disease

Emerging diseases are those that have only recently been recognized, are increasing in humans, or are likely to spread to new geographical areas in the near future. The most pervasive emerging disease is the HIV virus, which is believed to have originated in central Africa. Diseases may also reemerge later in a slightly mutated form that is resistant to the previous methods of treatment. Viruses and bacteria are capable of endless alterations and even a simple change may enable them to become stronger or more deadly. Another reason why emerging and recurring disease is a growing problem in the world is the infiltration of civilization into previously uninhabited territories; people are encountering millions of microbes that have never been encountered before.

Communicable and non-communicable diseases

Communicable diseases are those that are caused by microorganisms and can be transferred from one infected person or animal to a previously uninfected person or animal. Although some diseases are passed on by direct contact with an infected individual, many can be spread through close proximity: airborne bacteria or viruses account for most communication of disease. Some examples of communicable disease are measles, smallpox, influenza, and scarlet fever. Some communicable diseases require specific circumstances for transmission; for instance, tetanus requires the presence of infected soil or dirt. Any disease that cannot be transferred from one person or animal to another is considered non-communicable.

HIV and AIDS

Although the number of people suffering from human immunodeficiency virus (HIV) or acquired immunodeficiency syndrome (AIDS) has declined in the United States in recent years, there is still a tremendous health risk associated with the virus. Although the disease was once linked with homosexual males, the highest rates of growth are currently among heterosexuals in developing countries. HIV is generally spread through vaginal sexual contact, although it is also possible to spread the disease through anal or oral sex if either partner loses some blood during the act. HIV is also commonly spread among drug users through contaminated needles. Other, rarer ways of contracting HIV are through blood transfusions, blood products, and organ transplants.

Individuals who have previously been diagnosed with HIV may be diagnosed with AIDS if they develop a severe or debilitating illness or if their immune system has become extremely impaired. AIDS victims may suffer from persistent bouts of pneumonia, fever, or diarrhea. They may also begin to experience neurological problems like dementia and impaired motor skills. It is important to note that people do not actually die from the AIDS virus; rather, they succumb to another infection after AIDS has weakened their immune system. The most common secondary infections are pneumonia, tuberculosis, and thrush; secondary cancers commonly associated with AIDS include Kaposi's sarcoma and cervical cancer.

HPV

The human papilloma virus (HPV), which is known to cause genital warts, is the most common viral STD. HPV is typically transmitted through vaginal, anal, or oral sex. Over half the people infected with this virus will never display any symptoms. The rest will develop genital warts in the period between 3 weeks and 18 months after contact. HPV is known to cause urinary obstruction and bleeding, and in women, it may contribute to cervical cancer. There is at present no way to fully eliminate HPV, though some intensive treatments have been known to discourage recurrence. There is, however, an effective test to determine whether an individual has HPV, even when it is latent.

Sexually transmitted diseases

Sexually transmitted diseases (STD), otherwise known as venereal diseases, are among the top ten most frequently reported diseases in the United States. Although any sexually active individual is at risk of contracting an STD, the most frequently infected populations are young adults and homosexual males. In addition, unborn children can catch an STD from their mother. Although STDs are currently at their highest ever rate in the United States, they are even more prevalent in developing countries because of low-grade prevention measures, poor access to treatment, and inadequate health care. All of the STD pathogens can inhabit the warm, viscous surfaces of the body and are repelled by light, cold, and dryness. It is quite possible to have more than one STD at a time.

Vaginal infections

There are three main types of vaginal infection: trichmoniasis, candidiasis, and bacterial vaginosis. Trichmoniasis is suffered when protozoa in the vagina multiply quickly, creating burning, itching, and painful discharge. Males may carry this infection without displaying any of the symptoms. The infection known as candidiasis begins when a normal yeast found in the vagina becomes too abundant, causing burning, itching, and a whitish discharge. There are numerous over-the-counter treatments for this infection. Bacterial vaginosis occurs when the microorganisms that live in the vagina are altered, the result being a whitish-gray discharge and a fishy aroma. This infection most often affects women who have numerous sexual partners.

Allergies

An allergy is a hypersensitivity or overreaction to some substance in a person's environment or diet; it is the most common kind of immune disorder. There are many different symptoms of an allergic reaction, but the most common are sneezing, hives, eye irritation, vomiting, and nasal congestion. In some extreme cases, the person may collapse and even die. Allergic triggers, or allergens, can be anything from peanuts to pollen, from insect bites to mold. Although there is no way to reverse or eliminate a personal allergy, science has made progress in treating the allergic reaction. These days, it is possible to be treated for an allergic reaction without becoming drowsy or sluggish.

Chronic fatigue syndrome

There are a wide range of conditions that fall under the heading of Chronic Fatigue Syndrome. Individuals may have CFS if they suffer from chills, low fever, persistent weakness that does not improve with rest, muscle pain, headaches, joint pain, and sleep disorders. These symptoms may last for a period of years. After a while, they are usually accompanied by anxiety attacks and low-grade depression. Scientists have a number of theories for the persistent failure of the immune system to fight off these symptoms: some feel it is the result of many small viruses attacking the system, while others blame it on the Epstein-Barr virus, which can cause mononucleosis and is latent in most people. There is neither a definitive test for CFS nor is there any specific treatment.

Common cold

The common cold is one of the most pesky and irritating of viruses, though it is rarely a great risk to long-term health. One reason the cold is so difficult to fight is that there are over 200 varieties of the virus, so the body is never able to develop a comprehensive immunity. The cold virus is typically spread through the air or through contact. There is no completely effective medical treatment, either. Indeed, doctors warn that taking aspirin and acetaminophen may actually suppress the antibodies that the body needs to fight the infection and may therefore contribute to some symptoms. There is also no conclusive evidence to support taking vitamin C in large doses. Antihistamines, which many people credit with relieving the symptoms of the common cold, may make the user drowsy.

Pneumonia

Pneumonia can be caused by bacteria, virus, or by foreign particles in the air. When it is contracted, fluid fills the intricate network of spongy tissue in the lungs. When it is contracted in its bacterial form, the symptoms are shortness of breath, fever, and general weakness. Symptoms related to every variety include coughing, high fever, chills, and abundant phlegm. Antibiotics can be used to treat bacterial pneumonia if they are administered quickly enough. Individuals who have had pneumonia in the past are advised to get a vaccination for it, especially if they are over the age of 50. Pneumonia may develop very slowly, or it may occur so fast that it greatly endangers health.

Hepatitis

There are five varieties of hepatitis (A, B, C, Delta, and E), which is a virus that causes inflammation of the liver. Many people die each year as a result of the hepatitis infection. The symptoms include headaches, fever, fatigue, nausea, and vomiting. The liver will enlarge and become sensitive to the touch, and the person's skin may develop the yellowish tinge of jaundice. The best way to treat hepatitis is to get plenty of rest and to avoid alcohol and drugs that will put the liver to work. In order to avoid contracting hepatitis in the first place, one should practice good hygiene and avoid using illegal drugs or engaging in risky sex. There are available vaccinations for hepatitis A and B. Hepatitis B is responsible for most of the hepatitis-related deaths.

Lyme disease

Lyme disease is a bacterial infection spread by ticks. The most common symptoms of the infection are joint inflammation, heart arrhythmia, severe headaches, and memory lapses. In pregnant women, Lyme disease may cause birth defects and miscarriages. For obvious reasons, hunters, campers, and people who spend a great deal of time in the outdoors are the most likely to contract Lyme disease. It is important, therefore, always to check yourself for ticks, which may be very tiny, every time you have been in a wooded area. Most people who are infected will notice some skin lesions, often a red blotch around the area of the bite. If you spot a tick already on your body, remove it quickly with a pair of tweezers, making sure that the head does not stay embedded below the skin.

Strep infections

Although a sore throat is a common symptom of a winter cold, if the symptom is actually the result of group A streptococcus bacteria, it can be much more serious. Strep bacteria will eventually travel to the kidneys, liver, and heart if they are not treated promptly with antibiotics. Once there, they will cause rheumatic fever, an inflammation of the heart that can lead to joint pain and an irregular heartbeat. There are tests currently available that can diagnose strep throat in moments. Group B streptococcus, on the other hand, only affects pregnant women and their newborn children. Very young women and those with poor health are the most likely victims of this disease, which causes scores of infant deaths each year. Doctors recommend that pregnant women be screened for group B strep.

Mononucleosis

Mononucleosis is a viral disease most commonly found in people who are 15 to 24years of age. It is spread by kissing or other close contact. The symptoms of mononucleosis include a sore throat, headache, fever, nausea, and, most characteristically, prolonged periods of weakness. These symptoms may last a month or more. There is no great long-term risk to a person's health from mononucleosis, although trying to exercise vigorously may cause the spleen to rupture. It is also possible for the liver to become inflamed, though this is rare. At present, there is no good treatment for mononucleosis; individuals who suspect that they have it should see their doctor for a blood test.

Heart attack

The clinical name for a heart attack is myocardial infarction. If the myocardial cells, which surround the heart and cause it to contract, do not get enough oxygen, they may begin to die. This happens when the arteries that supply the myocardium are blocked by plaque or a clot. Even though heart attacks are commonly thought of as sudden events, they are actually a long time in coming. The common signs of heart attack are anxiety, shortness of breath, dizziness, a squeezing pain in the center of the chest, and pain that radiates out to the shoulder, arm, jaw, or neck. The period immediately after the beginning of these symptoms is the most important, though many victims try to ignore the signs. If an individual receives treatment immediately for a heart attack, he or she is much more likely to survive this very deadly ordeal.

Angina pectoris

When the heart experiences a sudden, temporary drop in the flow of oxygen to the heart tissue, it is called angina pectoris. This condition is usually accompanied by discomfort in the chest. Individuals are at a greater risk of angina when they place great demands on their heart, for instance, when they are under stress or exercising. If angina becomes severe and persistent, the individual should seek medical treatment, as he or she may be at greater risk of a heart attack. Many people, however, have been known to suffer from angina pectoris for years without ever having any further heart trouble. When angina is diagnosed, doctors typically prescribe beta blockers, calcium channel blockers, or nitrates.

Congestive heart failure

If the heart is not pumping out enough blood, fluid will begin to build up in the lungs, hands, and feet. As the fluid builds up in the lungs, it may become difficult to breathe, and the individual is said to be suffering from pulmonary congestion and heart failure. In the other afflicted parts of the body, the fluid will soak through the capillary walls and cause swelling, particularly in the legs and ankles. The clinical term for this swelling is edema. This set of problems, known collectively as congestive heart failure, typically occurs when an individual has suffered a myocardial infarction, although they may also occur because of rheumatic fever, birth defects, or hypertension. The only way to treat a congestive heart failure is to lower the intake of salt, take drugs to remove the excess fluid, and to reduce the workload on the heart.

Treating heart problems

Most of the time, doctors use diuretics, beta blockers, calcium channel blockers, and angiotensin converting enzyme inhibitors to treat individuals with heart trouble. These last drugs, known as ACE inhibitors, prevent the release of a hormone that contributes to high blood pressure. Beta blockers are drugs that alter the nervous system and thereby reduce the amount of blood required by the heart. Calcium channel blockers slow the flow of calcium ions into the heart. This is beneficial because scientists have found that excess amounts of calcium can cause the heart to violently contract, blocking arterial passages. Many of these heart medications are accompanied by some side effects, like lethargy and chest pain, and they may all be dangerous if they are not taken under close medical supervision.

Heart surgery

One of the most common surgical procedures performed on the human heart is the coronary bypass. In this procedure, an artery is taken from the leg of the patient and grafted onto a coronary artery that is blocked. Blood can then travel around the blocked area and reach its destination. These surgeries are performed often, but they do not always have the desired effect and may affect mental functioning. Percutaneous transluminal coronary angioplasty (PTCA), also known as balloon angioplasty, is the most frequently performed heart surgery. It is done to open arteries that have been narrowed by plaque buildup; doctors insert a catheter with a tiny balloon affixed, and then they inflate the balloon temporarily in the narrowed area.

Transient ischemic attacks

Some people do not ever suffer a massive stroke but instead are victims of a series of tiny strokes known as transient ischemic attacks (TIA). Sometimes these TIAs warn that a larger stroke is coming. They can be divided into two classes: transient monocular blindness, in which the individual blacks out or has some other visual problems; or transient hemispheral attack, in which a reduced blood flow to one side of the brain cause a numbness or weakness on one side of the body. Most TIAs are caused by a narrowing of arteries in the neck as a result of plaque buildup. Some individuals will benefit from a surgery that broadens these carotid arteries, while others may reduce their risk of TIA by taking aspirin.

Strokes

Many strokes are caused by a blood clot (also known as a thrombus) in a brain artery. These clots typically form between deposits that cling to the arterial walls. On occasion, a free-floating clot will lodge into one of the cerebral arteries, creating what is known as a cerebral embolism. Strokes may also be caused by the rupture of any diseased artery in the brain. When this happens, the cells that depend on this artery will be unable to function. Similar hemorrhaging can also be caused by the rupture of an aneurysm, a pouch of blood that extends outward from the wall of an artery. If brain tissue begins to die, the individual will immediately lose memory, motor skills, or the use of language. This damage may be permanent and even fatal.

A stroke occurs when the blood supply to any portion of the brain is blocked. After heart disease and cancer, strokes are the third leading cause of death in the United States. Although the number of strokes has risen in recent years, most doctors attribute this to advances in treating heart disease that have made it possible for more people to live long enough to eventually suffer strokes. In order to minimize the risk of a stroke, individuals can exercise and quit smoking, both of which reduce deposits in the blood vessels that can contribute to a stroke. Also, maintaining low blood pressure by eating a low-fat diet can reduce the risk of stroke. Obesity puts a heavy strain on the heart and may reduce its ability to get blood to all portions of the brain.

Stroke risk factors

Any individual who has suffered a transient ischemic attack (TIA) is very likely to suffer a larger stroke. Men are more likely to have a stroke than women, although women will increase their odds significantly if they take an oral contraceptive. African Americans and Hispanics are both more likely to suffer strokes than whites. The risk of stroke increases as a person gets older, develops high blood pressure, or suffers from heart disease. Also, individuals who are found to have a high red blood cell count or a high level of blood fats (specifically low-density lipoproteins) are more likely to suffer a stroke. Finally, individuals who suffer from diabetes mellitus are more likely to suffer strokes.

Stroke treatment

Many people take aspirin every day to help reduce the risk of strokes caused by rapid beating of the heart. Besides aspirin, doctors are experimenting with nimodipine and other drugs that may be able to prevent brain damage during a stroke. Many doctors believe that thrombolytic drugs, which are typically reserved for victims of heart attack, may quickly restore blood flow after a stroke. Many people at risk for strokes have their carotid arteries cleaned out surgically, which enables blood to flow freely up the neck to the brain. There are also experimental procedures in which tiny "clothespins" are used to stop hemorrhaging while doctors suction up the rest of the blood.

Tuberculosis

At one time, tuberculosis (TB) was the leading cause of death in the United States. Indeed, it is so common that even today one-third the world's population is infected with the disease, although not all of these people will develop the active form of the disease. TB is extremely contagious, and when it does emerge, it typically does so on a large scale, often contaminating entire populations in a brief period. The symptoms most commonly associated with TB are fatigue, chills, loss of appetite, coughing, and night sweats. Although most TB patients recover fully after about 6 months, it is best to take steps to avoid the disease. If you think you may be infected, you should see your doctor immediately and ask for a TB test.

Basics of cancer

Cancer is the uncontrolled growth and spread throughout the body of abnormal cells. Cancer cells, unlike the regular cells of the body, do not follow the instructions encoded in the body's DNA. Instead, these cells reproduce themselves quickly, creating neoplasms, or tumors. A tumor may be either benign, when it is not considered dangerous, or malignant (cancerous). Unless they are stopped, cancer cells continue to grow, crowding out normal cells in a process called infiltration. Cancer cells can also metastasize, or spread to the other parts of the body by entering the bloodstream or lymphatic system. The gradual overtaking of the body by these cancer cells will eventually make it impossible to sustain human life.

Cancer development

For a long time, researchers have puzzled over how normal cells can turn into cancer cells. A great deal has been learned about this process by studying oncogenes, the genes that normally control growth but have begun behaving abnormally. For unknown reasons, the

DNA in these genes becomes altered. Cancer can also result when cells fail to effectively deploy their tumor-suppressing genes, which should stop excessive growth. Genetic and environmental factors can also contribute to the appearance of cancer. Some individuals inherit genes that are more likely to develop into certain kinds of cancer, and other individuals may increase their chances of developing cancer by consuming a high-fat diet or exposing themselves to harmful radiation.

Race, culture and cancer

Interestingly, the rates of cancer vary markedly between different ethnic and racial groups. In the United States, the cancer rate among African Americans is higher than among whites, and more African Americans who get cancer die from the disease. Many critics assert that there are socioeconomic reasons for this last statistic. In addition, much of the cancer literature provided to the public is not available in Spanish, so Hispanics are generally less aware of the warning signs that they may be developing cancer. Similarly, Vietnamese American women, even though they are three times as likely to develop cervical cancer as whites, are much less likely to receive frequent Pap smears and checkups.

Types of Cancer

Skin cancer
Most cases of skin cancer are the result of overexposure to direct sunlight, especially the B range of ultraviolet light (UVB). It is also possible for tanning salons to produce this harmful radiation. The two most common kinds of skin cancer are basal-cell and squamous-cell. Basal-cell cancer involves the base of the epidermis, which is the outermost layer of skin; squamous-cell cancer affects the cells in the epidermis itself. Both of these cancers can be treated with surgery if they are caught early. Malignant melanoma is the deadliest form of skin cancer and is known to especially target individuals with blond or red hair, freckles on the upper back, and rough red bumps on the skin (known as actinic keratoses). Individuals who spend a great deal of time in the sun should have their skin checked regularly by a dermatologist.

Testicular cancer
Testicular cancer is not especially common, but it can be quite dangerous, particularly because it most often affects seemingly healthy men between the ages of 18 and 35. Men are at a greater risk if they have an undescended testicle. Testicular cancer usually is accompanied by a swelling or tenderness in one of the testes, so men who experience this condition should seek medical attention immediately. Although it may be necessary to remove a testicle that becomes cancerous, this will not impede a man's sexual function or potency. Testosterone injections may be required if both testicles are removed. If testicular cancer is diagnosed early on, it is very unlikely that the individual will suffer any long-term health problems.

Breast cancer
Though it is possible for men to develop breast cancer, it is still a disease that primarily affects women. Women are considered to be particularly at risk if they are over the age of 50, have a family history of the disease, have no children, have experienced late menopause, or are obese. In order to guard against this threat, women should perform regular self-examinations for lumps or alterations in their breasts, as well as receiving frequent mammograms (a diagnostic X-ray of the breast). If these procedures discover an abnormal

growth, a biopsy will be performed to determine its character. Doctors may then opt to perform a lumpectomy (removal of tumor and surrounding tissue), quadrantectomy (removal of a larger area around the breast), or mastectomy (removal of the entire breast).

Cervical and ovarian

Women are considered to be prone to cervical cancer if they had intercourse at an early age, have had multiple sex partners, have genital herpes, or have been exposed to environmental smoke. The standard test for cervical cancer is the Pap smear. Women are advised to have this test performed regularly and to watch out for irregular vaginal discharge or bleeding. Women are considered to be at risk for ovarian cancer if they have a family history of the disease, are infertile, or are obese. Unfortunately, some women may not develop any signs of ovarian cancer until it is quite advanced; at that point, they will develop irregular bleeding, digestive or urinary trouble, bloating, and weight gain. Doctors recommend an annual pelvic and rectal exam to help guard against ovarian cancer.

Leukemia, lung and oral

Leukemia is a cancer of the blood that frequently targets individuals with Down syndrome or those who have been exposed to large amounts of radiation. Leukemia may be difficult to diagnose because its early symptoms are very similar to those of the flu. Lung cancer is caused primarily by cigarette smoking, although it can also be caused by inhalation of asbestos or exposure to radiation. Like leukemia, lung cancer is difficult to spot early. Its common warning signs are persistent cough and bloody mucus. Oral cancer is most frequently associated with the use of smokeless tobacco or pipes, although it can also develop as a result of alcoholism. Anyone with a persistent mouth sore, a reddish or whitish patch in the mouth, or difficulty chewing or swallowing should consult a doctor without delay and undergo testing for oral cancer

Prostate

Except for skin cancer, prostate cancer is the most common form of cancer in men. The following factors increase a man's risk for prostate cancer: increasing age, a family history of the disease, exposure to large amounts of cadmium, a large number of sexual partners, and a past history of several sexually transmitted diseases. A high intake of saturated fats is also thought to contribute to prostate cancer. In recent years, doctors have been able to create a test that measures the level of prostate-specific antigen, the substance created by the body to fight prostate cancer. This has made it possible to accurately determine prostate health during an annual checkup. All men are advised to get an annual prostate exam.

Colon and rectal

Individuals are considered to be at a high risk of developing colon or rectal cancer if they have a personal history of the disease or if they have polyps (growths) in the colon or rectum. Typically, an individual who has one of these cancers will notice bleeding from the rectum, bloody stool, or a general change in bowel habits. Since these cancers primarily affect people who are above the age of 50, doctors recommend that every individual of the appropriate age have an annual exam to check for blood in the feces and a digital rectal exam. This is especially important for women because they are more likely than men to develop these kinds of cancer. When an individual is diagnosed with colon or rectal cancer, the treatment usually includes surgery, radiation therapy, chemotherapy, or a combination of these.

Cancer therapies

The more common treatments for cancer are surgery, radiation therapy, chemotherapy, and immunotherapy. Surgery is usually performed to remove the tumor as well as the cells that surround it. This approach is most successful when it is applied to small, contained cancers. Radiation therapy entails exposing the body to powerful radiation, which will destroy cancer cells. Radiation is often administered along with chemotherapy, which requires the injection of powerful drugs into the body. The goal of radiation and chemotherapy is to stall the development of cancer. Immunotherapy tries to rally the body's immune system to fight the cancer. This is often done by injecting antibodies and helpful proteins into the bloodstream.

Alcoholism

The National Council on Alcoholism and Drug Dependence considers alcoholism as a disease that is influenced by social, environmental, and genetic factors. The common features of alcoholism are the inability to control consumption, continued drinking despite negative consequences, and distorted thinking patterns (like irrational denial). It is important to note that alcoholism is not simply the result of a weak will but is a physiological state that requires medical treatment so that it can be controlled. Many individuals may have a problem with alcoholism but not realize it if they are still functioning well overall and only drink in social situations. Alcoholics tend to be those who, even when they aren't drinking, place an undue amount of psychological emphasis on alcohol.

Effects of alcohol

Alcohol has a number of effects on behavior and judgment. It is known to impair sensory perceptions: the eye is less able to adjust to bright lights, and the ear has difficulty distinguishing sounds. The senses of smell and taste are also diminished by excessive consumption of alcohol. Alcohol will decrease sensitivity in general, making it possible for individuals to feel comfortable in extreme temperatures that may be hazardous to their health. Intoxication typically causes an impairment of motor skills, meaning that activities performed with the muscles cannot be done with any precision or coordination. Intoxication usually has a negative effect on sexual performance, even though it may increase interest in sexual activity.

From the moment it is consumed, and even before the individual notices any of the psychological effects, alcohol is at work in the human body. It is almost immediately absorbed into the bloodstream through the walls of the stomach and the upper intestine. Typically, it takes about 15 minutes for the alcohol in a drink to reach the bloodstream and, usually, about 1 hour for the alcohol to reach its peak. Once in the bloodstream, alcohol is carried to the liver, heart, and brain. Although alcohol cannot leave the body until it is metabolized by the liver, it is a diuretic that accelerates the removal of other liquids from the body; thus, alcohol has a dehydrating effect. Alcohol also lowers the temperature of the body.

Alchohol and the brain

When consumed in low volume, alcohol alters the areas of the brain that influence behavior in a way that makes the individual feel more relaxed and less inhibited. Of course, this is accompanied by deficits in concentration, memory, judgment, and motor control. Heavy drinkers may experience long-term intelligence and memory impairment. This occurs because alcohol depresses the central nervous system and slows down the activity of the neurons in the brain. This dulling of mental reactions increases in proportion to the amount of alcohol consumed and can culminate in unconsciousness, coma, or even death. Although one or two drinks may have a pleasant tranquilizing effect, many more can entirely snuff out central nervous system activity.

Response to alcohol

Several things determine the severity of an individual's response to alcohol. Obviously, the more alcohol consumed, the higher the individual's blood-alcohol concentration will be. Also, since the liver can only process half an ounce of alcohol every hour, heavy drinking results in a higher level of intoxication than moderate drinking. More potent forms of alcohol, like liquor and fortified wine, get into the bloodstream more quickly than less concentrated beverages, like beer, especially if the liquor is accompanied by a carbonated beverage. Heavy individuals tend to get drunk more slowly as they have an excess of water with which to dilute the incoming alcohol. Typically, women tolerate alcohol less well than men because they have less of the stomach enzyme that neutralizes alcohol. Older individuals tend to have less water and so are more affected by alcohol. The effects of alcohol are seen more quickly if it is taken on an empty stomach, if tolerance to it has not been built up, or if it is accompanied by a prescription medication.

Recommended level of alcohol consumption

Alcohol is not entirely bad for the body; in fact, there is consistent evidence that suggests a single drink every day can reduce an individual's risk of heart disease. This is more true for men than for women. The National Institute of Alcohol and Alcohol Abuse suggests that men should have no more than two drinks every day, and women should have no more than one. This amount should be adjusted, depending on an individual's weight or age. Many individuals, including pregnant women, people with ulcers, people on certain prescription medications, or those operating heavy machinery, shouldn't drink at all. The health risks associated with alcohol increase in proportion to the amount of alcohol that is consumed.

Alcohol and the cardiovascular and immune systems

Alcohol is thought to have some positive effects on the cardiovascular system. Light drinkers seem to have healthier hearts, fewer heart attacks, lower cholesterol levels, and, thus, a lower risk for heart disease than those who abstain altogether. In contrast, excessive drinking will weaken the heart muscle, and this is particularly true if alcohol is used in combination with tobacco and cocaine. Chronic alcohol use will inhibit the creation of white blood cells (which help fight infection) and of red blood cells (which carry oxygen around the body). It is dangerous for a person suffering from an infection (like a cold or the flu), to drink alcohol because it will suppress the immune system's ability to fight the infection.

Alcohol and the digestive system

The first stop for alcohol is the stomach. It is partially broken down there, and the remainder of it is absorbed into the bloodstream through the stomach lining. While in the stomach, alcohol stimulates the release of certain chemicals that tend to irritate the lining; it is for this reason that heavy drinking often causes nausea and chronic drinking may contribute to ulcers. The alcohol in the bloodstream moves on to the liver where, for the most part, it will be converted into fat. If an individual consumes four or five drinks a day for a few weeks, the liver cells will accrue a large amount of fat. Heavy alcohol use may eventually cause white blood cells to attack the liver, which can cause irreparable damage.

Alcohol-related death

Alcohol can kill those who abuse it in various ways. The main cause of death is injury, generally sustained in auto accidents involving drunk driving. In fact, alcohol is involved in at least half of all traffic fatalities (as well as being involved in half of all homicides and a quarter of all suicides). After injury, the second most common cause of death related to alcohol is cirrhosis of the liver and other digestive disease. Health professionals believe that about half the people admitted to the hospital have a health problem related to alcohol. As would be expected, young drinkers are more likely to die from injury and older drinkers more likely to succumb to alcohol-related illness.

Alcohol when consumed with other drugs

The dangers of alcohol may be magnified greatly if it is consumed in combination with other drugs, whether legal or illegal. Indeed, more than half the most frequently prescribed drugs contain one or more ingredients that react with alcohol. In most cases, this is because the ingredient affects the same areas of the brain as alcohol, thus increasing the pharmacological effects. Particularly, the synergistic combination of alcohol and an antidepressant or anti-anxiety medication can be fatal. One commonly used drug that is thought to have negative consequences when taken with alcohol is aspirin. Although many people take aspirin to alleviate the negative consequences of drinking, research has shown that aspirin may diminish the stomach's ability to process alcohol.

Social drinking

Though there are no set standards for the varying degrees of alcohol consumption, there are a few basic patterns of drinking that are agreed upon by health professionals. Light drinking is usually defined as having three or fewer alcoholic beverages every week. Infrequent drinking is having less than one drink a month, but more than one drink in a year. Infrequent drinkers can often be those who rarely drink but, on the occasions when they do, are apt to drink four or more drinks. A moderate drinker is one who has approximately 12 drinks a week but is not impaired in any life domain. Social drinking is not defined by a particular quantity; rather, it is drinking at a level consistent with one's peer group, whether this level is high or low.

Reasons for alcohol consumption

Alcohol has been popular throughout history because it depresses the central nervous system and makes people feel more relaxed. People also often drink in celebration or when meeting with friends because alcohol tends to reduce inhibitions and make conversation easier. People who drink alcohol often report feeling smarter, sexier, or stronger, even if studies indicate the opposite. Alcohol is also used by many people as a way to escape personal problems or a bad mood. It is also true that many people drink because they are swayed by the massive advertising campaigns launched by brewers; indeed, the effects of alcohol advertising on underage consumers remains a controversial topic. Finally, many people drink in order to emulate people they admire, whether celebrities, family members, or peers.

Female alcoholism

Even though women are less likely to abuse alcohol than men, many women still drink too much. Furthermore, women tend to drink for different reasons than men. Many women have an increased susceptibility to alcohol written into their genes. Female alcoholics are more likely than male alcoholics to have a parent who drinks heavily, has psychiatric problems, or has attempted suicide. Approximately 25% of female alcoholics report that they were physically or sexually abused during childhood. Women are more likely than men to be depressed before and during a period of alcoholism. Women who are single, separated, or divorced tend to drink more than married women, though women who cohabitate with a man without being married are the most likely to be problem drinkers. Women tend to drink more when they lose a social role, e.g., when their children grow up and leave, they lose their job, or they are divorced.

Unfortunately, female alcoholics do not always receive the same quality of care and social support as male alcoholics. Often, this is because of women have lower incomes than men or because women are burdened with the responsibilities of raising children. Studies have also shown that women are more likely to blame their personal problems on anxiety or depression, whereas men more readily admit to a drinking problem. Female alcoholics are more likely to become addicted to prescription medications or to develop eating disorders and sexual dysfunctions. Many health professionals believe targeting the causes of female alcoholism, like low self-esteem and depression, is a promising approach to treatment. Other organizations, like Women for Sobriety, are working to ensure that female alcoholism is recognized as a serious problem that demands attention.

Binge drinking

The individuals who are at great risk of developing health problems from alcohol are those who follow the patterns known as problem drinking and binge drinking. Problem drinking is defined as any amount of drinking that interferes with a major part of the individual's life, whether safety, sleep, energy, family relationships, sexual activity, or health. Although some of the negative consequences associated with problem drinking are immediate (like bad judgment and physical impairment), other effects of consistent alcohol abuse may be evident only over the long term. Binge drinking is defined for a man as having five or more drinks in a sitting (the amount is four for a woman). Binge drinking is most common among young, single men.

Type I and Type II alcoholism

Over the past few decades, the health professionals working towards better prevention and treatment for alcoholism have developed a few different classes of the disease. Type I alcoholics are those who begin a pattern of heavy drinking sometime after the age of 25, often in response to some personal misfortune. These individuals are able to refrain from drinking for a long period of time and feel very conflicted about their drinking problem. Type II alcoholics, on the other hand, usually become dependent on alcohol before the age of 25 and are likely to have a close relative who also has an alcohol problem. These people tend to drink regardless of their personal situation and experience no feelings of guilt or fear regarding their alcoholism.

Factors for alcoholism

It is quite common for an alcoholic to begin drinking to escape psychological problems. Indeed, studies have shown that approximately half the individuals who are diagnosed with alcoholism have another mental disorder. Alcohol is frequently linked with both depression and anxiety disorders. Another common cause of alcoholism is having a parent who abuses alcohol. It has been documented that the children of alcoholics are about five times as likely to develop alcoholism themselves. Perhaps, this is because the children have become accustomed to problems associated with alcoholism, such as poor interpersonal performance, unstable family life, and antisocial tendencies.

Drinking and driving

The most common crime in the United States is drinking and driving. In order to combat this menace to public safety, many communities offer free rides to people who have had too much to drink. Police frequently set up checkpoints along major roads so they can check drivers for the signs of intoxication. There has also been a move to increase the legal consequences of a drunk-driving ticket, and many states revoke a license for the first offense. At present, the National Commission Against Drunk Driving defines a drunk driver as one with a blood-alcohol content above 0.15%, although most states will take a driver from behind the wheel for a BAC above 0.08%. Most drunk drivers are single men between the ages of 25 and 45.

Interventions

Brief interventions are short, intense training sessions that teach alcoholics the skills they will need to battle their drinking problem. These programs, which typically last about 8 weeks and center on topics like "assertiveness" and "self-esteem," are best suited for individuals who do not have a physical dependence on alcohol. Moderation training, another form of treatment, tries to equip drinkers with the skills to manage their drinking, by showing them ways to reduce consumption and avoid problematic situations. This method is somewhat controversial because critics assert that the only good choice for chronic alcohol abusers is abstinence. However, advocates of moderation training point out that their programs are designed for less severe cases and that their goals are more realistic than those found in other programs.

Detoxification

Whenever an individual with an alcohol problem begins treatment, the first step is detoxification, the gradual removal of alcohol from the system. Most of the time, detoxification does not produce major withdrawal symptoms. However, those who have been drinking heavily for a long period may develop severe symptoms, including seizures and delirium tremens (also known as DTs). Delirium tremens is a condition in which the individual becomes agitated and may have delusions, a rapid heartbeat, sweating, vivid hallucinations, fever, and trembling hands. This condition is most likely to strike those alcoholics who also suffer from malnutrition, depression, or fatigue and usually ceases after a few alcohol-free days.

Treatment of alcoholism

If alcoholism is caught in its early stages, doctors often prescribe antidepressant or anti-anxiety medication. These drugs increase the amount of serotonin in the brain and are believed to reduce painful cravings for alcohol. Doctors also recommend that recovering alcoholics take vitamin supplements to remedy the malnutrition that prolonged alcoholism may cause. For especially severe cases, doctors may prescribe Antabuse (the commercial name for the drug disulfiram), which causes an individual to become nauseous or ill when they consume alcohol. Individuals on this medication must also be careful to avoid foods that have been marinated or cooked in alcohol; indeed, some sensitive individuals may even have an adverse reaction to the alcohol in shaving lotion. Although Antabuse is effective in forcing an individual to stop drinking, it does not treat any of the psychological or social causes of drinking.

Inpatient and outpatient treatment for alcoholism

For a long time, a four-week stay at a psychiatric hospital or residential facility was considered necessary for a recovering alcoholic. This inpatient treatment was usually successful, too: over 70% of those who complete such a treatment remain sober for five years afterward, according to one study. Unfortunately, inpatient treatment is expensive, and insurance companies have been increasingly unwilling to pay for it. So outpatient treatments like group therapy, family therapy, interventions, and organizations like Alcoholics Anonymous have become more popular in recent years. Some studies have indicated that intensive outpatient treatment can be as effective as inpatient care, especially if the individual continues it for at least a year.

Recovery from alcoholism

Defeating alcoholism is often the most difficult challenge an individual will face in his or her lifetime. Relapse into drinking is common; some studies estimate that 90% of recovering alcoholics will drink again within a year after quitting. The people who tend to be successful at abstaining are those who have something to lose: that is, parents of children and people with important jobs. Almost every recovering alcoholic will experience mood swings and an occasional temptation to drink. More and more, relapse prevention is a part of treatment. Relapse prevention involves giving the individual the information and skills to cope with the temptations of alcohol, as well as providing a support network that the individual can rely on in times of stress. Exercise and a general reduction in stress seem to be the most helpful treatment techniques for creating a permanent life away from alcohol.

AA

The most famous self-help program for individuals battling a drinking problem is Alcoholics Anonymous (AA). This global organization seeks to force alcoholics to admit their problems and to rely on one another for support in solving them. Every member of AA will have a "sponsor," another member whom they can call upon if they are tempted to drink. AA also features a 12-step program in which members are forced to take responsibility, to own up to the problems that drinking causes, and to ask God for help. The 12-step model devised by AA has been used in many other self-help organizations. There are other self-help groups, such as Rational Recovery, that adhere to a similar philosophy as AA without the emphasis on spirituality.

Tobacco and nicotine

Smoking or otherwise ingesting tobacco creates an immediate effect on the body and brain. The primary active ingredient in tobacco is nicotine, a colorless, oily compound. Nicotine can be poisonous if it is ingested in a concentrated form. Inhaling cigarette smoke into the lungs causes about 90% of the nicotine to be absorbed into the body. Nicotine stimulates the cerebral cortex, enhancing mood and alertness, but, paradoxically, it can act as a sedative if taken in large doses. At the dose levels found in cigarettes, nicotine triggers the production of adrenaline, thereby increasing blood pressure and speeding up heart rate. Nicotine also decreases hunger, dulls the taste buds, and prevents the creation of urine. The FDA classifies nicotine as a dangerous and addictive drug because it is known to contribute to heart and respiratory disease.

Tobacco and respiratory disease

Respiratory function is one of the more immediate processes to be damaged by smoking. Even very new smokers can develop the breathlessness, cough, and excessive phlegm associated with heavy smoking. Smoking is known to contribute to instances of chronic obstructive lung disease, or COLD, a designation which includes both bronchitis and emphysema. These conditions are typically caused by a persistent inability to inhale enough air, which results in the destruction of air sacs and produces a strain on the heart. Chronic bronchitis is the condition in which the production of mucus increases and the bronchial tubes become inflamed, both of which help to narrow the air passages. In short, smoking is the most dangerous form of air pollution.

Tobacco link with cancer

By now, most Americans should be aware that the risk of developing cancer is increased more by cigarette smoking than by any other single behavior. Not only do cigarettes lead to lung cancer, but they also lead to cancer of the mouth, pharynx, larynx, esophagus, pancreas, and bladder. The risk of developing cancer is not limited to cigarettes: pipes, smokeless tobacco, and cigars all put a person at risk. Second-hand smoke has a similar effect; scientists have shown that individuals who are exposed to environmental smoke for more than 3 hours a day are three times more likely to develop cancer than those not exposed. In addition to tobacco, other acknowledged carcinogens are asbestos, dark hair dye, nickel, and vinyl chloride. Individuals should always try to make certain their living and working spaces are well ventilated to reduce the harmful substances in the air.

Tar and carbon

When it is burning, tobacco creates tar and carbon monoxide. Tar is a sticky, dark fluid made up of several hundred chemicals. Some of these chemicals are poisonous, and some are carcinogens. When tobacco smoke is inhaled, tar tends to settle in the bronchial tubes of the lungs where it damages the mucus and cilia that are charged with escorting harmful products out of the respiratory system. The smoke from burning tobacco also produces an amount of carbon monoxide about 400 times the amount considered safe by industry. Carbon monoxide is very bad for health: it prevents hemoglobin from carrying oxygen throughout the body, it impairs the nervous system, and is thought to be partly responsible for many heart attacks and strokes.

Tobacco and stroke

Although tobacco use is not usually associated with an increased risk of stroke, there is clear scientific evidence that links a long-term smoking habit with an increased risk of a debilitating or fatal stroke. Even when other risk factors are taken into consideration, smoking doubles the risk of stroke in men and women. Individuals suffering from hypertension (high blood pressure) exhibit the greatest benefits from quitting. Smoking seems to raise the risk of stroke by weakening the heart muscle, which in turn makes it more difficult for the body to clear blockages in the arteries that can eventually decrease the amount of blood to the brain. Individuals who quit smoking will reduce their risk of stroke, but it will never be quite as low as those who never took up the habit.

Tobacco and heart disease

Despite the attention given to lung cancer, heart disease is the leading cause of smoking-related death. Smoking doubles the risk of heart attack, and smokers are much less likely to recover from an attack. Smoking is considered to be more damaging to heart health than high blood pressure and high cholesterol, though it is even more dangerous when it is combined with one or both of those. Smoking is known to cause the condition cardiomyopathy, or the weakening of the heart's pumping action. Most doctors assume that it is either the tar or the nicotine in tobacco that creates this condition. Although some heart problems, like arteriosclerosis (hardening of the arteries), persist, smokers can immediately improve the health of their heart by quitting, no matter how long they have smoked.

Psychological addiction to tobacco

Tobacco creates in the user certain psychological changes that may become addictive over time. For instance, nicotine is known to stimulate the part of the brain that generates feelings of satisfaction or well-being. Nicotine is also known to temporarily enhance memory, the performance of repetitive tasks, and the tolerance of pain. It is also credited with reducing hunger and anxiety. Individuals suffering from depression may also seek relief through tobacco. Studies have consistently shown that depressed individuals are far more likely than others to develop a smoking habit. Even more troubling, the effects of depression make it much more difficult to quit smoking, so the interdependent relation between tobacco use and depression is likely to continue for a long time.

Miscellaneous problems caused by smoking

There are many ways in which smoking can damage health. Smokers are far more likely to develop gum disease or lose teeth. Even when a smoker practices good oral hygiene, he or she can still suffer from damage to the bones that support teeth. A smoking habit is known to contribute to the formation of mouth and stomach ulcers and cirrhosis of the liver. Smoking is blamed for a worsening in allergic reactions, diabetes, and hypertension. It is not uncommon for a man who smokes more than 10 cigarettes a day to become temporarily impotent. Overall, cigarette smokers tend to miss about one-third more days from work and school than do non-smokers, primarily from respiratory illness. There is also the danger of fires that begin when lit cigarettes are left unattended.

Risks to families of smokers

Even if they are not smokers themselves, the people who live with smokers are at an increased risk of developing serious health disorders. Secondhand smoke is known to contribute to asthma and bronchitis in children, as well as increasing the risk of sudden infant death syndrome (SIDS). The spouses of smokers are about 30% more likely to develop lung cancer than are other non-smokers. Similarly, children who grow up in homes where one or both parents smoke are several times more likely to develop lung cancer, heart disease, and stroke. Finally, opinion polls have discovered that most children object to their parents' smoking, worry about the health dangers posed to themselves by secondhand smoke, and dislike the odor of smoke in their hair and clothing.

Mainstream and sidestream smoke

Mainstream smoke is that smoke which is taken directly into the lungs by the smoker; sidestream smoke (otherwise known as secondhand smoke) is the smoke inhaled by everyone in the presence of a smoker. The smoking of a cigarette typically entails about eight or nine inhalations of mainstream smoke, each lasting for a few seconds. Sidestream smoke is actually different in composition from mainstream smoke: it has twice as much tar and nicotine and five times as much carbon monoxide. About 3,000 people develop lung cancer each year as a result of secondhand smoke. In terms of causing cancer, sidestream smoke is thought to be more dangerous than radon gas and most of the pollutants limited by federal law.

Quitting tobacco with group help

Studies have consistently shown that individuals who join support groups have a much higher chance of permanently ending a smoking addiction. Every year, the American Cancer Society offers about 1,500 clinics in which individuals get the training and the encouragement they need to quit smoking. The American Lung Association also organizes group therapy sessions for those who hope to quit, and they emphasize cooperation and group interdependence as a tool for avoiding tobacco.

Quitting tobacco alone

It is extremely difficult to quit smoking by oneself, though many people try. Some doctors think that a nicotine addiction is the most difficult addiction to break. Most smokers will have to try several times before they are able to quit successfully. When smokers try to quit all by themselves, they usually begin by throwing away all of their cigarettes, by cutting down on their intake, or by switching to a less potent brand. Successful quitters are usually those who develop some other hobby, often physical exercise, to take the place of smoking. It is also a good idea to explore various means of relaxation apart from tobacco so that kicking the habit will be a less stressful event.

Nicotine patches

Nicotine patches, formally known as nicotine transdermal delivery systems, are affixed to the skin and slowly provide a low level of nicotine to the body. Typically, patches are worn for between 6 and 16 weeks. Although the patch is known to minimize withdrawal symptoms, it has been most successful with those individuals who are highly motivated to quit, are enrolled in some kind of counseling program, and were smoking more than a pack of cigarettes every day. Doctors caution those who use the patch that, although it can help diminish the physical dependency on nicotine, it does not reduce the psychological addiction. Pregnant women and individuals with heart disease should not use the patch, and under no circumstances should any individual wear more than one patch at a time.

Nicotine gum

Nicotine gum, usually sold under the name Nicorette, is a chewing gum that gradually releases nicotine. This nicotine is absorbed through the mucous membranes of the mouth and, although it is not significant enough to produce the pleasant effects of a cigarette, will minimize the symptoms of withdrawal from smoking. This product is fairly expensive (a month's supply costs about $45) and has a somewhat bitter taste. Nicotine gum is not meant to become a long-term habit in its own right, and because it contains nicotine, it has many of the damaging effects on health as smoking. Pregnant women or individuals with heart disease should not use nicotine gum. Individuals who use nicotine gum should gradually reduce their consumption until they are entirely free of the nicotine addiction.

Hypnosis and acupuncture

Many individuals who have tried unsuccessfully to quit smoking in the past will consider hypnosis and acupuncture therapy. In hypnosis, the individual is put into a mild trance state and given suggestions that will hopefully persuade him or her to quit smoking. Hypnosis may not affect the physical dependence on nicotine, but it can create a good attitude for quitting successfully. When acupuncture therapy is given, the individual has a circular needle or staple inserted into the flap in front of his or her ear hole. This therapy is meant to stimulate the production of calming chemicals in the brain, and those who are given the therapy are encouraged to gently move the needle or staple when they feel a temptation to smoke.

Smokeless tobacco

As smoking becomes less and less acceptable in public places, sales of smokeless tobacco products are on the rise. The category smokeless tobacco includes snuff (a powdered tobacco that can be either sniffed or sucked) and chewing tobacco. With these products, nicotine is absorbed by the mucous membranes of the nose or mouth. Although smoking is considered to be a greater health risk, smokeless tobacco products still create a dependence on nicotine and are known to contribute to the formation of cancer. Snuff, in particular, is very high in nicotine and quadruples the user's risk of mouth cancer. Also, users of smokeless tobacco can suffer from bad breath, discolored teeth, cavities, and gum disease.

Drug abuse

A drug is any chemical substance that changes the way a person acts or feels. Drugs may affect a person's mental, physical, or emotional state. Though many drugs are taken to improve the condition of the body or to remedy personal problems, drugs can also undermine health by distorting a person's mind and weakening a person's body. According to the World Health Organization, drug abuse is any excessive drug use that is not approved by the medical profession. The use of some drugs in any quantity is considered abuse; other drugs must be taken in large quantities before they are considered to have been abused. There are health risks involved with the use of any drug, legal or illegal, insofar as they introduce a foreign substance into the balanced system of physical health.

Steroids

Many people looking to build strength and endurance have foolishly used anabolic steroids, which are synthetic derivatives of the male hormone testosterone. Though steroids will rapidly increase muscle strength and endurance, they are very bad for the liver, the brain, and the reproductive organs. Individuals who use steroids for long periods of time are more likely to develop heart disease. There are also harmful side effects associated with such steroid alternatives as human growth hormone (HGH) and gamma hydroxybutyrate (GHB). These substances both are known to cause medical complications like nausea, seizures, and even coma.

Drug toxicity

The toxicity level of a drug is the administered amount that will be poisonous to the body. A drug taken at a toxic level will cause either temporary or permanent damage to the body. Indeed, the enzymes in the liver that are responsible for breaking down drugs are called detoxification enzymes. Drugs may act locally, generally, or selectively. A drug acts locally when it only affects a specific area of the body. A drug acts generally when it affects an entire system of the body. A barbiturate, for instance, has a deadening effect on the entire nervous system. A drug acts selectively when it has a much greater effect on one organ or system than any other. Some anesthetics, for instance, will numb an isolated part of the body.

Prescription drugs

Every year, the Food and Drug Administration of the United States (FDA) grants permission for the production of about twenty new prescription drugs. Although these drugs can be very beneficial, they are frequently misused. The most common mistakes associated with prescription drug use are overdosing, under-dosing, omitting labeling information, ordering the wrong dose form (liquid instead of solid, for instance), and neglecting to recognize an allergic reaction to a drug. Failure to properly take a prescription medication can lead to recurrent infections, medical complications, and, even, death. Some patients endanger their own health by failing to adhere to the dosage schedule or failing to tell their doctor about side effects.

Sometimes, it is more difficult for patients to notice the psychological effects of a prescription medication than the physical side effects. The drugs most likely to cause noticeable psychological problems are those for depression, high blood pressure, epilepsy, asthma, insomnia, and arthritis. Doctors assert that psychological problems associated with drugs are more likely to affect people as they get older, especially if they are taking a large number of medications. Many of these drugs either induce depression by slowing the blood pressure or induce anxiety by overstimulating the nervous system. The best way to manage the psychological side effects of a prescription drug is to learn as much as possible about the drug and closely monitor yourself in consultation with a doctor.

Side effects of prescription drugs

There is no prescription drug that does not cause side effects, even if these go unnoticed by the patient. It is very common to have an allergic reaction to a drug. Patients frequently develop allergic reactions to penicillin and other antibiotics. These allergic responses may cause nausea, hives, a drop in blood pressure, constriction of the breathing passages, and even collapse. Patients who suffer an extreme reaction may require an immediate injection of adrenaline to maintain their vital processes. With other drugs, complications can include heart problems, blood disorders, birth defects, blindness, and memory problems. For these reasons, prescription drugs should only be taken under the close supervision of a doctor.

Over-the-counter drugs

In the United States, there are more than half a million health products that can be purchased without the approval of a doctor. Many of these over-the–counter drugs (OCD) (aspirin, for example) can have serious side effects. Some drugs that were obtained only with a doctor's permission in the past are now available for immediate purchase. Consumers should be aware that OCD products carry possible dangers. Nasal sprays, for instance, can have the opposite effect of what was intended if they are used too often. Laxatives can also do permanent damage to the body if they are taken too regularly. Eye drops may eventually make eyes redder if they are used habitually. Lastly, OCD sleep aids have not yet been adequately researched, and some doctors suspect they may have negative consequences for mental health.

Variables affecting drug use

The particular effects experienced by a drug user depend on a few different variables: dosage, individual characteristics, and setting. For most drugs, an increase in dosage will intensify the effects of the drug. There may also be a change in the effect experienced from a drug at a low dosage than from that same drug at a higher dosage. Every person will respond differently to a drug as well, depending on their psychological and physical state. The enzymes in the bloodstream play a major role in reducing drug levels in the blood, so an individual's drug experience will largely depend on the quality and quantity of his or her enzymes. Many people report a change in the effects of a drug related to their setting; a stressful situation, for instance, may cause the effects of some drugs to be more intense.

Drug interaction

There are four main ways in which drugs can interact: additive interaction, synergistic interaction, potentiating interaction, and antagonistic interaction.

In an additive interaction, the cumulative effect of all the drugs taken is simply the sum total of the individual effects of each drug.

In a synergistic interaction, however, the cumulative effect of all the drugs taken is greater than the effects of each individual drug. An example of a synergistic interaction is when barbiturates are mixed with alcohol, resulting in a greatly magnified depressant effect.

A drug interaction is referred to as potentiating when one drug increases the effect of another. Alcohol, for example, has a potentiating effect on some cold medicines.

Drugs are said to be antagonistic when they either neutralize or stifle the effects of one another.

Intoxication, withdrawal, polyabuse, and comorbidity

In clinical terms, intoxication is the behavioral, psychological, and physiological changes that occur in a drug user. In the beginning stages of drug addiction, the goal is usually intoxication. Later in the addiction process, however, the goal of use tends to be avoiding withdrawal symptoms. Withdrawal is any physiological distress that occurs because a drug is not taken. Many drug abusers take several different drugs, though they may prefer only one; this condition is known as polyabuse. Studies have also shown that there is a significant overlap between people with chemical dependencies and people with psychological disorders. This overlap is known as comorbidity and in part accounts for the profound problems that many drug abusers face in trying to escape their addictions.

Drug dependency

A psychological dependence on drugs may begin as a craving for the pleasurable feelings or relief from anxiety that the drug provides. However, this craving can soon turn into a dependency on the drug in order to perform normal mental operations. A physical dependency, on the other hand, is said to occur when the individual requires increasing amounts of the drug to get the desired effect. Many drugs, like marijuana or hallucinogens, do not cause withdrawal symptoms; others, like heroin or cocaine, may be extremely painful to stop using. Individuals with a severe chemical dependency will eventually use a drug like this simply to avoid experiencing the effects of withdrawal. Typically, an individual with a severe dependency will try to stop many times without success.

Amphetamines

For a long time, amphetamines were prescribed to control weight gain. Now, however, doctors have decided that these powerful stimulants can be extremely addictive and dangerous to health. Some common names of amphetamines are Benzedrine, Dexedrine, Methedrine. Other substances that are related to amphetamines include Ritalin, Cylert, and Preludin. Amphetamines are usually taken orally, though they may also be snorted, smoked, or injected. Some forms of methamphetamine are extremely addictive and can have effects lasting from 12 to 14 hours. These products all trigger the release of adrenaline, which stimulates the central nervous system and raises the heart rate.

Amphetamines make the user very alert and full of energy. Users typically report a feeling of well-being and confidence and a sense that they are thinking very clearly, even though research does not indicate that this is so. Amphetamine users are very talkative and animated, to the point of being uncomfortably restless. Large dosages will produce confusion, incoherent speech, anxiety, and even heart palpitations. In the short term, amphetamine use can cause heart trouble, a loss of coordination, anger, nausea, or chills. Over the long term, it may cause malnutrition, skin disorders, insomnia, depression, vitamin deficiencies, and brain damage affecting the areas controlling speech. Withdrawing from amphetamines can also be a very difficult and painful process.

Non-biological reasons for addiction

Some individuals are at a higher risk of addiction because they lack self-control, have no moral opposition to drugs, have low self-esteem, or are depressed. Research has also shown that individuals who live in isolation or in poverty are more likely to become addicted to drugs. People who associate with drug users are more likely to become users themselves. Drugs that produce a short-lived but intense state of intoxication (cocaine, for instance) are more likely to be addictive, as are those that have especially painful withdrawal symptoms. Most of the people who will experiment with drugs do so during adolescence. Although many have suggested that drugs like alcohol, tobacco, and marijuana lead to use of harder drugs, most research on this subject has been inconclusive.

Inhalants

Inhalants are those drugs that are taken into the body through vigorous inhalation, also known as huffing. They typically produce momentary hallucinations and a feeling of well-being. The effects of inhalants typically only last for a period of seconds. Inhalants have been blamed for dizziness, involuntary eye movements, nausea, lethargy, poor coordination, impaired motor skills, nosebleeds, loss of appetite, aggressiveness, and an increased risk of accident and injury. Furthermore, the chronic use of inhalants may lead to hepatitis, kidney failure, respiratory trouble, irregular heartbeat, bone problems, and heart failure. It is quite possible to die the first time you ever try an inhalant.

Barbiturates

Barbiturates are those drugs that slow down the central nervous system and, in the beginning stages of use, reduce physical and mental tension. Barbiturates are also known to decrease alertness and to induce drowsiness. Besides the obvious risks barbiturates pose to a driver, there is also the danger of slowed breathing, weak heartbeat, disrupted sleep, impaired vision, confusion, chronic lethargy, and irritability. Over a long period of time, many abusers of barbiturates will become dependent on the drug and may become virtually comatose. Indeed, excessively large doses of barbiturates can immediately result in coma, stupor, or death. There are tremendously painful withdrawal symptoms associated with barbiturates.

Phencyclidine

Phencyclidine, also known as PCP or angel dust, is one of the more dangerous drugs that are commonly abused. When it is taken, it immediately produces a profound change in perceptions, including hallucinations and delusions of personal strength. Individuals on PCP may incorrectly believe that they are invulnerable. Besides the obvious risks associated with this psychological condition, PCP users will experience flushing, an increase in heart rate, diminished sensitivity to pain, and impaired coordination and speech, and they can possibly be put into a stupor. The use of PCP can cause a psychosis, will increase the risk of danger to the user and those around the user, and can cause immediate coma and death.

Generic drugs

When doctors refer to the generic name of a drug, they are referring to a shortened version of the drug's exact chemical name. A particular drug may be sold under a variety of different brand names (trade names chosen by each manufacturer). When a brand name drug has lost its patent protection, a competing manufacturer copies the original drug and markets a generic version. It costs a great deal less than the brand name form of the drug. .Since most of the time, there is no substantial difference between the brand-name version of a drug and its generic counterpart, patients will save money by selecting the generic version. Patients should confer with their doctors about any changes that have occurred after starting a new medication to ensure that the prescribed dose is appropriate. It is also important that the patient learn how to store particular medications so that they do not diminish in effectiveness or become contaminated.

Chronic drug use

The effects of habitual drug use can be either chronic (resulting from long-term use) or acute (resulting from a single dose). Acute effects are usually determined by the particular drug; first-time users of stimulants, for instance, may be overcome with a powerful sense of anger. The effects of chronic drug use are more predictable. Over a long period of time, consistent drug users may feel tired, lose weight, have a nagging cough, and develop overall body aches. Drug abusers often suffer from blackouts and may undergo psychological turmoil and bouts of paranoia. Typically, the stress involved with supporting and maintaining a habit increases over time, and this stress adds to the damage done by the drug itself.

Caffeine

Caffeine is the most commonly used mind-altering (psychotropic) drug in the world. It is a stimulant, so it relieves drowsiness and aids in the performance of repetitive tasks. There is some anecdotal evidence to suggest that caffeine improves physical performance and endurance. On the other hand, overconsumption of caffeine can lead to anxiety, dizziness, insomnia, upset stomach, and addiction. Extremely high doses of caffeine can result in seizure and respiratory failure. Withdrawal from caffeine can be a painful process and should be done gradually. Caffeine does enter the tissues of a growing fetus, although there is no evidence to suggest that it causes birth defects.

Cocaine and crack

Cocaine and its deadly derivative, crack, are among the most addictive and deadly substances that are commonly abused. When they are taken, whether through inhalation or intravenous injection, they accelerate the mental and physical processes and create in the mind of the user a feeling of invulnerability and high energy. They may cause health problems in the short term, ranging from headaches and shaking to seizures, collapse, and death. Over the long term, cocaine and crack users usually have impaired sexual function, blood pressure problems, heart trouble, brain hemorrhaging, hepatitis, and malnutrition. Users of these drugs are also more likely to contract the HIV virus. Cocaine users frequently become paranoid, angry, and suspicious.

Cannabis

Cannabis, also known as marijuana or pot, is a commonly used substance abuse drug. When taken, it relaxes the mind and body, affects the mood, and heightens sensory perceptions. Cannabis use speeds up heart rate, dries out the mouth and throat, impairs the ability to react to external stimuli, and causes lethargy. In large doses, cannabis may cause hallucinations and panic attacks. Long-term users of cannabis exhibit decreased motivation and laziness. The general risks of prolonged cannabis use are psychological dependence, impaired memory and cognitive abilities, increased blood pressure, lung cancer, emphysema, impaired coordination, and diminished fertility.

Ecstasy

The complex chemical MDMA, popularly known as Ecstasy, has emerged as one of the most common and dangerous drugs of the past decade. Originally developed as a solution to social anxiety and depression, Ecstasy has become popular as a recreational drug among young people. Although users of the drug report that it causes a feeling of happiness and euphoria, they, also report some troubling side effects. Ecstasy has been linked with insomnia, nausea, fatigue, and problems in concentrating. It is particularly dangerous to take the drug in a chaotic and hot environment, like a dance club, because it causes dehydration to a dangerous degree. There have been scores of deaths blamed on Ecstasy; most of the time, this was because the user raised their body temperature to around 110º Fahrenheit.

Opioids

The opioid family of narcotics relaxes the central nervous system and provides a temporary relief to physical pain. They also produce a short-term sense of mental well-being and satisfaction. They have serious health consequences, however. Opioids are blamed for restlessness, nausea, weight loss, loss of sex drive, slurred speech, sweating, drowsiness, and impaired judgment, attention, and memory. Over time, many individuals will become extremely addicted to opioids and will suffer from malnutrition, an impaired immune system, infections of the heart and lungs, hepatitis, tetanus, depression, skin abscesses, and even the HIV virus. It is also possible to overdose on opioids and lapse into a coma or die.

12-step programs

Though it was first introduced by Alcoholics Anonymous, the 12-step method of recovery has become the model for rehabilitation in over 200 organizations. The basic tenet of a 12-step program is that the user is powerless to control his or her own addiction. In order to be a part of the program, the individual must want to quit. Then he or she will get in touch with a group and attend meetings. One of the fundamental parts of the 12-step program is the cooperation among members; when one feels tempted to relapse into the former behavior, he or she is supposed to call on other members for support. Individuals are ultimately responsible for themselves, however, and are not required to pay dues or to attend any meeting if they do not desire.

Relapse prevention

Most substance abusers will relapse several times after kicking the habit. This is important for both the user and the user's support group to know so that they do not become too frustrated at the setbacks on the road to recovery. Some therapists even say that these relapses can strengthen self-understanding and make it more likely that future relapses can be avoided. Over time, substance abusers should be able to recognize the stimuli that make them susceptible to using drugs, and they should learn to avoid these people, places, and situations. It is also important to make the distinction between a minor and a major relapse; often, it is a huge victory for a recovering addict to keep a minor relapse from turning into a major one.

Infectious disease

Emerging diseases are those that have only recently been recognized, are increasing in humans, or are likely to spread to new geographical areas in the near future. The most pervasive emerging disease is the HIV virus, which is believed to have originated in central Africa. Diseases may also reemerge later in a slightly mutated form that is resistant to the previous methods of treatment. Viruses and bacteria are capable of endless alterations and even a simple change may enable them to become stronger or more deadly. Another reason why emerging and recurring disease is a growing problem in the world is the infiltration of civilization into previously uninhabited territories; people are encountering millions of microbes that have never been encountered before.

Immune system

The body uses a number of different weapons to try to defeat infections. Most obviously, the skin repels most invaders. Many substances produced by the body (like mucus, saliva, and tears) also fight against infection. When these methods are ineffective, however, the immune system goes to work. The immune system consists of parts of the lymphatic system, like the spleen, thymus gland, and lymph nodes, and vessels called lymphatics that work to filter impurities out of the body. The spleen is where antibodies are made, as well as the place where old red blood cells are disposed. The thymus gland fortifies white blood cells with the ability to find and destroy invaders. The lymph nodes filter our bacteria and other pathogens.

Aiding the immune system

There are a few steps that every person can take to ensure the optimal performance of his or her immune system. By eating a balanced diet, a person can prevent vitamin deficiencies that slow the reactions of the immune system. In particular, a low-fat diet has been shown to speed up the activity of immune cells as they travel throughout the body. Unless a person gets enough sleep, the body will not be able to maintain and renew its immune system. Smoking will decrease the reserve levels of some immune cells, but regular exercise will boost the production of immune cells. Finally, alcoholism will lower the number of defender cells and will slow down the normal immune responses of the body.

Basic immune response

Whenever an antigen, or infecting substance, enters the body, the immune system immediately goes to work to defeat it. To begin with, the T cells fight the antigen, assisted by macrophages (cells that scavenge for foreign or weakened cells). While this battle is raging, the B cells create antibodies to join in. Many pathogens will be transported to the lymph nodes, where a reserve store of antibodies will eliminate them. It is for this reason that the lymph nodes often become swollen during cold and flu season. If the antigens find some success, the body will rush a greater blood supply to the infected area, enriching the supply of oxygen and nutrients. In the event that the pathogens are able to contaminate the blood stream, the infection becomes systemic and much more dangerous.

Immunity and stress relationship

There is a well-documented link between an increased level of stress and the diminished activity of the immune system. Whenever a person becomes stressed out, certain chemicals are released by the body in order to organize the response to the stressful event. These chemicals, however, dampen the effectiveness of the immune system. This is evidenced by research that indicates people who have recently suffered a personal loss are more likely to contract an infection. Persistent stress also gradually weakens an individual's response to pathogens. On the other hand, research suggests that a low-stress life, coupled with support from friends and family, can have a bolstering effect on the immune system.

Immunizations

Despite the overwhelming evidence supporting the use of immunization in preventing potentially life-threatening diseases, many Americans still neglect to get the basic immunizations. At present, the American Academy of Pediatrics recommends that every child be immunized against measles, mumps, smallpox, rubella, diphtheria, tetanus, and hepatitis B. Some vaccinations will need to be repeated on a certain schedule. Basically, a vaccination is the intentional introduction of a small amount of an antigen into the body. This stimulates the immune system to learn how to fight that particular antigen. There are certain vaccinations that a pregnant woman should not get, and a person should never be vaccinated if he or she is sick.

Autoimmune disorders and immune deficiencies

Although they are less common than allergies, autoimmune disorders and immune deficiencies are two fairly common kinds of immune disorders. In an autoimmune disorder, the immune system mistakes normal body tissue for a foreign invader and attacks it. Unfortunately, these infections are most likely to strike women during the childbearing period. These conditions also tend to get worse with time, and though they can be treated with drugs that suppress the immune system, this treatment leaves the body vulnerable to real invaders. Immune deficiencies, on the other hand, occur when a person has a naturally weak immune system. Scientists are still working on genetic therapies to allow individuals with immune deficiencies to lead normal lives.

Basic first-aid tips and supplies

Since it is necessary to act fast when an emergency happens, it is a good idea to think ahead and have a plan in place. If you are in a public place, you may want to begin by shouting for help to see if a doctor is available. Someone should immediately dial 911. Do not attempt any resuscitation techniques unless you are trained. If you have a car and it is appropriate, you should immediately take the victim to the nearest hospital. Furthermore, every home should have some basic first-aid supplies. A good first-aid kit will include bandages, sterile gauze pads, scissors, adhesive tape, calamine lotion, cotton balls, thermometer, ipecac syrup (to induce vomiting), a sharp needle, and safety pins.

Treating various ailments

Open wound
When treating an open wound, a person should apply direct pressure to the wounded area after covering it entirely with sterile gauze or a clean cloth. Apply steady pressure for between 5 and 15 minutes. If possible, elevate the wound above the heart to slow bleeding. Placing a plastic bag of ice or cold water on top of the protective gauze will also help to slow the bleeding. If, after 15 minutes, there is no sign that the blood loss is decreasing or the injury appears serious, the victim should see a doctor for further treatment. If bleeding has stopped within 15 minutes, care from a doctor may still be needed. This is the case if stitches will be required to keep the wound closed or if the victim has not had a tetanus shot within the last 10 years.

Broken bone
If you think someone may have broken a bone, restrict the person from moving unless there is some immediate danger. First, ensure that the person is breathing normally. If the person is bleeding, apply pressure to the wound before assessing the potentially broken bone. Never try to push a broken bone back into place, especially if it is protruding from the skin. If possible, apply a moist compress to any exposed bone. Moisture prevents drying and may promote better healing. Never try to straighten a fracture, and never allow the victim of a broken bone to walk. Any unstable fractures should be placed in a splint to prevent painful motions.

Internal bleeding
If you suspect that a person is bleeding internally (for instance, if they cough or vomit up blood or if they pass blood in their waste matter), do not allow the person to take any fluids or medication because these could get in the way if surgery is necessary. Lay the victim flat and cover the victim with a light blanket; then seek medical attention immediately. If a person is experiencing a bloody nose, have them sit down, leaning slightly forward. The victim should spit out any blood in the nose or mouth. Apply light but steady pressure to the area for about 10 minutes and then, if the bleeding continues, pack the nose with gauze. If there is a foreign object lodged in the nose, do not attempt to remove it.

Choking victim
Never slap a person's back if the person appears to be choking; this can make the situation worse. If the victim is conscious but cannot cough, speak, or breathe, perform the Heimlich maneuver. Begin by standing behind the victim, wrapping your arms around the victim's waist. Make a fist with one hand and place the fist just above the victim's navel. Grab the fist with your other hand and pull upward sharply, trying not to exert too much pressure against the rib cage with your forearms. Repeat this procedure until the victim is either no longer choking or has lost consciousness. This procedure can be performed on oneself, either with one's fist or by pressing sharply against some stationary object, like the back of a chair.

Unconscious choking victim
If a person is choking and has lost consciousness, lay the person on the ground and perform mouth-to-mouth resuscitation. If this does not seem to work, give the person a few abdominal thrusts, as in the Heimlich maneuver. Repeat this from six to ten times if necessary. Next, try to clear the victim's airway: tilt the head back, use your thumb to depress the tongue, and gently sweep a hooked finger through the back of the throat to

remove any objects. Repeat the sequence of abdominal thrusts, probing of the mouth, and mouth-to-mouth resuscitation as many times as necessary. If the victim suddenly is revived but nothing has come out of the mouth, go to the hospital. Hard matter can damage the internal organs as it passes through the body.

Burns

If a person has been burned by fire, cool the burned area with water as soon as possible. This will help to stop the burn process. Next, remove the victim's garments and jewelry and cover the victim with clean sheets or towels. Once the victim is secure, call for emergency medical assistance. If burns have been caused by chemicals, wash the affected area immediately with cool water. Affected areas should be washed for at least 20 minutes. When the eyes are burned by chemicals, the victim will require immediate medical attention even after the eyes have been washed with cool water for 20 minutes.

Drowning victim

A person who has drowned can die 4 to 6 minutes after breathing stops. Get the victim out of the water immediately. Place the victim on his or her back and, if not breathing, immediately begin performing mouth-to-mouth resuscitation. Continue this treatment either until the victim begins breathing normally or help arrives. It should be noted that it can take as long as 2 hours for a drowning victim to regain independent breathing. Never leave a victim of drowning alone. Once the victim has begun breathing normally, simply wait nearby until professional help arrives. Resuscitation efforts can be suspended if the individual begins coughing.

Poisoning

If you feel an individual has been poisoned, you should be prepared to call 911 and the Poison Control Center and tell them the kind and quantity of poison that has been ingested, as well as the symptoms. Do not administer any medications unless you are instructed to do so by a professional. If a poisoned child is conscious, give him or her a little bit of water to dilute the poison. If a victim of poisoning is unconscious, make sure the person is breathing and, if not, perform mouth-to-mouth resuscitation. If the victim is vomiting, make sure they do not choke. Even though vomiting is the easiest way to remove poisons from the body, never try to induce vomiting when an individual has swallowed acid or an alkaline substance.

Heart attack

An individual may be suffering from a heart attack if he or she has an intense clenching pain in the chest, has shortness of breath, sweats heavily, is nauseous, has an irregular pulse, has pale or bluish skin, and is beset by severe anxiety. If you believe someone may be having a heart attack, immediately call 911. Have the person sit up and loosen any tight clothing. Try to keep the person comfortably warm. If the person is on medication for angina pectoris, help him or her take it. If the person is unconscious and you are trained to perform CPR, then do so after checking for a pulse at the wrist or neck. If there is no pulse, perform CPR along with mouth-to-mouth resuscitation. Even if you are untrained, performing chest compressions until help arrives is recommended for victims of a heart attack.

Breathing problems

If an unconscious victim is either not breathing or shows no signs of breath, lay the person on his back on the ground. Loosen any clothing that may be constricting some part of the body. Immediately check the air passages for any foreign objects, and then open the air passage by tilting the head back and lifting the chin up. Pinch the nostrils shut with thumb and index finger, then deliver two deep breaths directly into the victim's mouth. Each of these breaths should last from one to ten seconds. After each, look at the victim's chest to see if it rises. Repeat this process once every five seconds until medical help arrives. If your breaths do not seem to raise the victim's chest, tilt the head back farther and check for signs of choking.

Administering drugs

Drugs can be introduced to the body through different means. The most common way of taking a drug is by oral administration, i.e., swallowing it in a solid, liquid, or plasma form. Drugs may be injected directly into the bloodstream, a method that produces faster results than oral administration. Drugs may be inhaled; inhalants that are placed in a plastic bag and breathed are said to be huffed. There are different types of injections: intravenous injections are made directly into a vein; intramuscular injections are made into muscle tissue; and subcutaneous injections are made below the skin. Of these, intravenous injection is the fastest acting, while the effects of a subcutaneous injection may not be felt for 10 minutes or more.

Resource Management and Community Health

Health maintenance organizations

Health maintenance organizations, commonly known as HMOs, are managed-care plans in which a member makes a standard monthly payment for basic medical services. More than a quarter of the United States population receives health care as a member of a HMO. The cost of belonging to a HMO is generally small, with members not having to pay a deductible or a large co-payment. The main criticism of HMOs is that they limit the consumer to a small network of doctors and hospitals. In answer to this criticism, open-ended HMO plans have been introduced which allow the consumer to receive treatment at a facility and from a doctor of their choice. These plans are slightly more expensive, however.

Basic medical tests

A chest X-ray is sometimes used to diagnose abnormalities in a person's heart or lungs. Smokers and individuals with a family history of heart disease are often encouraged to get a regular chest X-ray. Doctors may also recommend an electrocardiogram, in which the electrical activity of the heart is measured. An electrocardiogram can indicate damage of the heart muscle as well as hardening of the arteries. Many doctors will also perform a routine urinalysis, in which the patient's urine is assessed in a laboratory. If the urine has too much glucose, for instance, it may be an indication of diabetes.

Basic medical exam

Female patients are likely to receive a pelvic examination when they make a routine trip to the doctor, especially the gynecologist (for many women, a gynecologist is their primary care physician). During a pelvic exam, the woman reclines with her heels raised in stirrups at the edge of the table. The doctor will then inspect the labia, clitoris, and vaginal opening. Using a lubricated, gloved finger, the doctor will also examine the vagina, looking for abnormalities in it, as well as in the uterus, fallopian tubes, and ovaries. Most doctors have a nurse in attendance during this procedure in order to make the patient feel more comfortable. Many women also insist that this procedure be performed by a female doctor.

During a basic medical examination, a doctor will touch and prod the skin of the patient's abdomen, searching for tender spots or irregularities that may signal problems in the liver or other organs. Certain deformities may indicate alcoholism, hepatitis, or a hernia. A doctor may use a gloved hand to check the rectum for hemorrhoids and other growths. Many male patients will receive rectal exams to check for a swollen prostate gland. During this part of the examination, it is typical for a doctor to check a male patient's testicles and spermatic cords for any abnormalities. A doctor will also check the patient's pulse in several different areas to ensure that circulation is good. Checking the blood pressure is another routine part of any medical exam.

Head, neck, and chest exams

During a basic medical examination, a doctor will typically use a small, concentrated flashlight called an ophthalmoscope to inspect the lens, retina, and blood vessels of the patient's eyes. After this, the doctor will inspect the ears, mouth, tongue, teeth, and gums. The doctor will also palpate the patient's neck, checking to see if the lymph glands are swollen, if there are any lumps in the thyroid gland, and if there are any signs that a stroke might be coming. The doctor will use a stethoscope to listen to the noises made by the heart, making sure that there are no signs of heart murmur or irregular contractions. The stethoscope is also used to listen to the lungs, particularly for the signs of asthma or emphysema. Tapping on the chest and back can indicate the size and condition of the heart and lungs.

Medical exam involving the extremities

During the course of a basic medical exam, a doctor will examine the reflexes of the patient. This is done by striking certain places on the body with a rubber hammer and observing the response. Abnormal reflexes may indicate a disorder of the nerves. A doctor will also examine the patient's skin for color, moisture, and elasticity. Abnormalities of the skin may indicate malnutrition, diabetes, or a potential skin cancer. An examination of the hair and nails of the patient can help a doctor determine the presence of blood disorders or other internal problems. Finally, doctors will always check the condition of the patient's ankles because swollen ankles can be a sign of heart, kidney, or lung disease.

Medical history and patient conduct

During a basic medical examination, a doctor should have a summary of your medical history, including any major illnesses or injuries, allergies, and past treatments. Sometimes, a physician may need to know information that the patient considers private, like sexual history. Unless there is a particular reason for withholding such information, patients can be confident that a doctor will not divulge confidential matters. A patient has to be honest so that the doctor will be able to make an accurate diagnosis and determine what medication may be needed. It is important for the patient to point out to the doctor any unusual bumps, rashes, pains, or other conditions that have appeared since the last examination. If necessary, patients should write out a summary of their current health so that they will be prepared to present all the important information.

Medical confidentiality

In the United States, the information to a physician by a patient cannot be accessed by any other person or group, including the government, unless there is a clear danger to some other individual or group. This means that the conversations between patient and doctor cannot be used in a court of law. This is called physician-patient privilege. This confidentiality exists even if the patient confesses a crime, as well as if the patient has suffered an injury that may result in a civil action. The laws of patient-physician privilege vary in their force from state to state. Though some states restrict this privilege to the conversations between a psychiatrist and patient, most states include all physicians in their confidentiality legislation.

Accessing valid health information

One of the core responsibilities for health educators, as outlined by the National Commission for Health Education Counseling (NCHEC), is being able to access accurate and appropriate health information. This is more difficult than it might seem because of the large amount of false or unsubstantiated health data in circulation. In order for health educators to stay afloat in this sea of information, the NCHEC recommends that they subscribe to major health journals, maintain membership in professional organizations, and be familiar with the major health databases. Moreover, the NCHEC recommends that health educators cultivate relationships with other health professionals in the community so that they will receive information from these specialized sources as well.

Disease reporting

In order to stay abreast of any outbreaks of disease, the government has made it mandatory for health agencies to report certain diseases to their state department of health. Diseases that must be reported immediately by phone include anthrax, botulism, rabies, plague, and smallpox. Other disease, including AIDS, E.Coli, and gonorrhea, are to be reported within 1 business day. These laws apply to physicians, health care facilities, medical laboratories, and, in some circumstances, veterinarians. These individuals or groups also need to send a report to the government any time they treat a pregnant woman for a chronic infection, like AIDS. For diseases that are less contagious or severe, the government provides forms for reporting.

Receiving good health care

Individuals can improve the quality of their health care if they abide by a few simple rules. First, they should try to remain informed on the health issues that are relevant to their lives. They should also try to find a primary care physician who listens to their complaints and concerns. It is never a bad idea to get a second opinion, though, especially for important decisions. It is important to ascertain that medical decisions are made on the basis of scientific evaluation rather than on the basis of the doctor's opinion. Patients should always be prepared to speak up and ask questions if they are unsure about a diagnosis. Finally, many patients take notes while they are at the doctor so they can research things later or confer with a knowledgeable friend.

Home health care

As it becomes less financially viable to remain in a hospital for a long period of time, more individuals are receiving treatment while they recuperate and rest at home. Many treatments that once could only be performed in hospitals (for instance kidney dialysis, chemotherapy, and traction) can now be administered in a private residence. Doctors are even beginning to make house calls again. Most of the time, the people who oversee the release of hospital patients (known in the industry as discharge planners) will arrange a program of home health care for those who need it. Also, individuals who desire home health care can contact their local health care professionals to ask if that service is provided. Most health insurance policies will cover a reasonable amount of home health care.

Outpatient treatment centers

Many procedures that at one time required overnight hospitalization can now be performed at outpatient centers. Outpatient centers can be freestanding and self-sustaining, or they can be affiliated with a larger medical center. Outpatient centers have become the preferred place to get a tonsillectomy, cataract removal, breast biopsy, vasectomy, or plastic surgery procedure. Because they have much lower overhead costs, outpatient facilities are able to provide services for a fraction of the cost for a similar procedure at a hospital. For this reason, insurance companies encourage their clients to have minor surgery performed at outpatient centers. A popular spin-off of the outpatient treatment center is the freestanding emergency center, where people can receive treatment for minor illness or injury in a somewhat shorter amount of time.

Primary, secondary, and tertiary care

Individuals seeking medical treatment have a number of options from which to choose. Primary care, otherwise known as ambulatory or outpatient care, is generally provided by a primary care physician in an office, an emergency room, or a clinic. Secondary care is generally provided by the specialists or subspecialists in a hospital. Secondary care may be provided in an inpatient or outpatient setting. Tertiary care includes most major procedures, e.g., open-heart surgery, kidney dialysis, and organ transplants. Tertiary care is generally conducted at regional specialty hospitals and at university-affiliated hospitals, where specialists in the particular disease or treatment carry out both clinical and teaching responsibilities.

Hospital evaluation

If you have the time, it is a good idea to compare various hospitals before determining where to receive treatment. One easy way to collect information is to ask your doctors which hospitals they would recommend, and why. Another way to evaluate hospitals is to inquire about the ratio of nurses to patients; many hospitals that are trying to cut costs provide fewer than the standard number of nurses. If you are having a rare procedure performed, you should ask whether the hospital has performed the procedure recently and what their success rate has been. If it is possible to do so, you should tour the various hospitals, checking to ensure that they are clean and orderly and have a courteous staff.

Kinds of hospitals

There are several different kinds of hospitals. Private (or community) hospitals are those that have between 50 and 400 beds and provide more personalized care than do public hospitals. Private hospitals may be run either for profit or as a nonprofit business. In public hospitals, the care is administered by the health service of the city, county, military, or Veterans Administration. Whereas the quality of care in a private hospital is determined by the skill of the doctors, the quality of care in a public hospital is more dependent on the general state of the institution that runs it. In the United States, there are approximately 300 hospitals that are directly affiliated with university medical schools. These hospitals often offer the most advanced treatments because the doctors there are required to stay abreast of all developments in their respective fields.

Self-care

Most individuals, even if they have no medical training, are constantly diagnosing themselves and changing their behavior and diet accordingly. This can include taking aspirin for a headache, taking a nap to combat fatigue, or eating a piece of fruit to stimulate the digestive system. Doctors recommend that individuals perform basic tests (like breast, testicular, and skin examinations) on themselves to determine whether they may need consultation with the doctor. Other tests, like those for pregnancy or blood pressure, require some diagnostic equipment but can be performed easily by untrained individuals, nevertheless. The most important skill to have when performing self-care, of course, is to know when to seek professional opinion.

Leadership roles

Each of these activities--guiding students effectively in health decisions, coordinating school-wide health programs, and setting a good example for students in health behavior--are listed as important roles for health educators, according to the National Commission for Health Education Credentialing (NCHEC). The Code of Ethics for health educators suggests that health educators are obligated by their position to stay abreast of all developments in the field of health so that they can serve as mediators in case of disputes. Health educators are also obliged to take every opportunity to use their training and knowledge to promote public health. The NCHEC suggests that health educators can most effectively lead when they set a good example with their own health behavior.

Physician training

In the United States, it takes at least 3 years of premedical studies (with an emphasis on physics, biology, and chemistry) followed by 4 (occasionally 3 or 5) years of medical school before a student can become a physician. The first 2 years are devoted to basic subjects: anatomy, embryology, pharmacology, and others. In the next 2 years, aspiring physicians begin clinical work in cooperation with practicing physicians in hospitals. After this, they must pass a series of national board examinations and complete a one-year hospital internship. Finally, they will have to finish a period of residency, which can last from 2 to 5 years. During their residency, doctors become trained and certified in one of the specialty branches of medicine.

Nurse training

In order to become a registered nurse, individuals must undergo rigorous training and graduate from a school of nursing that is approved by the state. Registered nurses may take basic science courses at a college or university and obtain a bachelor's or associate's degree along with their nursing degree. Nurses may choose to specialize in certain areas, such as intensive care or midwifery. If they receive extra training, they may become nurse practitioners, who are qualified to run a community clinic or even go into private practice. A licensed practical nurse, also known as a licensed vocational nurse, is licensed by the state and can work alongside either a registered nurse or a physician. Nursing aides and orderlies are those individuals who help nurses to perform their duties, usually by providing comfort directly to patients.

Physician certification

The majority of certified physicians are either specialists or subspecialists who focus almost exclusively on one part of the body, system of organs, type of disease, or type of treatment. For a long time, these specialists were better paid and more esteemed in the medical community. However, recent changes in the structure of health care in the United States have put more emphasis on the work of so-called primary care physicians, specifically, family practitioners and pediatricians. These physicians typically provide routine checkups, treat common ailments, and prescribe basic medications. Increasingly, primary care physicians are responsible for determining whether a patient should seek the aid of a specialist.

Psychiatrists and psychologists

Many people confuse the two most common types of mental health professionals: psychiatrists and psychologists. A psychiatrist has a degree in medicine and has received specialized training in treating mental illness. This qualifies a psychiatrist to prescribe medication and make other medical decisions. Many psychiatrists specialize in treating individuals in a particular age range or those with a certain mental condition. Psychologists, on the other hand, have completed a graduate program in mental functioning, usually receiving a doctorate and having post-doctoral training in a particular area of treatment. They must to be licensed by a state board in order to have a clinical practice. Many psychologists specialize in working with children or families. However, psychologists cannot prescribe medication and often work collaboratively with psychiatrists.

Chiropractic training

The study of chiropractics suggests that most human ailments are caused by a misalignment of the bones. Chiropractors are especially attentive to the vertebrae in the back, as they believe damage to the nerve tissue in the back can create problems in other parts of the body. In order to become a chiropractor, an individual must complete 2 years of college-level training and then spend 4 years in a special school for chiropractors. Chiropractors must be licensed by the state in which they practice. Chiropractors are known for advocating preventive care and wellness training, rather than surgery or medication. Although X-rays are often used in making chiropractic diagnoses, most chiropractic treatment relies simply on the manipulation of bones.

Dental problems

Since the introduction of fluoridated water and fluoridated toothpaste, dental health in the United States has improved markedly. There are a few dental conditions that require personal monitoring,, however. Gum disease is an inflammation of the gum and the bone that holds teeth in place; it is caused by plaque, a film of bacteria that can accrue on the teeth. The early stage of gum disease is called gingivitis. If gingivitis goes untreated, it can lead to periodontitis, the condition in which infection has spread to the roots of the teeth. Gum disease may be present if the gums bleed while an individual is brushing or flossing or if the gums are red or puffy; other signs are bad breath or shifting teeth. Individuals who are developing gum disease should visit a dentist to have their teeth scraped and have a further evaluation.

Dental care

In order to maintain good dental health, individuals should brush their teeth every morning and night; bacterial buildup is greatest while a person is sleeping, so it is imperative to clean the teeth soon after waking up. It is a good idea to use a toothbrush with soft, rounded bristles that carries the certification of the American Dental Association. It is also essential to floss every day to remove the plaque that a toothbrush can't reach. Cleaning slowly between teeth removes plaque and food that can be destructive to dental health if they are allowed to accumulate. If possible, every person should see a dentist twice a year for a cleaning and general examination. Many forms of health insurance include provisions for these visits.

Dental training

In order to become a dentist, an individual must complete a bachelor's degree with an emphasis in biology and chemistry and then graduate from dental school. Dental school is a 4-year venture; the first 2 years focus on general science, and the second 2 years focus on clinical work in dentistry. After this program is finished, the individual will be either a Doctor of Dental Surgery (DDS) or Doctor of Medical Dentistry (DMD). At this point, a prospective dentist will have to pass a written and clinical examination to receive a license to practice. Successful candidates can either become specialists in some area of dentistry or begin a general practice. One of the most common dental specialties is orthodontics, the straightening of the teeth.

Life guarding certification

The American Red Cross offers a comprehensive training program for individuals seeking to become lifeguards. The training program includes basic surveillance skills, water and land rescue, first aid and cardiopulmonary resuscitation (CPR), and the professional lifeguard's responsibilities, i.e., encouraging public safety and handling unruly swimmers. Many lifeguards will also benefit from becoming certified to use an automated external defibrillator (AED) and being trained to prevent disease transmission. Individuals must be at least 15 years old to receive certification as a trained lifeguard. Many of the skills learned during lifeguard training can be used in emergency situations away from the water.

Medical advertising

Prescription medicine has become big business in the past few decades, and pharmaceutical companies now make lavish expenditures on advertising that directly presents their products to the consumer. It is important that consumers be equipped with the skills to interpret and judge medical advertising. First of all, one should isolate the claims made by the advertising; some prescription medications are not allowed by law to declare what they will do, so this may be trickier than it sounds. Next, one should consider the sources cited by the advertising, if any are cited at all. Are these sources reputable? Advertising can be a positive influence if it helps a consumer learn more about what new products are available; still, all final decisions regarding medication should be made in consultation with a licensed physician.

Quackery

Quackery is the informal name given to any medical advice or information that is given by someone who is either unqualified or incompetent in that field. There is a long history of quackery in medicine. The United States government attempts to curtail quackery through legislation for the licensing of practicing physicians and the regulation of drug development and marketing. At present, the products considered quackery by medical experts are the so-called "natural" remedies sold in health food stores. Quackery continues to have some standing with the public because of general ignorance about health issues, the occurrence of a placebo effect (patients report positive effects because they expect them), and the distrust of modern medicine.

CDC findings

Drug abuse
The Center for Disease Control maintains that adolescent drug abuse is an ongoing problem that needs to be addressed. Besides the health risks associated with the drugs themselves, the CDC asserts that persistent drug use contributes to failure in school, fights, antisocial behavior, and unintentional injuries. Prolonged drug use can also be responsible for depression and anxiety. The CDC also maintains that drug use contributes to the HIV epidemic, insofar as those who share needles are liable to contract the virus, and drug users in general tend to engage in risky sexual behaviors. The statistics kept by the CDC state that marijuana use among teenagers decreased from 26% to 22% between 1997 and 2003.

Alcohol abuse
The Center for Disease Control not only considers alcohol destructive to adolescent health in itself, but believes that it contributes to other behaviors that are damaging to adolescent health. Specifically, the CDC suggests that alcohol contributes to unintentional injuries, fights, academic problems, and illegal behaviors. Over time, alcohol may lead to liver disease, cancer, cardiovascular disease, neurological damage, depression, anxiety, and antisocial tendencies. The rate of alcohol abuse among adolescents has fluctuated a bit in the past years: whereas 50% of high school students admitted to regular drinking in 1999, only 45% said that they were regular drinkers in 2003. Of these, 28% stated that they engaged in regular heavy drinking.

Unintended pregnancy
According to the CDC, teens who become pregnant immediately decrease their chances for success in life. Teen mothers have a reduced chance of finishing high school, and are more likely to spend their lives in poverty. The good news on this subject is that better contraceptive practices and more responsible behavior by adolescents have led to a reduction in the number of teen pregnancies, abortions, and birth rates over the past decade. However, these rates are still higher in the United States than in other developed countries, and they are especially high among African-Americans and Hispanics. The CDC has approved a number of programs that they say do a good job of educating and encouraging teens to make less risky decisions.

Tobacco
According to the Center for Disease Control, every day about 4000 American teenagers try smoking for the first time. Assuming that conditions remain as they are today, about 6.4 million of today's children will eventually die from a smoking-related illness. The CDC

reports that in 2003 22% of high school students smoked cigarettes regularly, and 15% smoked cigars on a regular basis. In addition, about 10% of high school students were users of smokeless tobacco. For the most part, students seem to be more likely to smoke cigarettes if they are from a poor background and if they have parents or friends who are smokers. White males are far more likely to use smokeless tobacco than are any other demographic group.

Sexually transmitted disease

Because they are more likely to engage in risky sexual activity with multiple partners, adolescents are more likely to contract a sexually transmitted disease. The CDC believes that adolescents are particularly at risk if they are frequent drug users and if they do not have access to contraceptives or to sex education. In order to meet the ongoing needs, the CDC has developed programs to present important information to adolescents so that they can protect themselves, as well as so that they can seek treatment if they do contract an STD. Part of the CDC's mission is to increase the level of parental involvement in the lives of adolescents. The CDC has published a number of statistics indicating that when parents actively supervise their children's lives, the children are less likely to engage in dangerous sexual behavior.

Managing nutrition services

The CDC offers some suggestions for how schools can manage the nutrition services provided to students and staff. First, health education at the high school should include some instruction on basic nutrition. Most high schools benefit from participating in the USDA National School Lunch Program, and many of these participate in the breakfast program as well. Schools should make sure to order the following healthy foods: skim or low-fat milk, fruit juice, vegetables, baked goods that are low in fat, and fresh fruits. In order to best serve students, schools should employ a full-time nutritionist and food service manager. All food-service employees should receive some training in nutrition.

School-provided health services

In order to provide adequate health services, the CDC recommends that every school have a coordinator of health services, a full-time physician, a nurse, and health aides. Schools should have policies in place to deal with students who have HIV/AIDS. Staff should be allowed to administer medication to students, provided students have the appropriate documentation. Moreover, students should be allowed to self-medicate with prescription inhalers and insulin injections as long as they are supervised by staff and have filled out the necessary paperwork. In order to fully serve students, many schools will need to form partnerships with local health agencies, organizations, or health professionals.

Mental health and social services

The Centers for Disease Control has provided some basic guidelines for schools seeking to provide adequate mental health care and social services to students. It is recommended that each school have an employee to oversee mental health and social services; some schools may benefit from having a guidance counselor, psychologist, or social worker. Many states require schools to provide a Student Assistance Program (SAP) for all students. Schools that lack either the population or money for such services should partner with local health agencies. Schools that can provide counseling services to students may benefit from offering assessments as well as family, individual, and group counseling.

Health promotion

The Centers for Disease Control outlines a few ways for schools to promote the health of the faculty and staff. Many schools have an employee in charge of overseeing health promotion for faculty and staff. Most schools allow the faculty and staff to use the exercise facilities maintained for students. Unfortunately, too many schools fail to provide physical examinations to employees. If possible, employees should also receive a tuberculosis test and screening for illegal drugs. Many school districts provide funding for alcohol treatment, HIV testing, nutrition counseling, stress management therapy, and weight management therapy for employees.

Family and community health

The Centers for Disease Control has issued some basic guidelines for schools to incorporate families and the community into school health programs. First, schools need to communicate their health programs and services to families. It is important for parents to know what materials and services are available to their children. Many schools have a specific employee charged with acting as a liaison between the school and the community. A number of schools benefit from a close working relationship with external health organizations and professionals. Many schools also open up school exercise facilities to members of the community. Schools should have a protocol in place in the event that a health educator needs to contact a student's family immediately.

Amount of exercise

According to the Centers for Disease Control, individuals should engage in a minimum of 30 minutes of moderate exercise at least five days per week. By "moderate," the CDC means any level of activity in which oxygen consumption is increased to between three and six times the amount required during rest. Thirty minutes of moderate physical activity is roughly equivalent to a fast walk of about 2 miles. Fulfilling this exercise requirement does not necessarily mean starting a planned, regimented fitness program; a person can get 30 minutes of exercise simply by playing with a child or pet or by cleaning vigorously. Indeed, it may be better for individuals who are out of shape to get used to exercise gradually by introducing it into their normal lives.

Code of Ethics for the Health Education Profession

Preamble

The preamble to the Coalition of National Health Education Organization's Code of Ethics states that the health education profession is dedicated to promoting individual, family, and community health. Furthermore, it states that health educators should embrace a multicultural perspective and respect the worth of all students. The fundamental values underlying the Code of Ethics are respect for autonomy, promotion of social justice, promotion of good, and avoidance of harm.

Article 1

Health teachers are responsible for educating the general public about good health practices. In order to do this, they must support the rights of individuals to make informed decisions; encourage social policies that promote health; communicate the consequences of health services and programs; act on issues that can damage public health; be honest regarding their qualifications and limitations; protect the dignity and privacy of individuals; and actively work to involve individuals, groups, and communities in the educational process so that health issues are understood by all.

Article 2

Health educators are responsible for their own professional behavior, for the reputation of their profession, and for promoting ethical conduct in the profession. In order to do so, health educators must continuously maintain and expand their professional competence through study and training; join professional organizations; model and encourage nondiscriminatory behavior; encourage critical discourse that protects and enhances the profession; share the processes and results of their work; avoid conflicts of interest; and avoid violating the rights of others.

Article 3

Health educators must recognize the boundaries of their own professional competence and be accountable for their own activities and actions. In order to do this, they must accurately represent their qualifications and the qualifications of those they recommend; use appropriate standards, theories, and guidelines when carrying out professional duties; accurately represent potential outcomes to employers; anticipate and disclose competing commitments, conflicts of interest, and endorsement of products; openly communicate any job expectations that conflict with professional ethics; and maintain competence in their areas of practice.

Article 4

Health teachers must exercise ethical behavior in the delivery of health education. Health educators need to respect the rights, confidentiality, and worth of all people by adapting effective strategies for a diverse community. In order to do this, health educators must be sensitive to social and cultural diversity and in accordance with the law; stay informed of the latest advances in theory, research, and practice; stay committed to program evaluation and the methods used to achieve results; empower individuals to adopt healthy lifestyles; and communicate the potential outcomes of proposed services, strategies, and decisions to all relevant individuals.

Article 5

Health educators must contribute to the health of the population through research and evaluation and do so in accordance with federal and state law. They should support research practices that do no harm to individuals or the environment; ensure that participation in research is based on informed consent; respect the privacy and dignity of research participants; treat all information received from participants as confidential unless otherwise required by law; take credit only for work they themselves have performed; discuss the results of research or evaluation only with those for whom the service is performed, unless withholding information would jeopardize someone's health or safety; and report the results of research objectively, accurately, and in a timely manner.

Article 6

Health educators who are involved in the training of new health educators are required to provide their students with a quality education that benefits both the profession and the public. Health educators must select students based on merit and on a system of equal opportunity; strive to make the educational environment and culture conducive to overall health; engage in adequate and effective preparation; present up-to-date and appropriate material; give fair feedback to students; state reasonable objectives; conduct fair assessments; provide objective counseling; and provide adequate supervision and meaningful opportunities for professional development.

Laws

Individualized Education Program

The Individuals with Disabilities Education Act mandates that any disabled student will have an Individualized Education Program (IEP) created specifically for him or her. IEPs are created by teams of specialists, including school psychologists, parents, and special education teachers. The point of an IEP is to assess the student's performance and determine appropriate goals and methods for further schooling. Typically, it will include schedule modifications, necessary accommodations for transportation, and a vision statement indicating hopes for the student's future. For many students, an IEP will include the critical health information teachers may need to know in case of an in-class emergency.

Controlled substances law

For the most part, the law of the United States takes a stern view of the growth, use, and distribution of controlled substances, such as marijuana, cocaine, and heroin. These drugs are illegal in any quantity, and individuals carrying a certain minimum amount can be charged with possession with intent to sell, which carries a much stiffer penalty. Individuals will also receive a much stiffer penalty if they are discovered carrying drugs across state lines. The minimum age for purchasing tobacco products is 18 years of age in most states. Retail carriers can be fined substantially for selling to underage individuals. Moreover, more places are becoming off-limits to smoking every year; recently, the city of New York banned smoking in all of its bars and restaurants.

American disability law

For the most part, American disability law is regulated by the Americans with Disabilities Act of 1990 (ADA). This law prevents discrimination against disabled individuals with respect to housing, employment, education, and access to public services. Interestingly, the ADA includes alcoholism as a disability. The ADA asks that reasonable accommodations be made to provide equal opportunities to disabled individuals. States are not forbidden from passing their own disability laws, so long as they do not contradict the ADA. A number of other acts have been created as spin-offs to the ADA, eg, the Fair Housing Act, the Air Carrier Access Act, and the Individuals with Disabilities Education Act.

Immunization laws

Every state sets specific immunization laws for children seeking to attend public school. Most states require children to be immunized for diphtheria, tetanus, pertussis, influenza, measles, mumps, rubella, polio, and hepatitis B. Some states will also require immunization against chickenpox. Though many schools offer these immunizations on-site, parents can also have them performed elsewhere and then provide documentation. There are no mandatory immunizations for adults, unless they are entering the military service. Individuals seeking to permanently migrate to the United States must receive immunization for every disease which is preventable by vaccine.

Inclusion and Public Law 94-142

A great deal of time is spent trying to equip teachers to handle students labeled "exceptional" for one reason or another. Furthermore, Public Law 94-142 mandates that schools must identify those students that require special treatment, whether for being extremely gifted or because of a disability. Many schools, however, feel that the best way to handle exceptional students is simply to include them in the regular classroom. Advocates of this program assert that specialists can come into the class and help exceptional students as necessary and that otherwise these students will benefit from being in contact with students from a wide range of abilities. However, this approach can overwhelm classroom teachers.

Mainstreaming

United States law indicates that students are to be educated in the least restrictive environment possible; that is, they should be allowed to join the highest level class in which they can participate. For many high-functioning disabled students, this means being "mainstreamed," or put into a class with normally-functioning students. The success or failure of such students often has a great deal to do with the expectations of the teacher; students who are ignored or who are made to feel they do not belong are more likely to have trouble. The AAHPERD states that it is "cruel" to place students in activities they are not equipped to handle, but it is "criminal" to exclude them from those in which they could contribute. The best strategy for teachers is to learn as much as possible about students and their disabilities before determining their level of participation.

Affirmative action

Affirmative action is the set of programs that have been developed in the United States to try and offset the discrimination of the past. This policy was put into action by various government agencies after the passage of the Civil Rights Act in 1964, and is currently enforced by the Equal Employment Opportunity Commission. Specifically, affirmative action policies allocate jobs and resources to specific groups that were discriminated against in the past, such as minorities and women. In the profession of physical education, this means not only that schools are prohibited from discriminating against formerly-oppressed groups, but that schools are required to hire qualified members of these groups whenever possible. This has led some to charge that affirmative action creates reverse discrimination. This issue has been batted about in the courts for decades, although affirmative action continues to apply.

OSHA

In the United States, work safety is overseen by the Occupational Safety and Health Administration (OSHA), which was created in 1970 by the Occupational Safety and Health Act. The major changes that have been effected by OSHA are placement of guards on all moving parts in industrial operations, regulation of chemical exposure to employees, enforcement of employee dress codes including protective equipment, mandatory disconnection of electrical equipment before repair, and specific requirements governing procedures for working in enclosed spaces. OSHA sets many other guidelines for specific businesses and routinely inspects worksites to ensure that they are safe for employees and visitors.

Types of negligence

Several types of negligence are chargeable offenses. Malfeasance occurs when the teacher has committed some act which is against the law. Misfeasance, on the other hand, occurs when the teacher obeys the law but not well enough to prevent injury. Nonfeasance occurs when a teacher has failed to perform some act which could have prevented an injury to a student. Contributory negligence occurs when the injured student is, in part, to blame for the injury. Finally, comparative (or shared) negligence is said to have occurred when both the injured student and the teacher are to blame. In this latter situation, the student must prove that the teacher was more to blame in order to receive compensation from the teacher.

Lawsuit

No matter how responsible and cautious they are, many physical educators will be charged with negligence for a student injury at some point in their career. In order to avoid having their professional life seriously damaged by such allegations, teachers should make sure that they have liability insurance. This is typically provided by the school district. Often, a good liability insurance policy allows the teacher to settle cases out of court. Teachers should also be sure to keep good records of any accidents, as records are vital to a legal defense. Finally, teachers should create and maintain a comprehensive checklist of safety and emergency care guidelines so that they will be prepared in the event of any injury and can demonstrate an intention to protect students.

Secret Key #1 - Time is Your Greatest Enemy

Pace Yourself

Wear a watch. At the beginning of the test, check the time (or start a chronometer on your watch to count the minutes), and check the time after every few questions to make sure you are "on schedule."

If you are forced to speed up, do it efficiently. Usually one or more answer choices can be eliminated without too much difficulty. Above all, don't panic. Don't speed up and just begin guessing at random choices. By pacing yourself, and continually monitoring your progress against your watch, you will always know exactly how far ahead or behind you are with your available time. If you find that you are one minute behind on the test, don't skip one question without spending any time on it, just to catch back up. Take 15 fewer seconds on the next four questions, and after four questions you'll have caught back up. Once you catch back up, you can continue working each problem at your normal pace.

Furthermore, don't dwell on the problems that you were rushed on. If a problem was taking up too much time and you made a hurried guess, it must be difficult. The difficult questions are the ones you are most likely to miss anyway, so it isn't a big loss. It is better to end with more time than you need than to run out of time.

Lastly, sometimes it is beneficial to slow down if you are constantly getting ahead of time. You are always more likely to catch a careless mistake by working more slowly than quickly, and among very high-scoring test takers (those who are likely to have lots of time left over), careless errors affect the score more than mastery of material.

Secret Key #2 - Guessing is not Guesswork

You probably know that guessing is a good idea. Unlike other standardized tests, there is no penalty for getting a wrong answer. Even if you have no idea about a question, you still have a 20-25% chance of getting it right.

Most test takers do not understand the impact that proper guessing can have on their score. Unless you score extremely high, guessing will significantly contribute to your final score.

Monkeys Take the Test

What most test takers don't realize is that to insure that 20-25% chance, you have to guess randomly. If you put 20 monkeys in a room to take this test, assuming they answered once per question and behaved themselves, on average they would get 20-25% of the questions correct. Put 20 test takers in the room, and the average will be much lower among guessed questions. Why?

1. The test writers intentionally write deceptive answer choices that "look" right. A test taker has no idea about a question, so he picks the "best looking" answer, which is often wrong. The monkey has no idea what looks good and what doesn't, so it will consistently be right about 20-25% of the time.
2. Test takers will eliminate answer choices from the guessing pool based on a hunch or intuition. Simple but correct answers often get excluded, leaving a 0% chance of being correct. The monkey has no clue, and often gets lucky with the best choice.

This is why the process of elimination endorsed by most test courses is flawed and detrimental to your performance. Test takers don't guess; they make an ignorant stab in the dark that is usually worse than random.

$5 Challenge

Let me introduce one of the most valuable ideas of this course—the $5 challenge:
- *You only mark your "best guess" if you are willing to bet $5 on it.*
- *You only eliminate choices from guessing if you are willing to bet $5 on it.*

Why $5? Five dollars is an amount of money that is small yet not insignificant, and can really add up fast (20 questions could cost you $100). Likewise, each answer choice on one question of the test will have a small impact on your overall score, but it can really add up to a lot of points in the end.

The process of elimination IS valuable. The following shows your chance of guessing it right:

If you eliminate wrong answer choices until only this many remain:	Chance of getting it correct:
1	100%
2	50%
3	33%

However, if you accidentally eliminate the right answer or go on a hunch for an incorrect answer, your chances drop dramatically—to 0%. By guessing among all the answer choices, you are GUARANTEED to have a shot at the right answer.

That's why the $5 test is so valuable. If you give up the advantage and safety of a pure guess, it had better be worth the risk.

What we still haven't covered is how to be sure that whatever guess you make is truly random. Here's the easiest way:
- *Always pick the first answer choice among those remaining.*

Such a technique means that you have decided, **before you see a single test question**, exactly how you are going to guess, and since the order of choices tells you nothing about which one is correct, this guessing technique is perfectly random.

This section is not meant to scare you away from making educated guesses or eliminating choices; you just need to define when a choice is worth eliminating. The $5 test, along with a pre-defined random guessing strategy, is the best way to make sure you reap all of the benefits of guessing.

Secret Key #3 - Practice Smarter, Not Harder

Many test takers delay the test preparation process because they dread the awful amounts of practice time they think necessary to succeed on the test. We have refined an effective method that will take you only a fraction of the time.

There are a number of "obstacles" in the path to success. Among these are answering questions, finishing in time, and mastering test-taking strategies. All must be executed on the day of the test at peak performance, or your score will suffer. The test is a mental marathon that has a large impact on your future.

Just like a marathon runner, it is important to work your way up to the full challenge. So first you just worry about questions, and then time, and finally strategy:

Success Strategy

1. Find a good source for practice tests.
2. If you are willing to make a larger time investment, consider using more than one study guide. Often the different approaches of multiple authors will help you "get" difficult concepts.
3. Take a practice test with no time constraints, with all study helps, "open book." Take your time with questions and focus on applying strategies.
4. Take a practice test with time constraints, with all guides, "open book."
5. Take a final practice test without open material and with time limits.

If you have time to take more practice tests, just repeat step 5. By gradually exposing yourself to the full rigors of the test environment, you will condition your mind to the stress of test day and maximize your success.

Secret Key #4 - Prepare, Don't Procrastinate

Let me state an obvious fact: if you take the test three times, you will probably get three different scores. This is due to the way you feel on test day, the level of preparedness you have, and the version of the test you see. Despite the test writers' claims to the contrary, some versions of the test WILL be easier for you than others.

Since your future depends so much on your score, you should maximize your chances of success. In order to maximize the likelihood of success, you've got to prepare in advance. This means taking practice tests and spending time learning the information and test taking strategies you will need to succeed.

Never go take the actual test as a "practice" test, expecting that you can just take it again if you need to. Take all the practice tests you can on your own, but when you go to take the official test, be prepared, be focused, and do your best the first time!

Secret Key #5 - Test Yourself

Everyone knows that time is money. There is no need to spend too much of your time or too little of your time preparing for the test. You should only spend as much of your precious time preparing as is necessary for you to get the score you need.

Once you have taken a practice test under real conditions of time constraints, then you will know if you are ready for the test or not.

If you have scored extremely high the first time that you take the practice test, then there is not much point in spending countless hours studying. You are already there.

Benchmark your abilities by retaking practice tests and seeing how much you have improved. Once you consistently score high enough to guarantee success, then you are ready.

If you have scored well below where you need, then knuckle down and begin studying in earnest. Check your improvement regularly through the use of practice tests under real conditions. Above all, don't worry, panic, or give up. The key is perseverance!

Then, when you go to take the test, remain confident and remember how well you did on the practice tests. If you can score high enough on a practice test, then you can do the same on the real thing.

General Strategies

The most important thing you can do is to ignore your fears and jump into the test immediately. Do not be overwhelmed by any strange-sounding terms. You have to jump into the test like jumping into a pool—all at once is the easiest way.

Make Predictions

As you read and understand the question, try to guess what the answer will be. Remember that several of the answer choices are wrong, and once you begin reading them, your mind will immediately become cluttered with answer choices designed to throw you off. Your mind is typically the most focused immediately after you have read the question and digested its contents. If you can, try to predict what the correct answer will be. You may be surprised at what you can predict.

Quickly scan the choices and see if your prediction is in the listed answer choices. If it is, then you can be quite confident that you have the right answer. It still won't hurt to check the other answer choices, but most of the time, you've got it!

Answer the Question

It may seem obvious to only pick answer choices that answer the question, but the test writers can create some excellent answer choices that are wrong. Don't pick an answer just because it sounds right, or you believe it to be true. It MUST answer the question. Once you've made your selection, always go back and check it against the question and make sure that you didn't misread the question and that the answer choice does answer the question posed.

Benchmark

After you read the first answer choice, decide if you think it sounds correct or not. If it doesn't, move on to the next answer choice. If it does, mentally mark that answer choice. This doesn't mean that you've definitely selected it as your answer choice, it just means that it's the best you've seen thus far. Go ahead and read the next choice. If the next choice is worse than the one you've already selected, keep going to the next answer choice. If the next choice is better than the choice you've already selected, mentally mark the new answer choice as your best guess.

The first answer choice that you select becomes your standard. Every other answer choice must be benchmarked against that standard. That choice is correct until proven otherwise by another answer choice beating it out. Once you've decided that no other answer choice seems as good, do one final check to ensure that your answer choice answers the question posed.

Valid Information

Don't discount any of the information provided in the question. Every piece of information may be necessary to determine the correct answer. None of the information in the question is there to throw you off (while the answer choices will certainly have information to throw you off). If two seemingly unrelated topics are discussed, don't ignore either. You can be confident there is a relationship, or it wouldn't be included in the question, and you are probably going to have to determine what is that relationship to find the answer.

Avoid "Fact Traps"

Don't get distracted by a choice that is factually true. Your search is for the answer that answers the question. Stay focused and don't fall for an answer that is true but irrelevant. Always go back to the question and make sure you're choosing an answer that actually answers the question and is not just a true statement. An answer can be factually correct, but it MUST answer the question asked. Additionally, two answers can both be seemingly correct, so be sure to read all of the answer choices, and make sure that you get the one that BEST answers the question.

Milk the Question

Some of the questions may throw you completely off. They might deal with a subject you have not been exposed to, or one that you haven't reviewed in years. While your lack of knowledge about the subject will be a hindrance, the question itself can give you many clues that will help you find the correct answer. Read the question carefully and look for clues. Watch particularly for adjectives and nouns describing difficult terms or words that you don't recognize. Regardless of whether you completely understand a word or not, replacing it with a synonym, either provided or one you more familiar with, may help you to understand what the questions are asking. Rather than wracking your mind about specific detailed information concerning a difficult term or word, try to use mental substitutes that are easier to understand.

The Trap of Familiarity

Don't just choose a word because you recognize it. On difficult questions, you may not recognize a number of words in the answer choices. The test writers don't put "make-believe" words on the test, so don't think that just because you only recognize all the words in one answer choice that that answer choice must be correct. If you only recognize words in one answer choice, then focus on that one. Is it correct? Try your best to determine if it is correct. If it is, that's great. If not, eliminate it. Each word and answer choice you eliminate increases your chances of getting the question correct, even if you then have to guess among the unfamiliar choices.

Eliminate Answers

Eliminate choices as soon as you realize they are wrong. But be careful! Make sure you consider all of the possible answer choices. Just because one appears right, doesn't mean that the next one won't be even better! The test writers will usually put more than one good answer choice for every question, so read all of them. Don't worry if you are stuck between two that seem right. By getting down to just two remaining possible choices, your odds are now 50/50. Rather than wasting too much time, play the odds. You are guessing, but guessing wisely because you've been able to knock out some of the answer choices that you know are wrong. If you are eliminating choices and realize that the last answer choice you are left with is also obviously wrong, don't panic. Start over and consider each choice again. There may easily be something that you missed the first time and will realize on the second pass.

Tough Questions

If you are stumped on a problem or it appears too hard or too difficult, don't waste time. Move on! Remember though, if you can quickly check for obviously incorrect answer choices, your chances of guessing correctly are greatly improved. Before you completely give up, at least try to knock out a couple of possible answers. Eliminate what you can and then guess at the remaining answer choices before moving on.

Brainstorm

If you get stuck on a difficult question, spend a few seconds quickly brainstorming. Run through the complete list of possible answer choices. Look at each choice and ask yourself, "Could this answer the question satisfactorily?" Go through each answer choice and consider it independently of the others. By systematically going through all possibilities, you may find something that you would otherwise overlook. Remember though that when you get stuck, it's important to try to keep moving.

Read Carefully

Understand the problem. Read the question and answer choices carefully. Don't miss the question because you misread the terms. You have plenty of time to read each question thoroughly and make sure you understand what is being asked. Yet a happy medium must be attained, so don't waste too much time. You must read carefully, but efficiently.

Face Value

When in doubt, use common sense. Always accept the situation in the problem at face value. Don't read too much into it. These problems will not require you to make huge leaps of logic. The test writers aren't trying to throw you off with a cheap trick. If you have to go beyond creativity and make a leap of logic in order to have an answer choice answer the question, then you should look at the other answer choices. Don't overcomplicate the problem by creating theoretical relationships or explanations that will warp time or space. These are normal problems rooted in reality. It's just that the applicable relationship or explanation may not be readily apparent and you have to figure things out. Use your common sense to interpret anything that isn't clear.

Prefixes

If you're having trouble with a word in the question or answer choices, try dissecting it. Take advantage of every clue that the word might include. Prefixes and suffixes can be a huge help. Usually they allow you to determine a basic meaning. Pre- means before, post- means after, pro - is positive, de- is negative. From these prefixes and suffixes, you can get an idea of the general meaning of the word and try to put it into context. Beware though of any traps. Just because con- is the opposite of pro-, doesn't necessarily mean congress is the opposite of progress!

Hedge Phrases

Watch out for critical hedge phrases, led off with words such as "likely," "may," "can," "sometimes," "often," "almost," "mostly," "usually," "generally," "rarely," and "sometimes." Question writers insert these hedge phrases to cover every possibility. Often an answer choice will be wrong simply because it leaves no room for exception. Unless the situation calls for them, avoid answer choices that have definitive words like "exactly," and "always."

Switchback Words

Stay alert for "switchbacks." These are the words and phrases frequently used to alert you to shifts in thought. The most common switchback word is "but." Others include "although," "however," "nevertheless," "on the other hand," "even though," "while," "in spite of," "despite," and "regardless of."

New Information

Correct answer choices will rarely have completely new information included. Answer choices typically are straightforward reflections of the material asked about and will directly relate to the question. If a new piece of information is included in an answer choice that doesn't even seem to relate to the topic being asked about, then that answer choice is likely incorrect. All of the information needed to answer the question is usually provided for you in the question. You should not have to make guesses that are unsupported or choose answer choices that require unknown information that cannot be reasoned from what is given.

Time Management

On technical questions, don't get lost on the technical terms. Don't spend too much time on any one question. If you don't know what a term means, then odds are you aren't going to get much further since you don't have a dictionary. You should be able to immediately recognize whether or not you know a term. If you don't, work with the other clues that you have—the other answer choices and terms provided—but don't waste too much time trying to figure out a difficult term that you don't know.

Contextual Clues

Look for contextual clues. An answer can be right but not the correct answer. The contextual clues will help you find the answer that is most right and is correct. Understand the context in which a phrase or statement is made. This will help you make important distinctions.

Don't Panic

Panicking will not answer any questions for you; therefore, it isn't helpful. When you first see the question, if your mind goes blank, take a deep breath. Force yourself to mechanically go through the steps of solving the problem using the strategies you've learned.

Pace Yourself

Don't get clock fever. It's easy to be overwhelmed when you're looking at a page full of questions, your mind is full of random thoughts and feeling confused, and the clock is ticking down faster than you would like. Calm down and maintain the pace that you have set for yourself. As long as you are on track by monitoring your pace, you are guaranteed to have enough time for yourself. When you get to the last few minutes of the test, it may seem like you won't have enough time left, but if you only have as many questions as you should have left at that point, then you're right on track!

Answer Selection

The best way to pick an answer choice is to eliminate all of those that are wrong, until only one is left and confirm that is the correct answer. Sometimes though, an answer choice may immediately look right. Be careful! Take a second to make sure that the other choices are not equally obvious. Don't make a hasty mistake. There are only two times that you should stop before checking other answers. First is when you are positive that the answer choice you have selected is correct. Second is when time is almost out and you have to make a quick guess!

Check Your Work

Since you will probably not know every term listed and the answer to every question, it is important that you get credit for the ones that you do know. Don't miss any questions through careless mistakes. If at all possible, try to take a second to look back over your answer selection and make sure you've selected the correct answer choice and haven't made a costly careless mistake (such as marking an answer choice that you didn't mean to mark). The time it takes for this quick double check should more than pay for itself in caught mistakes.

Beware of Directly Quoted Answers

Sometimes an answer choice will repeat word for word a portion of the question or reference section. However, beware of such exact duplication. It may be a trap! More than likely, the correct choice will paraphrase or summarize a point, rather than being exactly the same wording.

Slang

Scientific sounding answers are better than slang ones. An answer choice that begins "To compare the outcomes…" is much more likely to be correct than one that begins "Because some people insisted…"

Extreme Statements

Avoid wild answers that throw out highly controversial ideas that are proclaimed as established fact. An answer choice that states the "process should used in certain situations, if…" is much more likely to be correct than one that states the "process should be discontinued completely." The first is a calm rational statement and doesn't even make a definitive, uncompromising stance, using a hedge word "if" to provide wiggle room, whereas the second choice is a radical idea and far more extreme.

Answer Choice Families

When you have two or more answer choices that are direct opposites or parallels, one of them is usually the correct answer. For instance, if one answer choice states "x increases" and another answer choice states "x decreases" or "y increases," then those two or three answer choices are very similar in construction and fall into the same family of answer choices. A family of answer choices consists of two or three answer choices, very similar in construction, but often with directly opposite meanings. Usually the correct answer choice will be in that family of answer choices. The "odd man out" or answer choice that doesn't seem to fit the parallel construction of the other answer choices is more likely to be incorrect.

Special Report: How to Overcome Test Anxiety

The very nature of tests caters to some level of anxiety, nervousness, or tension, just as we feel for any important event that occurs in our lives. A little bit of anxiety or nervousness can be a good thing. It helps us with motivation, and makes achievement just that much sweeter. However, too much anxiety can be a problem, especially if it hinders our ability to function and perform.

"Test anxiety," is the term that refers to the emotional reactions that some test-takers experience when faced with a test or exam. Having a fear of testing and exams is based upon a rational fear, since the test-taker's performance can shape the course of an academic career. Nevertheless, experiencing excessive fear of examinations will only interfere with the test-taker's ability to perform and chance to be successful.

There are a large variety of causes that can contribute to the development and sensation of test anxiety. These include, but are not limited to, lack of preparation and worrying about issues surrounding the test.

Lack of Preparation

Lack of preparation can be identified by the following behaviors or situations:
- Not scheduling enough time to study, and therefore cramming the night before the test or exam
- Managing time poorly, to create the sensation that there is not enough time to do everything
- Failing to organize the text information in advance, so that the study material consists of the entire text and not simply the pertinent information
- Poor overall studying habits

Worrying, on the other hand, can be related to both the test taker, or many other factors around him/her that will be affected by the results of the test. These include worrying about:
- Previous performances on similar exams, or exams in general
- How friends and other students are achieving
- The negative consequences that will result from a poor grade or failure

There are three primary elements to test anxiety. Physical components, which involve the same typical bodily reactions as those to acute anxiety (to be discussed below). Emotional factors have to do with fear or panic. Mental or cognitive issues concerning attention spans and memory abilities.

Physical Signals

There are many different symptoms of test anxiety, and these are not limited to mental and emotional strain. Frequently there are a range of physical signals that will let a test taker know that he/she is suffering from test anxiety. These bodily changes can include the following:

- Perspiring
- Sweaty palms
- Wet, trembling hands
- Nausea
- Dry mouth
- A knot in the stomach
- Headache
- Faintness
- Muscle tension
- Aching shoulders, back and neck
- Rapid heart beat
- Feeling too hot/cold

To recognize the sensation of test anxiety, a test-taker should monitor him/herself for the following sensations:

- The physical distress symptoms as listed above
- Emotional sensitivity, expressing emotional feelings such as the need to cry or laugh too much, or a sensation of anger or helplessness
- A decreased ability to think, causing the test-taker to blank out or have racing thoughts that are hard to organize or control.

Though most students will feel some level of anxiety when faced with a test or exam, the majority can cope with that anxiety and maintain it at a manageable level. However, those who cannot are faced with a very real and very serious condition, which can and should be controlled for the immeasurable benefit of this sufferer.

Naturally, these sensations lead to negative results for the testing experience. The most common effects of test anxiety have to do with nervousness and mental blocking.

Nervousness

Nervousness can appear in several different levels:

- The test-taker's difficulty, or even inability to read and understand the questions on the test
- The difficulty or inability to organize thoughts to a coherent form
- The difficulty or inability to recall key words and concepts relating to the testing questions (especially essays)
- The receipt of poor grades on a test, though the test material was well known by the test taker

Conversely, a person may also experience mental blocking, which involves:
- Blanking out on test questions
- Only remembering the correct answers to the questions when the test has already finished.

Fortunately for test anxiety sufferers, beating these feelings, to a large degree, has to do with proper preparation. When a test taker has a feeling of preparedness, then anxiety will be dramatically lessened.

The first step to resolving anxiety issues is to distinguish which of the two types of anxiety are being suffered. If the anxiety is a direct result of a lack of preparation, this should be considered a normal reaction, and the anxiety level (as opposed to the test results) shouldn't be anything to worry about. However, if, when adequately prepared, the test-taker still panics, blanks out, or seems to overreact, this is not a fully rational reaction. While this can be considered normal too, there are many ways to combat and overcome these effects.

Remember that anxiety cannot be entirely eliminated, however, there are ways to minimize it, to make the anxiety easier to manage. Preparation is one of the best ways to minimize test anxiety. Therefore the following techniques are wise in order to best fight off any anxiety that may want to build.

To begin with, try to avoid cramming before a test, whenever it is possible. By trying to memorize an entire term's worth of information in one day, you'll be shocking your system, and not giving yourself a very good chance to absorb the information. This is an easy path to anxiety, so for those who suffer from test anxiety, cramming should not even be considered an option.

Instead of cramming, work throughout the semester to combine all of the material which is presented throughout the semester, and work on it gradually as the course goes by, making sure to master the main concepts first, leaving minor details for a week or so before the test.

To study for the upcoming exam, be sure to pose questions that may be on the examination, to gauge the ability to answer them by integrating the ideas from your texts, notes and lectures, as well as any supplementary readings.

If it is truly impossible to cover all of the information that was covered in that particular term, concentrate on the most important portions, that can be covered very well. Learn these concepts as best as possible, so that when the test comes, a goal can be made to use these concepts as presentations of your knowledge.

In addition to study habits, changes in attitude are critical to beating a struggle with test anxiety. In fact, an improvement of the perspective over the entire test-taking experience can actually help a test taker to enjoy studying and therefore improve the overall experience. Be certain not to overemphasize the significance of the grade - know that the result of the test is neither a reflection of self worth, nor is it a measure of intelligence; one grade will not predict a person's future success.

To improve an overall testing outlook, the following steps should be tried:
- Keeping in mind that the most reasonable expectation for taking a test is to expect to try to demonstrate as much of what you know as you possibly can.
- Reminding ourselves that a test is only one test; this is not the only one, and there will be others.
- The thought of thinking of oneself in an irrational, all-or-nothing term should be avoided at all costs.
- A reward should be designated for after the test, so there's something to look forward to. Whether it be going to a movie, going out to eat, or simply visiting friends, schedule it in advance, and do it no matter what result is expected on the exam.

Test-takers should also keep in mind that the basics are some of the most important things, even beyond anti-anxiety techniques and studying. Never neglect the basic social, emotional and biological needs, in order to try to absorb information. In order to best achieve, these three factors must be held as just as important as the studying itself.

Study Steps

Remember the following important steps for studying:
- Maintain healthy nutrition and exercise habits. Continue both your recreational activities and social pass times. These both contribute to your physical and emotional well being.
- Be certain to get a good amount of sleep, especially the night before the test, because when you're overtired you are not able to perform to the best of your best ability.
- Keep the studying pace to a moderate level by taking breaks when they are needed, and varying the work whenever possible, to keep the mind fresh instead of getting bored.
- When enough studying has been done that all the material that can be learned has been learned, and the test taker is prepared for the test, stop studying and do something relaxing such as listening to music, watching a movie, or taking a warm bubble bath.

There are also many other techniques to minimize the uneasiness or apprehension that is experienced along with test anxiety before, during, or even after the examination. In fact, there are a great deal of things that can be done to stop anxiety from interfering with lifestyle and performance. Again, remember that anxiety will not be eliminated entirely, and it shouldn't be. Otherwise that "up" feeling for exams would not exist, and most of us depend on that sensation to perform better than usual. However, this anxiety has to be at a level that is manageable.

Of course, as we have just discussed, being prepared for the exam is half the battle right away. Attending all classes, finding out what knowledge will be expected on the exam, and knowing the exam schedules are easy steps to lowering anxiety. Keeping up with work will remove the need to cram, and efficient study habits will eliminate wasted time. Studying should be done in an ideal location for concentration, so that it is simple to become interested in the material and give it complete attention. A method such as

SQ3R (Survey, Question, Read, Recite, Review) is a wonderful key to follow to make sure that the study habits are as effective as possible, especially in the case of learning from a textbook. Flashcards are great techniques for memorization. Learning to take good notes will mean that notes will be full of useful information, so that less sifting will need to be done to seek out what is pertinent for studying. Reviewing notes after class and then again on occasion will keep the information fresh in the mind. From notes that have been taken summary sheets and outlines can be made for simpler reviewing.

A study group can also be a very motivational and helpful place to study, as there will be a sharing of ideas, all of the minds can work together, to make sure that everyone understands, and the studying will be made more interesting because it will be a social occasion. Basically, though, as long as the test-taker remains organized and self confident, with efficient study habits, less time will need to be spent studying, and higher grades will be achieved.

To become self confident, there are many useful steps. The first of these is "self talk." It has been shown through extensive research, that self-talk for students who suffer from test anxiety, should be well monitored, in order to make sure that it contributes to self confidence as opposed to sinking the student. Frequently the self talk of test-anxious students is negative or self-defeating, thinking that everyone else is smarter and faster, that they always mess up, and that if they don't do well, they'll fail the entire course. It is important to decreasing anxiety that awareness is made of self talk. Try writing any negative self thoughts and then disputing them with a positive statement instead. Begin self-encouragement as though it was a friend speaking. Repeat positive statements to help reprogram the mind to believing in successes instead of failures.

Helpful Techniques

Other extremely helpful techniques include:
- Self-visualization of doing well and reaching goals
- While aiming for an "A" level of understanding, don't try to "overprotect" by setting your expectations lower. This will only convince the mind to stop studying in order to meet the lower expectations.
- Don't make comparisons with the results or habits of other students. These are individual factors, and different things work for different people, causing different results.
- Strive to become an expert in learning what works well, and what can be done in order to improve. Consider collecting this data in a journal.
- Create rewards for after studying instead of doing things before studying that will only turn into avoidance behaviors.
- Make a practice of relaxing - by using methods such as progressive relaxation, self-hypnosis, guided imagery, etc - in order to make relaxation an automatic sensation.
- Work on creating a state of relaxed concentration so that concentrating will take on the focus of the mind, so that none will be wasted on worrying.
- Take good care of the physical self by eating well and getting enough sleep.
- Plan in time for exercise and stick to this plan.

Beyond these techniques, there are other methods to be used before, during and after the test that will help the test-taker perform well in addition to overcoming anxiety.

Before the exam comes the academic preparation. This involves establishing a study schedule and beginning at least one week before the actual date of the test. By doing this, the anxiety of not having enough time to study for the test will be automatically eliminated. Moreover, this will make the studying a much more effective experience, ensuring that the learning will be an easier process. This relieves much undue pressure on the test-taker.

Summary sheets, note cards, and flash cards with the main concepts and examples of these main concepts should be prepared in advance of the actual studying time. A topic should never be eliminated from this process. By omitting a topic because it isn't expected to be on the test is only setting up the test-taker for anxiety should it actually appear on the exam. Utilize the course syllabus for laying out the topics that should be studied. Carefully go over the notes that were made in class, paying special attention to any of the issues that the professor took special care to emphasize while lecturing in class. In the textbooks, use the chapter review, or if possible, the chapter tests, to begin your review.

It may even be possible to ask the instructor what information will be covered on the exam, or what the format of the exam will be (for example, multiple choice, essay, free form, true-false). Additionally, see if it is possible to find out how many questions will be on the test. If a review sheet or sample test has been offered by the professor, make good use of it, above anything else, for the preparation for the test. Another great resource for getting to know the examination is reviewing tests from previous semesters. Use these tests to review, and aim to achieve a 100% score on each of the possible topics. With a few exceptions, the goal that you set for yourself is the highest one that you will reach.

Take all of the questions that were assigned as homework, and rework them to any other possible course material. The more problems reworked, the more skill and confidence will form as a result. When forming the solution to a problem, write out each of the steps. Don't simply do head work. By doing as many steps on paper as possible, much clarification and therefore confidence will be formed. Do this with as many homework problems as possible, before checking the answers. By checking the answer after each problem, a reinforcement will exist, that will not be on the exam. Study situations should be as exam-like as possible, to prime the test-taker's system for the experience. By waiting to check the answers at the end, a psychological advantage will be formed, to decrease the stress factor.

Another fantastic reason for not cramming is the avoidance of confusion in concepts, especially when it comes to mathematics. 8-10 hours of study will become one hundred percent more effective if it is spread out over a week or at least several days, instead of doing it all in one sitting. Recognize that the human brain requires time in order to assimilate new material, so frequent breaks and a span of study time over several days will be much more beneficial.

Additionally, don't study right up until the point of the exam. Studying should stop a minimum of one hour before the exam begins. This allows the brain to rest and put

- 162 -

things in their proper order. This will also provide the time to become as relaxed as possible when going into the examination room. The test-taker will also have time to eat well and eat sensibly. Know that the brain needs food as much as the rest of the body. With enough food and enough sleep, as well as a relaxed attitude, the body and the mind are primed for success.

Avoid any anxious classmates who are talking about the exam. These students only spread anxiety, and are not worth sharing the anxious sentimentalities.

Before the test also involves creating a positive attitude, so mental preparation should also be a point of concentration. There are many keys to creating a positive attitude. Should fears become rushing in, make a visualization of taking the exam, doing well, and seeing an A written on the paper. Write out a list of affirmations that will bring a feeling of confidence, such as "I am doing well in my English class," "I studied well and know my material," "I enjoy this class." Even if the affirmations aren't believed at first, it sends a positive message to the subconscious which will result in an alteration of the overall belief system, which is the system that creates reality.

If a sensation of panic begins, work with the fear and imagine the very worst! Work through the entire scenario of not passing the test, failing the entire course, and dropping out of school, followed by not getting a job, and pushing a shopping cart through the dark alley where you'll live. This will place things into perspective! Then, practice deep breathing and create a visualization of the opposite situation - achieving an "A" on the exam, passing the entire course, receiving the degree at a graduation ceremony.

On the day of the test, there are many things to be done to ensure the best results, as well as the most calm outlook. The following stages are suggested in order to maximize test-taking potential:
- Begin the examination day with a moderate breakfast, and avoid any coffee or beverages with caffeine if the test taker is prone to jitters. Even people who are used to managing caffeine can feel jittery or light-headed when it is taken on a test day.
- Attempt to do something that is relaxing before the examination begins. As last minute cramming clouds the mastering of overall concepts, it is better to use this time to create a calming outlook.
- Be certain to arrive at the test location well in advance, in order to provide time to select a location that is away from doors, windows and other distractions, as well as giving enough time to relax before the test begins.
- Keep away from anxiety generating classmates who will upset the sensation of stability and relaxation that is being attempted before the exam.
- Should the waiting period before the exam begins cause anxiety, create a self-distraction by reading a light magazine or something else that is relaxing and simple.

During the exam itself, read the entire exam from beginning to end, and find out how much time should be allotted to each individual problem. Once writing the exam, should more time be taken for a problem, it should be abandoned, in order to begin another problem. If there is time at the end, the unfinished problem can always be returned to and completed.

Read the instructions very carefully - twice - so that unpleasant surprises won't follow during or after the exam has ended.

When writing the exam, pretend that the situation is actually simply the completion of homework within a library, or at home. This will assist in forming a relaxed atmosphere, and will allow the brain extra focus for the complex thinking function.

Begin the exam with all of the questions with which the most confidence is felt. This will build the confidence level regarding the entire exam and will begin a quality momentum. This will also create encouragement for trying the problems where uncertainty resides.

Going with the "gut instinct" is always the way to go when solving a problem. Second guessing should be avoided at all costs. Have confidence in the ability to do well.

For essay questions, create an outline in advance that will keep the mind organized and make certain that all of the points are remembered. For multiple choice, read every answer, even if the correct one has been spotted - a better one may exist.

Continue at a pace that is reasonable and not rushed, in order to be able to work carefully. Provide enough time to go over the answers at the end, to check for small errors that can be corrected.

Should a feeling of panic begin, breathe deeply, and think of the feeling of the body releasing sand through its pores. Visualize a calm, peaceful place, and include all of the sights, sounds and sensations of this image. Continue the deep breathing, and take a few minutes to continue this with closed eyes. When all is well again, return to the test.

If a "blanking" occurs for a certain question, skip it and move on to the next question. There will be time to return to the other question later. Get everything done that can be done, first, to guarantee all the grades that can be compiled, and to build all of the confidence possible. Then return to the weaker questions to build the marks from there.

Remember, one's own reality can be created, so as long as the belief is there, success will follow. And remember: anxiety can happen later, right now, there's an exam to be written!

After the examination is complete, whether there is a feeling for a good grade or a bad grade, don't dwell on the exam, and be certain to follow through on the reward that was promised...and enjoy it! Don't dwell on any mistakes that have been made, as there is nothing that can be done at this point anyway.

Additionally, don't begin to study for the next test right away. Do something relaxing for a while, and let the mind relax and prepare itself to begin absorbing information again.

From the results of the exam - both the grade and the entire experience, be certain to learn from what has gone on. Perfect studying habits and work some more on confidence in order to make the next examination experience even better than the last one.

Learn to avoid places where openings occurred for laziness, procrastination and day dreaming.

Use the time between this exam and the next one to better learn to relax, even learning to relax on cue, so that any anxiety can be controlled during the next exam. Learn how to relax the body. Slouch in your chair if that helps. Tighten and then relax all of the different muscle groups, one group at a time, beginning with the feet and then working all the way up to the neck and face. This will ultimately relax the muscles more than they were to begin with. Learn how to breathe deeply and comfortably, and focus on this breathing going in and out as a relaxing thought. With every exhale, repeat the word "relax."

As common as test anxiety is, it is very possible to overcome it. Make yourself one of the test-takers who overcome this frustrating hindrance.

Practice Test and Additional Bonus Material

Due to our efforts to try to keep this book to a manageable length, we've created a link that will give you access to all of your additional bonus material.

Please visit http://www.mometrix.com/bonus948/mtelhealthed to access the information.